SPECIAL KIDS
Problem Solver

KENNETH SHORE, Psy. D.

JOSSEY-BASS
A Wiley Imprint
www.josseybass.com

Published by Jossey-Bass
A Wiley Imprint
989 Market Street, San Francisco, CA 94103-1741   www.josseybass.com

Jossey-Bass books and products are available through most bookstores. To contact Jossey-Bass
directly call our Customer Care Department within the U.S. at (800) 956-7739, outside the U.S.
at (317) 572-3986 or fax (317) 572-4002.

Every effort has been made to ensure that the information provided in this publication is both accurate and current. The addresses and phone numbers of the various organizations listed were veri-
fied at time of publication. Given the dynamic nature of telecommunications as well as ongoing
educational research, the publisher and author do not guarantee the accuracy and completeness of
any information and are not responsible for errors, omissions, or results obtained from using the
information.

Jossey-Bass also publishes its books in a variety of electronic formats. Some content that appears
in print may not be available in electronic books.

Library of Congress Cataloging-in-Publication Data:
Shore, Kenneth.
  Special kids problem solver : ready-to-use interventions for
helping all students with academic, behavioral & physical problems /
Kenneth Shore.
      p. cm.
  Includes bibliographical references.
  ISBN 0-13-632-530-0
  ISBN 0-7879-6619-3 (layflat)
    1. Special education—Handbooks, manuals, etc. 2. Handicapped
children—Education—Handbooks, manuals, etc. 3. Learning disabled
children—Education—Handbooks, manuals, etc. 4. Problem children—
Education—Handbooks, manuals, etc. I. Title.
LC3969.S37 1998
371.9—dc21   98-26715

Printed in the United States of America
FIRST EDITION
HB Printing 10 9 8 7 6 5 4 3

TO MELISSA AND REBECCA

ABOUT THE AUTHOR

Dr. Kenneth Shore, a school psychologist for over 20 years, has helped teachers with school-related problems by providing practical strategies which take into account the pressures and constraints teachers face daily in their classrooms. He is also a family counselor who has assisted parents in helping their children succeed at school and at home.

He has written two books as well as many articles for professional journals and parenting magazines. His first book, *The Special Education Handbook: A Comprehensive Guide for Parents and Educators,* was published by Teachers College Press of Columbia University in 1986 and republished by Warner Books in 1988. His most recent book, *The Parents' Public School Handbook: How to Make the Most of Your Child's Education, from Kindergarten through Middle School,* was published by Simon & Schuster in 1994.

Dr. Shore has given many talks and appeared on numerous radio and television programs, including a wide-ranging interview on CNN and a PBS television series called *Raising Kids.*

INTRODUCTION

A teacher affects eternity; he never knows where his influence stops.
—Henry Adams

Teaching in today's classroom can be a daunting experience. The responsibilities of teachers seem to be increasing at the same time that resources for education are diminishing. In recent years, teachers have been expected more than ever to deal with a wide range of problems—from students with severe academic deficiencies to students whose first language is other than English to students suffering the effects of parental substance abuse. With the current trend toward inclusion, namely placing special education students in regular classes, teachers may find they are instructing students with problems for which they have little training or preparation.

This book is intended to fill that gap by giving teachers the tools to cope with common yet challenging classroom problems in the form of key information and practical strategies. While this book aims to help teachers resolve the problems of students with special needs, it is not a book about special education as much as it is about effective education. Indeed, many of the problems discussed are commonly found in regular education classrooms. This book is also not just for regular and special education teachers although that is the primary audience. It should also prove useful to others working with children in an educational context: principals, guidance counselors, school psychologists, learning specialists, school nurses, speech-language pathologists, classroom aides, and even camp personnel. In addition, parents of children with special needs may find the information and strategies helpful in making sure their children receive appropriate classroom instruction and support.

In determining what information to include, I used a need-to-know standard: What do teachers need to know to help the student perform or adjust better in class? Each chapter tackles a different problem, providing key information about the problem as well as a menu of classroom strategies. I have tried to select strategies that have proven useful to teachers and can be practically implemented in the classroom given the constraint of time and the demands of other students. Not every strategy will apply to every student with the problem. Some are appropriate for elementary students while others are better suited to secondary students. Some are to be used with students presenting the problem while others are intended to prevent the problem from occurring. Some can be implemented in regular classrooms while others are more feasible in special education classrooms. Use the strategies that suit your and the student's particular needs, and are compatible with your teaching values.

A few words about the organization of this book. It is divided into three sections: academic problems, behavioral problems, and physical problems. Because problems are multi-dimensional, the assignment of a problem to a section was to some extent arbitrary; some of the problems could have been placed in more than one section. Each chapter includes a list of references on the specific problem area and, if applicable, a list of relevant organizations. In addition, a See Also listing refers the reader to other chapters on related topics. In terms of writing style, I have tried to write with a maximum of clarity and a minimum of jargon. I have chosen to alternate the use of *he* and *she* when referring to students.

I want to acknowledge some people who have made important contributions to this book. First, I am indebted to the many educators with whom I have worked over the years and who have provided me with a special education in ways of working with students with special needs. The staff at Prentice Hall has been first-rate. I cannot imagine a better editor to work with than Susan Kolwicz, who has been involved with this book from the very beginning. She has been a model of professionalism, moving the book through the various stages of production with efficiency and always with consideration for my views. Her judgment has been impeccable and her insight invaluable. I am also grateful to Evan Holstrom for the clarity and precision that she brought to the editing of this book. In addition, my children, Melissa and Rebecca, deserve my thanks for their understanding during the times I was unavailable. Finally, I wish to express my appreciation to my wife Maxine, who provided unceasing encouragement and support during the writing of this book.

Kenneth Shore

CONTENTS

☞ SECTION 2 ☞
BEHAVIORAL PROBLEMS

➤ SECTION 3 ➤

PHYSICAL PROBLEMS

CEREBRAL PALSY / 275

CYSTIC FIBROSIS / 287

DIABETES / 293

EPILEPSY / 305

Hearing Impairment / 317

Spina Bifida / 328

Tourette Syndrome / 334

Visual Impairment / 341

ACADEMIC PROBLEMS

This section describes a variety of common problems that may affect students' academic performance. In some cases, these problems are specific to an academic subject (for example, reading disability or math anxiety) and in others they are in areas that support academic performance (for example, auditory processing or speech and language). A chapter has also been included on gifted students not because they display problems, but rather because they often require special accommodations by the teacher.

Your goal in working with these students is not simply to reinforce academic skills. It is also to help them become confident and eager learners. With their likely history of frustration, students with academic problems may be sensitive to their deficiencies and are at risk for losing confidence and being turned off to academic subjects. They may need emotional support and experience with success to help break this cycle of frustration and failure. In considering how to help them, make sure to take advantage of the expertise of school specialists (for example, the ESL teacher, the reading teacher, the gifted and talented teacher, or the speech-language pathologist).

The key to preventing student discouragement is to tailor instruction to their academic development rather than their chronological development, to where they are rather than how old they are. This requires giving them tasks that they can complete successfully as well as providing a feeling of satisfaction. In addition to structuring learning activities so they experience success, it is also vital to convey confidence in their ability to be successful to give them the courage to take risks.

Auditory Processing Problem

Good listening is an essential skill for students. Indeed, the majority of what children learn in school is acquired through the auditory channel. Some students, however, have a problem in their ability to listen. They may have what is called an auditory processing problem—namely, difficulty in understanding spoken language in the absence of a hearing problem. Auditory processing may go by other names such as central auditory processing, auditory comprehension, auditory perception, and receptive language.

Auditory processing is different from hearing. In fact, a student who has difficulty processing auditory information typically hears normally. She hears the sounds accurately but her brain has difficulty making sense of what her ear is telling it. Just as a child with a reading disability typically has good visual acuity but a problem interpreting visual symbols, a child with an auditory processing problem usually has adequate hearing but difficulty interpreting auditory information.

A student with an auditory processing problem may struggle in school, especially if listening conditions are less than optimal. She may misunderstand what you say or confuse one word for another. You may give her directions, and she may stare at you blankly, having little idea of what she is supposed to do. Or she may respond immediately and confidently, only to do the wrong thing. Questions may elicit irrelevant responses. The problem is likely to be accentuated when the message is long, complicated, or spoken rapidly, or when there is a lot of background noise.

Children with auditory processing problems are typically of normal intelligence but they are prone to learning problems, especially in the areas of reading, spelling, and writing. A student who has difficulty telling speech sounds apart (for example, *ba* and *da*) is at risk for a reading disability. This is not surprising, since the ability to sound out words requires that a child be able to clearly hear the sounds that letters make. For some students, the sounds of the vowels and consonants may come at them too quickly for them to process accurately. A novel treatment approach that has shown promise in improving reading skills for students with this problem involves using computers to slow down and exaggerate different sounds, enabling them to discriminate sounds and decode words more accurately.

An auditory processing problem can take various forms. A child can exhibit weakness in one or more of the following areas:

- *Auditory attention*: The child will have difficulty attending to information presented orally.

- *Auditory figure-ground*: The child will have difficulty understanding when there is background noise.

- *Auditory discrimination*: The child will have difficulty hearing the differences between sounds or words that are close to each other. As a result, she may have trouble learning letter sounds and names as well as names of people, places, and things. She may also struggle with reading, writing, and spelling.

- *Auditory memory*: The child will have difficulty remembering information that she hears such as letter names, names of classmates, her address and phone number, and directions. The information does not stick, so it is unavailable when she goes to retrieve it.

- *Auditory concepts*: The child will have difficulty understanding conceptual information presented orally, which may cause the student to have problems understanding riddles, grasping nuances from conversations, or comprehending abstract information.

Auditory processing problems may also vary in degree. The problem may be so mild that it does not surface until a child is well into school. Many children learn to compensate for these relatively minor problems by gaining meaning from the context, so the problem may become apparent only when they are exposed to complicated verbal messages. Or the problem may be at the other end of the spectrum. Students with severe auditory processing problems may have trouble understanding much of what they hear; they live in a virtual language fog, comparable to being in a foreign country with limited knowledge of the language. Some of these students may act out in class because of intense frustration and their lack of understanding of what to do.

IDENTIFYING AN AUDITORY PROCESSING PROBLEM

Identifying a child with an auditory processing problem can be tricky. Children may be poor listeners for a variety of reasons, not all of which are due to an auditory processing deficit. The following are characteristics of a child with an auditory processing problem:

- has difficulty following oral directions
- is often confused by questions
- responds to questions or comments with "what" or "huh"
- frequently asks for questions or directions to be repeated
- has difficulty understanding when there is background noise
- has trouble following conversations
- appears inattentive during class
- loses concentration easily as a result of random sounds
- struggles to understand abstract concepts presented orally
- often forgets what she has heard
- has problems with phonics and discriminating speech sounds

Some of these behaviors characterize students whose auditory processing skills are within the average range. For example, many students are distractible or need questions repeated on occasion. Children can be inattentive because they are bored with the subject or distressed about something. Also, keep in mind that some of these behaviors may signal the presence of other problems such as an ear infection, a hearing problem, an attention deficit disorder, or depression. You should be concerned about a possible auditory processing problem when a student demonstrates a consistent pattern of many of the above behaviors in different settings.

If one of your students is showing signs of an auditory processing problem, talk with your school's speech-language pathologist, who may observe the student in your class and conduct some tests to help pinpoint the nature of her difficulties. The procedure should be explained to parents, and their permission obtained, prior to the testing. The pathologist's testing of the student's expressive and receptive language skills will include her ability to follow directions and discriminate speech sounds. The pathologist may also recommend that further testing be done by an audiologist, a specialist in hearing and auditory processing. The hearing screening by the school nurse is a limited and superficial diagnostic tool; the student with suspected auditory problems will need a more comprehensive evaluation.

An audiologist will examine the student's hearing acuity and middle ear functioning. In addition, she or he will probably test the child's ability to understand spoken language with background noise and competing speech. The audiologist will test the child's auditory skills from the time the sound is heard by the external ear to the point at which it reaches the auditory cortex of the brain.

HOW TEACHERS CAN HELP

Taking steps to promote good listening skills presents a challenge to any teacher, but you can help students understand spoken language by varying the way you communicate and making subtle changes in the classroom setting. Simply telling the student with an auditory processing problem to "listen" or "pay attention" is usually not sufficient. The following strategies will not only help the student with an auditory processing deficit but may also assist other students with poor listening skills.

1. Seat the Student to Maximize Understanding

Place the student near you and the chalkboard, and avoid seating her near the hallway door or next to the window. In this way, she will be better able to understand your instruction and less vulnerable to distraction. Avoid standing in front of the window on a sunny day while talking to your class, because it will be more difficult for students to see your face clearly.

2. Minimize Auditory and Visual Distractions

Do not place the student in an open classroom, because the distractions will impede her concentration. Closed classrooms, of course, are not free of distractions either. The student's attention may be diverted by noises from the pencil sharpener, shuffling of chairs, reading groups, students moving around class, and classroom conversation. Even mild noises like the hum of a heater may be distracting. While you certainly cannot eliminate all distractions, you may be able to lessen them by seating her away from major sources of noise and keeping classroom chatter to a minimum. Suggest to the student that she consider using ear plugs or a study carrel to block out distractions.

3. Gain the Student's Attention before You Speak to Her

This is especially important when you are giving assignments or directions, or introducing new ideas. If necessary, alert the student that you are about to begin speaking by calling her name or gently tapping her on the shoulder. Face the student and make sure she has eye contact with you. Vary your tone and volume as a way of maintaining the student's attention.

4. Speak in a Slow, Distinct Manner, Using Simple Vocabulary

Make directions and questions simple, brief, and concrete. Do not give the student more than one or two directions at a time, allowing her to complete those directions before giving more. If you must repeat directions, rephrase what you said rather than repeating them word for word. Emphasize key words, and try to use vocabulary consistently to lessen confusion. Present directions in the order to be done and introduce each direction with words to facilitate understanding such as *first*, *next*, or *last*. You will have to walk a fine line here. While you want to speak in a manner that the student can readily understand, at the same time you want to avoid overexaggerating or seeming to talk down to her.

5. Use Gestures to Reinforce What You Are Saying

Gestures and facial expressions serve to clarify and support your meaning. Make sure the gestures reinforce the key aspects of your communication. For example, if you want students to write down three examples of a noun, hold three fingers up.

6. Give the Student Extra Time to Process Information Presented Orally

The student may take somewhat longer to absorb and think about questions or directions, and thus may require more *wait time* from you than do other students.

7. Supplement Orally Presented Information with Written Information

This is especially important if you are giving lengthy or multistep directions. The student with auditory memory problems may remember the first or last step but lose the others. Write down the directions or assignments, or at least the key words, on the board, or provide a handout with the information. If you are presenting a lecture to your class, you may want to distribute outlines to your students or list the topics and key points on the board. You may also help students understand and remember what you say by the use of visual aids.

8. Explain Transitions Clearly

When shifting from one subject to another, make it clear that you are changing topics by saying, for example, "That ends our discussion of (name of topic). Now let's move on to talk about (name of new topic)." In discussing the new topic, begin by summarizing the main points. When finished with your lesson, review the main ideas. Also, review previously learned material prior to new lessons.

9. Monitor the Student's Understanding

Check the student's understanding periodically by having her repeat back your statements or asking her questions to assess her grasp of what you have said. Make sure that she really understands and is not just parroting what she has heard. If she has not understood, repeat what you have said, but simplify the syntax, grammar, and vocabulary. You might assign another student to regularly check her understanding of directions and assignments.

10. Show Patience with the Student Who Confuses Easily

Becoming frustrated with a student who has difficulty processing what you say will only compound her problem. Your impatience will increase her anxiety and make it more difficult for her to focus. Be understanding of her difficulty, and allow her to take occasional breaks from schoolwork to help her relax. Students with auditory processing problems must put forth more effort than their classmates to attend and listen in class, and can be fatigued and stressed by the effort. Give them some relief from classroom instruction by allowing them to get a drink of water, go to the bathroom, pass out papers, or serve as messengers.

11. Encourage the Student to Speak Up When She Is Unclear

Let her know that you expect her to tell you when she is confused or uncertain about directions or assignments. Make sure, however, that she does not abuse this by not paying attention when she first hears your instructions.

12. Give Students a Task to Foster Attention

If you are reading a story to your students, you can promote concentration and enhance comprehension by having them listen for specific information. For example, you might show the students three possible names of a book (one of which is the real title) prior to reading it and then ask them to guess the real title after hearing the story.

13. Find an Alternative to Taking Notes

The student with an auditory processing problem may have difficulty writing and listening at the same time. If so, you might photocopy your notes, or arrange for another student to take notes for the student with the difficulty. Another possible solution is a notebook with lined, three-holed paper that provides duplicate copies of each page. You can also allow the student to audiotape the class.

14. Help the Student Remember What She Hears

Speaking in short sentences and talking relatively slowly will enhance the student's ability to recall what you have said. Repeating what you have said or having the student repeat it to you or rehearse it will also help, as will having the student write the information down. If the student has difficulty remembering math facts, consider allowing her to use a calculator during tests or assignments. If she has problems recalling answers to specific questions you pose in class, give her possible answers to choose from, or ask questions with a number of correct answers.

15. In Severe Cases, Consider Using an FM Trainer

This is a wireless amplification device that transmits speech directly from a microphone worn by the teacher to an earpiece worn by the student, without interference from classroom noise. While this device is typically used for students with hearing impairments, it may also be helpful to students with auditory processing problems, whose hearing is intact.

16. Refer the Student for Speech and Language Therapy

While speech-language pathologists typically see students with speech articulation or expressive language problems, they may also work with students with auditory processing deficits. In an effort to improve the student's ability to understand spoken language, the speech-language pathologist may give the student exercises to improve her ability to understand directions of increasing length and complexity, to discriminate sounds, and to listen more effectively with background noise. Training these skills in isolation, however, may not help the student as much as teaching the student (and teacher) strategies to use in the classroom setting—as well as teaching the student functional language skills (for example, vocabulary, grammar, and conversational ability).

FOR FURTHER INFORMATION

Chermak, G. D., and Musiek, F. E. (1997). *Central Auditory Processing Disorders: New Perspectives.* San Diego: Singular Publishing.

Friedman, P. G. (1986). *Listening Processes: Attention, Understanding, Evaluation* (2d ed.). Washington, DC: National Education Association.

Gillet, P. (1993). *Auditory Processes* (rev. ed.). Novato, CA: Academic Therapy Publications.

Wolvin, A. D., and Coakley, C. G. (1995). *Listening* (5th ed.). Dubuque, IA: Brown & Benchmark.

ORGANIZATIONS

American Speech-Language-Hearing Association
10801 Rockville Pike
Rockville, MD 20852
1-800-638-8255

See also:
    Attention Deficit Disorder
    Cerebral Palsy
    Speech and Language Problems
    Hearing Impairment
    Stuttering

THE ESL STUDENT

With the increasing diversity of America's schools, teachers are educating more and more students for whom English is a second language (ESL). Students from different cultures make up a substantial percentage of the school population nationwide. There are almost 3 million ESL students in this country, and the number is growing. By one estimate, the number of students who speak English as a second language is increasing two and a half times as fast as those who speak English as their primary language. These students offer schools an opportunity to celebrate cultural diversity, but they also present challenges for teachers.

While schools have always played a special role in helping children from other cultures learn to speak English and assimilate into society, the demands upon schools to educate students with limited English proficiency have never been greater. Teachers face four primary challenges in working with ESL students: to help them gain academic skills; to support their learning of the English language; to help them adapt to the educational setting; and to help them adjust to the American culture without lessening their connection to their own cultural heritage.

Schools have not always succeeded in this mission, however. Indeed, the approach of schools for many years was to assume that students with limited English proficiency would naturally pick up the language by being exposed to it in the classroom, without formal language instruction. While some students were able to adapt to this approach, many did not. Even today, when formal language programs are more readily available, ESL students may have school adjustment difficulties and are at risk for dropping out. Students who quit school and fail to learn the language put themselves at a significant disadvantage; they have little ability to obtain meaningful employment and limited access to other opportunities in society.

To teach ESL students effectively, it is helpful to understand the experience of being educated in an unfamiliar language in an unfamiliar culture. These students may understand only a portion of what they hear, causing them to feel stupid, lonely, and out of touch. They may look different from their classmates, accentuating their feelings of being different and out of place—and socially they may feel out of step. They may lack not only the words to relate to peers but the appropriate social protocol.

This experience is even more daunting for the student who has recently arrived from another country. This student is facing an overwhelming set of obstacles that can send her into culture shock: a new country, a new language, a new home, unfamiliar customs, and strange food. With time, many learn to adjust and feel more comfortable, but the adjustment can be greatly eased by school staff who make a concerted effort to make them feel welcome, and convey confidence in their ability to succeed.

School is the primary place—and for some, may be the only place—where they learn to speak English. Outside school, they will spend time with friends and family, with whom they will typically speak in their native language. In school, their learning of English is not just confined to the English instruction classes; much of their language learning takes place as they interact with other students and listen to their teachers. Learning a language is as much a social process as it is an educational process. While formal language instruction is crucial, so, too, is using the language in social settings. Instruction in English cannot replace the experience of using English to communicate and express their needs, of practicing what they have learned. School is the place where this process happens. Your role is to try to structure the classroom experience in such a way that ESL students are interacting with those who speak English, to promote their language skills.

Having limited proficiency in English will complicate the learning of academic skills for ESL students; reading comprehension requires a good understanding of the language. While ESL students can typically learn to decode words capably, understanding what they read is a different matter. Even math can be difficult for the ESL student; you must use language to teach math, and the student must understand language to do word problems.

EDUCATIONAL PROGRAMS

Most ESL students receive some formal instruction in spoken English. This usually takes place in an ESL program or a bilingual education program. ESL instruction, which is offered in most school districts across the country, differs from bilingual education in the degree of exposure to English. In a typical ESL program, students may spend as much as one or two hours a day in a small group learning to speak English. They attend regular English-speaking classes for the remainder of the day. The goal is to help students master the language as quickly as possible by immersing them in English-speaking classes for the majority of the day and encouraging their use of the language with their classmates.

The goal of a bilingual program is not only to help students learn to speak English but also to preserve their facility in their native language, as well as their cultural heritage. Bilingual programs, which are most common in urban school districts, instruct students in both languages. Instruction in reading, writing, and math is provided in their native language so that they learn to master these basic skills on a par with their English-speaking peers. As their English skills improve, they should participate in more classes taught in English. The hope is that with time their English becomes good enough so they can attend all English-speaking classes. There is good reason for this: A child who is kept out of the mainstream of school is likely to be kept out of the mainstream of society. Some school districts with a large number of Spanish-speaking students have developed truly bilingual programs for students whose native language is English as well as for those whose native language is Spanish. With instruction provided in both languages, English-speaking students learn to speak Spanish and Spanish-speaking students learn to speak English.

Bilingual education has generated intense controversy. Supporters argue that it is critical for students to learn basic academic skills so they can do more advanced academic work. They claim that bilingual education fosters cultural parity by conveying respect for the customs and traditions of people from other countries. Critics contend that students stay in bilingual programs too long and thus do not become fluent in English. They maintain that the programs serve to divide students and prevent students who do not develop English fluency from participating in the mainstream of American life. Some have even taken the position that bilingual programs should be eliminated.

HOW TEACHERS CAN HELP

Having a student placed in your class who knows little English—and who may recently have come to this country—can be a daunting experience. In your efforts to understand and support these students, keep in mind that there is great variation among cultures and that ESL students may have very diverse educational needs. The strategies described below may help you in meeting these needs:

1. Pronounce the Student's Name Correctly

This may seem obvious, but mispronouncing her name may intensify her feelings of being a stranger in a strange land. Saying her name correctly will help the student feel welcome.

2. Recognize Any Biases You May Have

While we all like to consider ourselves fair-minded, it is the rare individual who does not have some stereotyped views of people from other cultures. There is a tendency to view differences as deficits. Be aware of your own cultural perceptions, and be careful that they do not limit your understanding of a child from that culture, or send biased messages to your other students. Be a positive role model for them in how to show respect and understanding for those from different cultures.

3. Assess the Student's English Proficiency

The ESL teacher or the parents may be able to help you determine how well the student speaks English. Keep a list of the vocabulary she has mastered as a way of gauging whether her English is improving. You might also use a tape recorder to record conversations with her periodically during the year, both to assess her progress and to show her how she has improved.

4. Have the Student Considered for an ESL or Bilingual Program

The ESL or bilingual instructor will probably give the student a test to assess her mastery of English. In considering the student's eligibility for these programs, it is important to make sure that she is actually proficient in another language and not just deficient in English. If the latter is the case, then she requires a remedial English class rather than bilingual or ESL instruction.

5. Find a Student or Staff Member Who Speaks the ESL Student's Native Language

If the ESL student speaks little or no English, this person will be available to interpret. In addition, knowing that another person in the school speaks the same language will lessen the student's feelings of isolation and give her somebody she can talk with easily. If no one in your school speaks the language, find a parent, community member, or student teacher from a nearby college who is willing to volunteer time periodically. This person will allow you to talk with the student and ask her questions, and thus show an interest in her and her background. This person might also talk with the class about the child's cultural heritage. If the student is willing, have her talk to the class and answer questions in her native language while the person translates.

6. Anticipate and Plan for Potential Trouble Spots

Review the student's school day, from the time she arrives in the morning until the time she boards the school bus to go home. Identify potential problem areas, and decide how you will deal with them. Be especially attentive to situations in which you are not available, such as the bus, lunch, and recess.

7. Arrange for Classmates to Help the ESL Student

Student "buddies" can free you from the need to constantly monitor the ESL student. In addition, she may be more open to receiving help from a classmate than from you. Assign students who are responsible, patient, and friendly. If possible, find students who speak the same language as the ESL student. You will have to find different buddies for different parts of the day. Select students to help out in the classroom, in the lunchroom, on the playground, and on the bus. Talk with each student about his or her specific responsibilities. The classroom buddy may have to point to the page that the class is on or use pictures to help the student understand instructions, or to assist the student during fire drills. The lunchroom helper may not only need to teach the ESL student about lunchroom protocol, but also may need to explain to her about unfamiliar foods. While you must be careful that you do not overburden the student helpers, most will enjoy the job and derive a sense of importance from helping a classmate.

8. Make the Student Feel Welcome

You can promote a sense of belonging and communicate acceptance by showing interest in the student's cultural heritage. If she seems receptive, ask her questions about her customs and invite her to bring in items of interest from her culture. Find out important holidays celebrated by the student, and avoid scheduling special events on those dates. You might put up signs in the classroom in the student's native language with some welcoming messages as well as a map of her country. Schools can do the same for parents by displaying signs greeting parents in the various languages of the school community.

9. Show Respect for Cultural Differences

Understanding cultural differences will allow you to make sense of the student's actions, and to respond in a sensitive and respectful manner. In many cultures (for example, Haiti, some Hispanic cultures, and Japan), it is a sign of disrespect for a child to make eye contact with the teacher. Similarly, children from some cultures may be more likely to nod or smile than speak to a teacher because talking directly to an adult may be perceived as a sign of disrespect. If you apply American standards to these behaviors, you might conclude that the students are shy or inattentive, when in fact they are conforming to the standards of their culture. As another example of the influence of cultural experience, children from countries that have been devastated by war and revolution may not be permitted to go on school overnights because of parental fears related to tragic events in their native countries. Failure of teachers to understand these cultural differences may give rise to inadvertent acts of disrespect, as has happened, for example, with teachers who have touched Vietnamese children on the tops of their heads—an inappropriate act in that culture. You can learn about these cultural do's and don'ts by talking with people familiar with that culture, such as the ESL or bilingual teacher, parents, community members, or other students.

10. Encourage Your Students to Learn about Their Own Cultural Heritage

While having someone from another culture offers a valuable learning experience for the whole class, it is also enriching to have students examine their own cultural heritage. If you have your students investigate their own backgrounds, they will see firsthand that they all come from different places around the world, and the ESL student will come to appreciate that she is more like other students. As the year goes along, find opportunities to refer to the different countries of origin represented in the classroom and to celebrate the contributions of people from various cultures. The following examples of classroom projects or assignments can help your students connect with their own cultural heritage:

- Put a map of the world on your bulletin board, and have students place pushpins on their countries of origin, with their names under the pins. This gives meaning to the study of geography.

- Ask students to interview a relative about their family origins, and have them prepare a written or oral report.

- Have students do a family tree or compile a family scrapbook, noting the countries of origin of family members.

- Assign students to do a report on a famous person from their country of origin and bring in pictures of the person that can be displayed on the classroom wall.

- Have students draw or paint pictures on themes related to their country of origin or culture. Make a collage of these pictures for display in the school.

- Ask students to bring in items of interest from their cultural heritage and create a multicultural display.

- Plan an international food festival, and ask students to bring in a dish representative of their cultural heritage.

- Use folklore to foster cultural understanding. Other countries have their own versions of stories well known to American students. For example, there are Russian, Chinese, and Vietnamese versions of *Cinderella*.

- Read books to the class from different countries and cultures. You will find that the themes resonate with your students, conveying the message that children in different cultures have many of the same interests, desires, and concerns.

11. Help Your Students Appreciate the Experience of an ESL Student

Arrange for an adult who speaks the student's native language to present a short lesson in that language. Have the ESL student help her classmates in understanding the lesson. This will help them to understand the difficulties of being an ESL student and to realize that failure to understand language is not due to lack of intelligence. After the lesson, discuss with the students how they felt, being educated in a language they did not understand.

12. Give the Student a Chance to Shine

A child who speaks English poorly or not at all may be perceived as incompetent by her classmates. Give them a chance to see her in a different light by having her read a story in her native language or teach her classmates some words in her own language. You might suggest that older students write an article for the school newspaper in their native language. Look for other areas where the student can shine. Is she talented at art? Does she sing well? Is she a skilled soccer player? Find opportunities to showcase the student's talents.

13. Teach Your Students Vocabulary in the ESL Student's Native Language

Conducting a lesson in the student's native language will validate the importance of her language and convey a sense of acceptance. It may even foster friendships by encouraging classmates to interact with her. If you lead the lesson, you will, of course, have to learn some vocabulary in the student's language. If the student feels comfortable, she can help instruct her classmates. You may prefer to have a person familiar with the language, such as a colleague, a community member, another student, or even the parents conduct the lesson. Consider having the students write some phrases in the ESL student's language, to give them a sense of what it is like to write in another language. Students will find it especially eye-opening to write in another alphabet.

14. Teach the ESL Student Practical Vocabulary

Knowing key words will ease her adjustment to school. Make sure she learns early such words as *student, teacher, principal, nurse, book, reading, math, writing, spelling, cafeteria, lunch, playground, recess,* and *bell.* You might label important objects in the classroom, such as the clock or chalkboard. Draw pictures on 4″ by 6″ index cards, or cut out pictures from magazines (or have classmates or parent volunteers help out with this), and put the name of the picture on the back. Maintain a box with the cards in the classroom, and keep adding to it with new cards. As the box grows, you may have to separate the cards by categories. As an alternative, encourage the student to create her own picture dictionary in a three-ring binder. Have her draw pictures or cut out pictures from magazines and glue them onto pages of the binder, writing the word under the picture in both languages.

15. Speak in a Normal Manner

Remember that you are not only teaching the student vocabulary when you speak to her; you are also modeling the way to speak. If you talk in an exaggerated manner for emphasis, you may find that the ESL student is doing the same.

16. Use Body Language to Teach Verbal Concepts

In teaching concepts such as *high* and *low* or *big* and *small*, reinforce what you say with gestures.

17. Assign Projects to Be Completed in Small Groups

When students are working together cooperatively, they must talk with one another. The ESL student may feel more comfortable speaking with peers in a small group. Choose carefully the students who will be in the group; you want students who do not dominate and give her a chance to participate.

18. Read to the Student as Often as Possible

If you have few opportunities to read to the student, arrange for other students or parent volunteers to do it. Find poems or stories to read that have patterns or rhythms, such as Dr. Seuss books. The child may join in stories with patterns, and they may hold her attention. Read books with pictures, which will help her understand the meaning. Find out what she prefers— whether it is poems, stories in areas of her interest, or articles from the news- paper—and do more of it.

19. Find Suitable Materials for the Student to Read on Her Own

ESL students with limited vocabulary and reading comprehension may be able to read books that are at a low reading level. Let the school li- brarian know the student's approximate reading level and areas of interest, and ask the librarian to identify appropriate high-interest, low-level books. You might also ask whether the library has any books in the student's native language.

20. Write Down Key Information

Because ESL students may miss oral directions, write important infor- mation on the board—homework assignments, details of special events, and items the student needs to bring home. If you expect your students to take notes, you may have to arrange for the ESL student to obtain notes from another student, or provide her with photocopies of your notes or overheads.

21. Don't Be Concerned if the Student Is Quiet

Students with limited proficiency in English may be reticent in class until they feel confident speaking up. This does not mean that they are not learning or that they are upset. In fact, they are probably observing very closely and absorbing new words and concepts. On the other hand, some ESL students may be naturally shy, so they may be less inclined to use English with their classmates than more sociable ESL students. These students will need special attention and encouragement from you.

22. Make Use of Computer Software with Speech Capability

Have the student use computer software that employs speech—both to give instructions and to repeat her responses. Many software programs offer the user a choice of languages so that the student can do the program in her native language and then repeat it in English. CD-ROM programs are available that allow students not only to read texts but to hear them spoken.

23. Build Trust and Rapport with the Student's Parents

Parents who speak little or no English are often reluctant to become involved in schools because of their lack of familiarity with the language and their lack of comfort with school officials. Develop rapport with them by showing respect for their concerns and sensitivity to their values and customs. In this way, you will help the parents feel a connection with the school and engender trust in its staff, which may indirectly spur the child's academic performance.

24. Encourage the Student's Parents to Become Involved in Her Education

Because the parents may have limited English skills themselves and may be intimidated at the prospect of meeting with school staff, you will probably have to go above and beyond your normal procedures to encourage their involvement. Consider some of the following steps:

- Send home parent communications in the student's native language. Ask one of the school district's language teachers to do the translation. Include information about your expectations of the student, homework routines, procedures for contacting you, and volunteering opportunities in the classroom.

- Facilitate their attendance at parent-teacher conferences by providing child-care services, transportation to and from the school, and interpreters.

- Suggest to the parents activities that they can do at home with their children, including books they might read to them and television programs their children might watch.

- Help the parents locate community resources. In particular, ask the school social worker to investigate educational programs to help the parents improve their command of the English language. The children are likely to make more progress learning English if their parents are also making an effort to learn it.

FOR FURTHER INFORMATION

Carrasquillo, A., and Rodriguez, V. (1996). *Language Minority Students in the Mainstream Classroom.* Multilingual Matters UK, distributed by Alpenbooks, Mukilteo, WA.

Clegg, J. (ed.) (1996). *Mainstreaming ESL: Case Studies in Integrating ESL Students Into the Mainstream Curriculum.* Multilingual Matters UK, distributed by Alpenbooks, Mukilteo, WA.

Culturegrams are four-page pamphlets that describe the customs and traditions of various countries. They cost $4 each and can be obtained by calling Kennedy Center Publications in Provo, Utah, at 1-800-528-6279.

Fradd, S. H. (1993). *Educating Limited English Proficient Special Needs Students.* Upper Saddle River, NJ: Prentice Hall.

Lee, C. C. (ed.). (1995). *Counseling for Diversity: A Guide for School Counselors and Related Professionals.* Boston: Allyn & Bacon.

Spangenberg-Urbschat, K., and Pritchard, R. (1994). *Kids Come in All Languages: Reading Instruction for ESL Students.* Newark, DE: International Reading Association. (Call 1-800-336-READ, ext. 266 to obtain a copy. The cost is $20.95, plus $3 for shipping.)

ORGANIZATIONS

Council for Exceptional Children
Division for Culturally and Linguistically Diverse Exceptional Learners (DDEL)
1920 Association Drive
Reston, VA 22091
1-703-264-9435

National Clearinghouse for Bilingual Education
1118 22nd Street, NW
Washington, DC 20037
1-202-467-0867

Teachers of English to Speakers of Other Languages (TESOL)
1600 Cameron Street, Suite 300
Alexandria, VA 22314
1-703-836-0774

See also:
    The Shy Student
    Speech and Language Problems

THE GIFTED STUDENT

Approximately 3 to 5 percent of students nationwide are said to be academically gifted; these students can master school subjects at a much faster pace, and at a greater level of proficiency, than their classmates. Being gifted is not a problem per se, but gifted students do have special needs, and teaching them presents special challenges. While school districts often provide special programs for these students, most gifted students spend the majority of their day in regular classes. The responsibility of tailoring instruction to meet their academic needs thus falls largely on the regular classroom teacher.

Teaching gifted students in a mixed-ability class poses two basic challenges for teachers: The first is to provide appropriate and stimulating instruction for the gifted students while at the same time meeting the needs of the other students, and the second is to expose the gifted students to advanced concepts and materials while not segregating them from their classmates. Accomplishing these two goals is a formidable task for teachers, and can require much time and effort.

While the intellectual abilities of gifted students must be cultivated if their full potential is to be realized, schools may be remiss in this area. Academic gifts may go undetected and intellects unchallenged. Some educators may cling to the idea that gifted students can make it on their own, and thus do not need any help. In addition, teachers typically feel pressure to give attention to students who may have trouble attaining the achievement levels required by the state. They may even ask their gifted students to assist them in this effort by tutoring some of their classmates. If teachers do try to adapt instruction for their gifted students, the form of enrichment often is to give them the same work given to other students in a larger dose or at a faster pace.

The student with the greatest potential may benefit the least from classroom instruction; she may feel bored by the slow pace of teaching and frustrated by the tediousness of the assignments. This poor fit between the student's needs and the classroom instruction may give rise to inattentiveness, withdrawal, poor study habits, and even behavior problems. She may wage a silent protest against the lack of academic challenge by not completing assignments and not participating in class discussions. In some cases, a teacher may mistakenly conclude that the student has a learning problem—

as happened to Einstein at the age of 12. Some gifted students become so discouraged with school that they quit before obtaining a high school diploma. It is estimated that as many as 10 percent of students who drop out are gifted.

Gifted students may also struggle socially. Their interests may differ from those of their classmates, and their values may depart from the norm. Peer acceptance may be lacking, as their classmates view them as strange, and esteem them only for their brains. In an effort to gain acceptance, gifted students may disguise their academic abilities by purposely giving wrong answers or not responding when they know the right answers. Gifted students are constantly faced with the dilemma of choosing between using their ability to their utmost or trying to fit in with their peers. Gifted students may also have a tenuous relationship with school staff. Teachers may see them as disrespectful because they challenge rules—or threatening because they ask questions the teachers cannot answer. It is not surprising, then, that some gifted students feel disconnected from their peers and misunderstood by their teachers.

IDENTIFYING GIFTED STUDENTS

When people think of gifted students, they typically think of children with exceptional reasoning ability and high academic achievement. Children can, of course, demonstrate exceptional promise in other than academic areas, from art to drama to leadership to athletics. This broader view of giftedness is based on the premise that there are many different kinds of intelligence. In this chapter, we focus on the student who is academically gifted.

The regular classroom teacher is often the first person to identify gifted students, so it is important that you understand their characteristics. A student who is academically gifted will display above-average academic skills and typically excel in three areas: reasoning ability, creativity, and task commitment. In particular, gifted students will demonstrate many of the following characteristics:

- exhibits an enjoyment of learning and a desire for knowledge

- has unusual powers of concentration

- has an excellent memory and a wealth of information

- grasps ideas quickly and easily

- perceives connections between seemingly unconnected ideas or events

- understands cause-and-effect relationships easily

- expresses herself well, using advanced vocabulary and complex sentences

- asks probing questions

- offers original ideas in solving problems

- has a broad range of interests

- has an advanced understanding of justice

While there is not universal agreement on the best way to assess giftedness, most school districts continue to use the intelligence, or IQ, test as the primary measure for determining eligibility for gifted programs. Individually administered tests are preferred over group tests, because the results are more reliable and trustworthy. Districts often require that students score at or above 130 (equal to the 98th percentile) on an IQ test to qualify for a gifted program.

Using the IQ test as the sole measure of giftedness has generated much criticism—and for good reason. While it is a good measure of thinking, the IQ test tells us little about other characteristics of giftedness such as creativity and persistence. It predicts academic success better than it does life success. Indeed, the majority of adults with notable careers scored below the 95th percentile on standardized tests while in school. As a result, legitimate candidates for gifted programs—including late bloomers, minority students, and disabled children—may be overlooked by a reliance on the IQ test. While some argue that the intelligence test should not be used at all, at a minimum the intelligence test should be supplemented by other measures such as an achievement test, a creativity test, a portfolio review, a behavioral observation, and teacher assessment.

EDUCATIONAL PROGRAMS FOR THE GIFTED

The educational experience of many gifted students provides convincing evidence that they cannot be left to fend for themselves educationally. Schools have an obligation to challenge them to be their best. Because there is no federal mandate for gifted education, the programs provided to gifted students vary markedly from state to state and school district to school district.

If gifted students are to realize their full potential, they must be instructed at a pace consistent with their abilities, exposed to materials and concepts that challenge their intellect, and allowed to pursue areas of special interest. In addition, they must have the opportunity to interact with others with similar talents, which may lessen their feelings of being different while stimulating their thinking. The role of the teacher in working with gifted students is not just to provide information but also to nurture their talents by giving them opportunities to learn through guided exploration and discovery. If you do that, students will hone their critical-thinking skills, learn to understand and tackle problems from a variety of perspectives, and develop leadership ability.

Programs for the gifted have given rise to much controversy. Many criticize them for being elitist—for giving special treatment to a select group of students and sending a message of mediocrity to those not selected. While it is true that segregating one group of students from another undermines an important mission of education to help children of diverse characteristics get along with one another, it is also true that gifted students merit special attention. Trying to balance these concerns, many school districts have opted for a more inclusionary approach, in which gifted students spend most of their day in a regular class but are pulled out for one or more hours per week for an enrichment program.

Following is a description of the various kinds of gifted programs typically found in public schools:

- *Cluster Groups*: A cluster group is made up of four to eight students of high ability who attend the same regular class. This flexible-grouping arrangement keeps gifted students in regular classes with students of mixed ability, but allows them to be grouped with other exceptional students in their areas of strength for part of the day. A cluster group differs from tracking in that students who are tracked are typically grouped together for most of the day. Ideally, regular classroom teachers have some training in teaching gifted students, so they can adapt the level and pace of instruction to the abilities of the students in the cluster group. A secondary benefit of cluster groups is that you may learn techniques of instruction that can be applied to the larger class.

▪ *Acceleration*: Exceptional elementary school students may be sent to a higher grade for a specific subject, or even skipped to the next grade for all subjects. Gifted secondary school students may bypass subjects in which they can demonstrate proficiency. Some may even graduate early from high school. While you will, of course, want to consider the impact of acceleration on the student's social development and confidence, studies have shown that students who are accelerated generally adjust well to the change.

▪ *Pull-out Program*: A student may be pulled out of her regular class for one or more hours per week to work in a small group with a teacher of the gifted who provides enrichment activities. Make sure that the student has an opportunity to learn important lessons that she missed (unless she already knows them), and be alert to signs of stress from the additional workload.

▪ *Special Class*: Some gifted students attend special classes with other gifted students for the entire day. While these classes lessen the need for individualizing instruction, they have the disadvantage of removing positive role models from regular classes.

▪ *Advanced Courses*: Academically talented high school students may be placed in honors or advanced placement courses, or even college courses. Schools may also arrange mentorships with community members in the student's area of interest.

HOW TEACHERS CAN HELP

1. Avoid Labeling the Student as Gifted

Do not refer to the student as *gifted* in her presence, or in the presence of other students. Similarly, avoid talking about *gifted* or *G/T* programs; instead, describe them as enrichment classes or independent studies. The term places unnecessary pressure and hard-to-meet expectations on the student and builds a barrier between her and other students. Moreover, it may engender resentment and low self-esteem in students who are not in the program. Instead of placing barriers between students, find ways to build bridges. Encourage the gifted student to be friendly with and reach out to her

classmates. Help her learn to listen to and respect others' views when working in small groups.

2. Develop a Written Educational Plan for the Student

While this need not be an elaborate document, the process may help you
think through how you will adapt your instruction to the student's needs.
Consider sharing this plan with the student's parents to get their feedback.
The plan might include a description of the student's abilities and interests;
the methods to be used to assess her mastery of the regular curriculum; and
the nature of the advanced work she will be completing. If you have a group
of gifted students in your class, you might develop one plan for all the students. If the student is pursuing an independent study, you may want to develop a contract with the student describing the project or activity, her
responsibilities, and the way she will be evaluated.

3. Allow the Student to Bypass Topics She Has Already Mastered

Many gifted students spend time in school learning about topics or concepts they already know. While you should not assume the student's mastery
of the skills and concepts you plan to teach, you might assess her proficiency
of the material and allow her to skip or get credit for topics your assessment
indicates she has mastered. You might do this by giving her a pretest, unit
test, end-of-year test, or a test you have designed for this purpose. If she
passes the test to your satisfaction, excuse her from the assignments and tests
for the topics she has mastered, and provide her with more advanced work or
independent projects in that subject. As an example, you might give the student a quiz or test prior to beginning a new section and require that she obtain a grade of B or above to be exempt from the instruction and assignments
of that section. If she does not receive at least a B, have her participate in the
class until you begin the next section, when you may want to test her on the
new material.

4. Provide the Student with More Advanced Work in Her Areas of Strength

As much as possible, relieve the gifted student of the more mundane assignments covering skills or concepts she already knows, and give her tasks
that expand her understanding of the subject matter and emphasize critical
thinking. Keep in mind that a student should be accelerated only in subjects

in which she has excelled. Thus, a student may receive advanced work in math but follow the regular curriculum in other subjects. You can adapt the student's instruction in various ways. First, you can alter the pace of instruction by having her cover the same material as other students but in a shorter time, or by eliminating some of the material. This is called curriculum compacting. Most teachers can learn to compact the curriculum with as little as one hour of training. Curriculum compacting has proven especially effective in math and spelling. Second, you can alter the level of instruction by giving her a more in-depth understanding of the topic through exposure to new materials and more advanced concepts. Third, you can alter the instructional approach by, for example, having her do an independent study on a related topic (see item 5). Whatever strategy you pursue, monitor to ensure that the student is not feeling overwhelmed.

5. Allow the Student to Pursue a Topic of Interest to Her Through an Independent Project

The purpose of an independent study is to help the student become a self-starter and firsthand inquirer, and to promote resourcefulness. It also promotes self-esteem by endowing the student with the status of class expert on the topic. Begin by identifying the student's interests, and work with her to decide on a topic to investigate in depth. Depending on the age of the student, you may have to guide her in learning the research and library skills needed to pursue the project. As she works on this project, you will find that you are functioning less as an instructor and more as a facilitator of learning. Let her struggle with how to investigate the topic and manage her time, while encouraging her to ask for help when needed. Monitor the student's progress and offer suggestions, but refrain from taking over. The project may culminate in a presentation to the class or a school display.

6. Have the Student Tackle Real Problems

By grappling with practical issues and considering potential solutions, the student will find the project more meaningful and enjoyable. Rather than just feeding back information, she will be experimenting with ways of solving actual problems. For example, a student with a passion for science may be given the task of investigating and evaluating alternative energy sources. In an effort to promote concern and compassion for others, steer gifted students toward social issues affecting the local community or the larger society.

7. Promote Learning through Guided Exploration and Self-Discovery

Gifted students are usually excellent candidates for learning using the discovery method of instruction. Rather than lecturing to the student, you present her with situations or problems and ask a series of probing questions that lead to her discovery and understanding of important principles. You stimulate curiosity and thought by responding to the student's questions with answers that pose additional challenges. Television's Mr. Wizard used this discovery approach very effectively to teach students about science. The goal is to help the student become an independent, self-directed learner who can use critical thinking skills to learn important principles or information.

8. Supplement the Reading Texts with High-Quality Literature

The gifted student may be able to read by the time she enters school, so her reading instruction may have to be individualized. Failure to give her stimulating or challenging instruction may dampen her enthusiasm for reading. If you feel that she has mastered the basics of reading, ask the principal for permission to use literature in place of the regular basal readers. Allow the student to select books to read that reflect her interests, her preferred genre, and her favorite authors. If you want to exert some control over what she reads, have her choose from a group of challenging books that you or the librarian select, based on her interests and her reading ability. In discussing books with the student, talk about ideas and themes rather than just discussing facts and plot summaries. You might investigate using the Junior Great Books Program, which teaches students from grades 2 through 12 to apply critical thinking skills to the understanding of literature. The process of reading critically can be reinforced through the use of reading guides, which provide questions for the student to consider about issues, values, and techniques. For example, the student may be asked to identify strategies used by the writer to sway the reader's views, or to assess whether the conflict was resolved in a realistic manner.

9. Allow the Student Some Control over Educational Decisions

The gifted student is likely to be more invested in academic tasks if she has some say in helping to choose or design the assignment. For example, if the student has scored high on the spelling pretest given to your class, you might excuse her from studying those words, and instead let her select more advanced words to study. Allowing the student to make some decisions about the learning process is an expression of your trust in her, and helps her learn by seeing the consequences of her decisions. This, of course, does not mean that you should give the student total freedom. You can exert some control by having her choose from a range of options you present to her. While you should review the student's progress, also ask her to evaluate and critique her own work.

10. Consider Sending the Student to a Higher Grade in Her Strong Subject(s)

If you have a student who is particularly advanced in one subject, you may want to arrange for her to go to a higher grade for instruction in that subject. For example, a first grader might go to second grade for reading, but remain in first grade for all other subjects.

11. Find Alternate Settings for the Student to Pursue Her Talents

Talk with her parents about programs or activities in or out of school that might further develop her skills. This might include a school club, a science or art fair, a community program, private lessons, or a class at another school or institution.

12. Find a Mentor to Guide the Student

Mentoring, or pairing a student with an adult with expertise in her area of interest, can be an excellent learning experience. Arranging this will require some legwork on the school's part but it is likely to be time well spent. The mentor might be a teacher, administrator, or community member. The mentorship plan should be flexible, although it should include regularly scheduled meetings between the mentor and student, either during or after school. It should also include a written plan describing the goals and activities of the mentorship, the responsibilities of the mentor and the student, and the way in which the student will be evaluated.

13. Evaluate the Student's Progress in Nontraditional Ways

Consider evaluating the student's progress in her accelerated program or independent study in ways other than tests. For example, she might demonstrate what she has learned by making a presentation to the class, doing a project for school display, designing an invention, developing a game, creating a home page for the computer, writing a song or a play, or conducting a survey. Look for opportunities to showcase what the student has done. Gifted students often like the chance to show what they know.

14. Nurture the Student's Emotional as Well as Cognitive Development

You may have a student who started reading demanding novels in fourth grade or is able to multiply two-digit numbers in her head, but she probably has the same needs for emotional support and peer acceptance as her classmates. Be sensitive to the pressures the student may be feeling, and be aware that even gifted students may display little self-confidence and low self-esteem. It is not unusual for a gifted student to feel stress or pressure because of the high expectations she perceives from others, especially if her parents have focused on her need to fulfill her potential, or have boasted of or showcased her talents for others. As the great philosopher Linus said to Charlie Brown: "There's no heavier burden than great potential." Giftedness may also give rise to other problems that warrant your attention: isolation from peers, feelings of being misunderstood by teachers, and perfectionist tendencies.

15. Avoid Pigeonholing Girls Who Are Gifted

Even the most enlightened of teachers can engage in sexual stereotyping. This may take the form of steering students toward certain subjects or careers, or away from others. Boys who challenge the teacher's views and ask many questions may be viewed as assertive and confident, while girls who display the same behaviors may be seen as aggressive and even unfeminine. Show respect for the competency of girls—especially in areas that are typically male dominated. If they show an interest in math or science, for example, support and encourage them. Give attention to their performance, encourage their questions in class, and do not let boys dominate the class discussion. (Studies show that teachers tend to interact more with boys than girls in math and science classes.) Make sure that girls are not hesitant to speak up for fear of being embarrassed by a classmate. A few words of encouragement after class may help them feel more comfortable participating, and more confident in their abilities.

16. Encourage the Student to Take Risks

Some students of high ability are reluctant to take on challenges for fear of failing. As a result, they may lose out on worthwhile educational experiences, which may result in underachievement. Encourage them to take chances by expressing confidence in their abilities, but be available to support them if they fail. An experience of failure is not without value; it can help a student learn to cope with defeat and frustration, which may be a unique experience for gifted students. Remember to avoid talking about the student as gifted in her presence; the pressure to maintain that status may cause her to sidestep challenges out of fear that she will be exposed as not really gifted.

17. Expect the Student to Follow Your Rules

While gifted students may be more likely to challenge rules and seek explanations for them, they should be expected to abide by them. Similarly, they should be held to the same standards of courtesy that you have for all students. Avoid giving in to a student's arguments or pleas unless you believe they have genuine merit. If you do, you will be teaching her that rules are not to be respected.

18. Respect and Encourage the Student's Questions and Comments

Show interest in the student's thoughts by being respectful of her questions and comments—even those that are different or novel. The gifted student may ask some unusual or odd questions. Take them seriously, and do not let others make fun of her. If you cannot answer her questions, suggest to her ways of finding the answer by identifying potential resources. Allow the student to debate issues—to a point. Bright children often want to contest every point, and often do so with the skill of a Clarence Darrow. Once the student has had her say, allow a classmate to speak or bring the discussion to a close.

19. Obtain Help from a Specialist in Gifted Education

Your school's teacher of the gifted (sometimes called an enrichment specialist) is likely to be a good resource for you in adapting your instuction for a gifted student. The specialist should be able to suggest to you enrichment materials and special projects that you can pursue with the student. If your school does not have a teacher of the gifted, contact your state's department of education to seek help from a consultant in gifted education.

FOR FURTHER INFORMATION

Daniel, N., and Cox, J. (1988). *Flexible Pacing for Able Learners*. Reston, VA: Council for Exceptional Children.

Davis, G. A., and Rimm, S. B. (1997). *Education of the Gifted and Talented* (4th ed.). Old Tappan, NJ: Prentice-Hall/Allyn & Bacon.

Halsted, J. W. (1994). *Some of My Best Friends Are Books: Guiding Gifted Readers.* Scottsdale, AZ: Gifted Psychology Press.

Schmitz, C. C., and Galbraith, J. (1985). *Managing the Social and Emotional Needs of the Gifted: A Teacher's Survival Guide.* Minneapolis, MN: Free Spirit Publishing.

Winebrenner, S. (1992). *Teaching Gifted Kids in the Regular Classroom.* Minneapolis, MN: Free Spirit Publishing.

ORGANIZATIONS

The American Association for Gifted Children
Duke University
1121 W. Main Street, Suite 100
Durham, NC 27701
1-919-683-1400

Association for Gifted and Talented Students
P.O. Box 16037
Louisiana State University
Baton Rouge, LA 70893
1-800-626-8811
1-504-388-2469

National Research Center on the Gifted and Talented
University of Connecticut
362 Fairfield Road
Storrs, CT 06269-2007
1-860-486-4676

See also:
   The Perfectionist Student
   The Unmotivated Student

Handwriting Problem

In this age of computers, handwriting is struggling to maintain its place in the educational landscape. Teachers today devote less attention to handwriting instruction, and students spend less time practicing penmanship than in the past. This shift in focus may not pose difficulties for students for whom handwriting comes naturally; for students with fine-motor difficulties, however, it can spell problems. The student who exhibits poor handwriting may become exasperated with written tasks. In addition, his handwriting deficiency may interfere with his written expression. As a result, what he puts down on paper may reflect only a small part of what he knows. For this student, and many others, the ability to write legibly and fluently is essential to school success, and formal handwriting instruction continues to be an important part of their education.

IDENTIFYING A HANDWRITING PROBLEM

Handwriting has various components: size of letters, shape, spacing, slant, and proportion. The student with poor handwriting may have difficulty in one or more of these areas, which may decrease legibility. In particular, he may exhibit some of the following characteristics:

- expends much effort writing
- produces papers that are messy and difficult to read
- has a poor pencil grip
- uses too little or too much pencil pressure
- writes letters incorrectly (particularly a, e, r, and t)
- forms letters that are too small or too large
- slants cursive letters improperly
- uses upper- and/or lower-case letters incorrectly
- writes very quickly or very slowly
- allows too little space between words or letters

35

- uses both manuscript and cursive in the same assignment
- produces words that do not rest on the line
- erases excessively
- has trouble copying from the board or a book

Difficulty with handwriting, often called dysgraphia, may reflect problems with visual perception and memory, spatial relations, or fine-motor control. These problems may impede the student's ability to retain the shapes of letters or the sequence of strokes needed to make them, or interfere with his ability to execute them accurately. Children with attention deficit disorder, who exhibit impulsivity and inattention, and those with neurological problems, including cerebral palsy, are especially prone to handwriting problems. Of course, poor handwriting problems may also reflect inadequate or faulty teaching.

HANDWRITING INSTRUCTION

The goal of handwriting instruction is to teach students to write in a legible manner with reasonable speed. While formal instruction may not begin until first grade, kindergarten students will typically learn to write their names, most letters, and some numbers. First graders will focus on learning manuscript, or printing. At the end of second grade or the beginning of third, students will start to learn cursive writing. Little handwriting instruction is provided after third grade.

Many students welcome the introduction of cursive writing. They may perceive learning to write in script as a big step up in the world of school and a sign that they are growing up. Some students with learning problems may even find cursive easier than manuscript because of its rhythmical flow. Others, however, find it awkward, frustrating, and slow-going, and continue to use print.

In assessing the student's progress with handwriting, keep in mind that his ability to write legibly during handwriting exercises is not sufficient. He must also demonstrate legible handwriting in his daily work. It is not uncommon for a student to produce near-perfect penmanship during handwriting drills and barely legible handwriting on his assignments. This may occur because his head is working faster than his hand, causing him to write quickly and carelessly. You may see this with gifted students and those with attention deficit disorder. Pay attention to this in your instruction. As the student masters the formation of letters, encourage him to build up speed without lessening legibility.

HOW TEACHERS CAN HELP

In helping a student with handwriting problems, keep in mind that legibility is the most important goal. Because poor letter formation impedes legibility more than any other factor, it is important to teach the correct way of writing letters. This should be done as soon as the student is developmentally ready because of the difficulty in breaking him of bad handwriting habits. It is also important to pay attention to his level of frustration. The student who has come to dread writing tasks will find ways to avoid them. The following strategies should help improve his handwriting skills and ease his frustration:

1. Provide Young Students with Fine-Motor Activities

Be careful about giving writing tasks to students who are not ready for them. If they are struggling with basic writing skills and showing signs of frustration, take a step back and give them fine-motor tasks to promote eye-hand coordination and strengthen small-muscle control. To this end, you might have them color, paint, draw, cut with scissors, model with clay, string beads, engage in sewing or lacing activities, and play catch with a ball.

2. Attend to the Basics

Make sure the student is prepared to write properly. His desk and chair should be at a height that allows him to place his forearms on the desk and his feet on the floor. His elbows should be slightly extended. Show him how to hold a pencil—between his thumb and middle finger, with his index finger on top applying the pressure, and about an inch above the point. Also, demonstrate how to position the paper—straight in front of him for manuscript and slanted for cursive (to the left for a right-handed student and to the right for a left-handed student). You may have to put a piece of tape on his desk to guide him in the placement of the paper. Have him hold the top of the paper with his nonwriting hand; if necessary, tape the paper to the desk. Get the student in the habit of having a sharpened pencil and an eraser on his desk.

3. Communicate Your Writing Standards Clearly

Explain to the student the writing procedures you want him to follow, including the following:

- heading at top of the paper

- size of the margin

- space between items or problems

- whether to write on one or both sides

- whether to cross out, erase, or use editing marks (if they have been learned)

- what characteristics of his writing will cause you to require him to rewrite it

4. Reinforce Retention through a Multisensory Approach

Techniques of instruction that use more than one sense promote retention of letters and develop "muscle memory." In this way, the student comes to write letters automatically and effortlessly. The following are some examples of multisensory strategies:

- Create large letters on the floor, and have the student trace them with his body by walking on them.

- Have the student write letters in the air or on the back of a classmate. Have him write the letters with large arm movements initially, and then progress to much smaller movements. Small-muscle skills often are learned best when they are done with large muscles first.

- Have the student trace with his finger "raised" letters or letters that are textured, such as sandpaper letters. Tactile letters are also available; they feel smooth when traced in the right direction and rough when traced in the wrong direction.

- You can obtain molded plastic letters that allow the student to run his finger in their grooves to feel their shapes. The plastic letters may also come with a steel ball that, when nudged by the student, moves through the grooves while tracing the letters.

- Have the student write letters in materials such as sand, salt, or shaving cream placed in a shoebox or pan, or have him write letters while fingerpainting.

- Have the student form letters on the chalkboard using his finger or a flashlight beam.

- Have the student form letters using pipe cleaners, yarn, rope, or modeling clay.

As the student writes or traces these letters, have him describe his movements out loud, perhaps with your assistance.

5. Use Special Materials

In considering which materials to use in teaching handwriting, avoid adhering to rigid rules. Let the student's preferences and comfort level guide you. The following are some examples of materials you may want to use:

- *Pencil Grip*: Placing a grip on the pencil may enable the student to hold it more effectively. Grips come in different shapes. With older students, you might put a rubber band or tape around the pencil so it looks more adult.

- *Writing Implements*: Have the student change pencil types if his writing is too heavy or too light, or suggest that he use a mechanical pencil. If he is interested, have him use a beginner's pencil, which has a somewhat larger diameter. Let him make the choice; research does not indicate that children necessarily perform better with beginner's pencils. Allow him to switch to a ballpoint or felt-tipped pen around third grade if he finds that more comfortable.

- *Wide-Lined Paper*: Use this for a student at the beginning stages of learning printing and cursive. Phase out its use when he no longer needs it.

- *Computer Paper*: Using computer paper (with the alternating green and white lines) may help the student write letters at the correct height. It is also less fragile than the newsprint-quality paper often used in early elementary grades, and thus less likely to tear. (Have transparent tape handy to repair torn papers.) You can create regular paper out of computer paper by trimming it with a paper cutter and punching holes in it.

- *Other Papers*: Paper with raised lines is useful with a student whose letters tend to go above or below the line. In addition, paper with color-coded lines can help him stay within certain guidelines. For example, paper is available with lines of three colors: The green bottom line indicates where the student starts, the yellow midline is a caution line, and the red top line indicates where he stops. Graph paper works well if the student has spatial problems. You can add interest to writing exercises by using paper of different sizes, colors, and shapes. You might even have the student write on stationery that you have created on the computer.

- *Individual Chalkboards*: Chalkboards of varying sizes can be used by students to practice handwriting at their desk.

6. Model Good Handwriting

Show the student how to form letters correctly through your own handwriting—whether it is on the board, on worksheets, or on your comments on his papers.

7. Demonstrate Correct Handwriting While Describing Your Movements

As you model for the student the correct formation of letters, reinforce what he is seeing by verbalizing the sequence of strokes. You might begin by forming letters with large motions in the air and then demonstrating them on the board or with an overhead projector, perhaps placing the student's hand on yours as you form the letters. Have him go through a sequence of steps: tracing over the letter you have written on the board, copying the letter from your model, and finally writing the letter without a model. In each case, have him verbalize the motions as he does them. You may find that you need to guide the student by placing your hand over his hand as he forms the letter. You might give him cues by placing on your model a dot to indicate where to begin and arrows to indicate the direction to go in. Watch his performance to see if he is forming the letters correctly and making the strokes in the correct sequence. Provide corrective feedback, if necessary. Have him practice upper- and lower-case versions of a letter at the same time so he learns to associate them with each other.

8. Have the Student Practice Handwriting through Meaningful Writing

Handwriting is taught more effectively in the context of writing tasks than in isolated drills. As soon as the student is able, have him write words and sentences rather than individual letters. Also, have him write about themes that are personally meaningful to him. Begin with his name, and then move on to his address and the names of family members. You might also have him write sentences about topics he enjoys, for example, his pet or his baseball card collection.

9. Allow the Student to Write in Comfort

While the student with handwriting difficulties should be exposed to both manuscript and cursive, let him use the form of writing that is most comfortable for him. Students in secondary school often find cursive writing more awkward than manuscript; if so, allow them to print. In addition, do not make an issue of it if the student's style of writing deviates from the model you presented as long as it is legible. Almost all students develop their own unique style of writing.

10. Ease up on the Amount of Writing Required

Lessen the need for the student with handwriting problems to write by allowing him to record and present information in other than written form. Permit him to tape lessons in your class, or arrange for a student to take notes for him (see item 13). Also, allow him to demonstrate his knowledge in non-written form (for example, giving an oral report, doing a report on tape rather than on paper, or making an art project). If he tapes a report, try to arrange for someone to transcribe it, perhaps a parent volunteer or aide. You might also ease the student's writing demands by providing handouts with information rather than expecting him to write the information down (for example, directions for a long-term project). While you certainly don't want to excuse the student from all writing, make sure the content is meaningful and the length reasonable. Avoid written busywork.

11. Encourage Neatness, but Keep It in Perspective

If a student consistently produces messy work, talk with him about the importance of neatness. Let him know that a neat paper conveys a good impression and a sloppy paper suggests a lack of care or effort. Tell him that teachers are likely to evaluate his written reports more positively if they can be easily read. Give examples of real-life situations where sloppy writing may pose a problem for him in the future (for example, a college or job application). At the same time, do not emphasize neatness at the expense of content. Always keep in mind that the substance of his writing is more important than the form. When marking a paper, grade him on content, not neatness. Or consider giving him two grades, one for content and one for neatness, perhaps recording the latter with a plus or minus in your gradebook. Avoid having the student with a handwriting problem do the paper over if his writing is legible. His rewrite may not be any neater.

12. Encourage Students to Write with a Computer

The student who has difficulty writing legibly will benefit from learning to write with a computer. Even young children can be taught to type on a keyboard and use a word processing program. The student who uses a computer will be less distracted by the mechanics of writing and better able to focus on content. He may also be more motivated to write, especially because of access to graphics and a range of fonts—and, of course, his work will be easier to read. Allow students, particularly those in the upper grades, to hand in homework that is done on a computer, and permit older students to take notes in class using laptops. Voice-recognition software, which converts the spoken work into print, is becoming increasingly sophisticated and easier to use, and in the near future will very likely be a great asset to individuals with handwriting problems.

13. Arrange a Note Taker for the Student

The student with a handwriting problem may have difficulty taking notes and listening at the same time. In addition, copying notes from the board may take him much longer than it does his classmates. If so, photocopy your notes for the student, or arrange for a willing, conscientious classmate to take notes for him. You can obtain notebooks with lined, three-holed paper that provide duplicate copies of each page. NCR paper can also be used for this purpose. Do not simply tell the student to ask a classmate to take notes for him, especially if he has few friends in the class. Make the arrangements for him. You may want to tell the note taker that you would like a copy of his notes to assist another student without identifying the recipient. As an alternative, allow the student to audiotape the class.

14. Offer Alternatives to Written Tests

The student with handwriting problems may be at a disadvantage in taking tests. Consider the following accommodations so that his test results reflect his knowledge more than his handwriting ability:

- Allow the student to take oral exams instead of written exams.

- Allow the student to take oral exams in addition to written exams, and then combine the scores to obtain one grade.

- Allow the student to take tests on a computer.

- Provide the student with tests that require minimal writing (for example, a fill-in-the-blank or multiple-choice test).

- On some standardized tests, the student with visual perceptual problems may have difficulty moving his eyes from the question to the appropriate response box. Have him use a ruler to place under the question to guide him to the correct response box.

15. Make Accommodations in Math

Handwriting problems can cause the student difficulty on math assignments or tests. He may have trouble copying problems on paper accurately, lining up columns of numbers correctly, or using allotted space efficiently. If he has problems copying, give him handouts with the problems on them. If he has problems lining up columns, have him use graph paper or regular lined paper that is turned sideways so the lines are vertical. If he has problems using space, have him leave three or four lines between problems, have him fold the paper into quarters or eighths and place a different problem in each folded area, or give him a worksheet with boxes for each problem.

16. Show the Student Evidence of His Progress

Keep samples of the student's handwriting from early in the year, and periodically compare his current efforts with the earlier samples to show him how he has improved. Recognize his handwriting successes by praising specific aspects of his performance and posting his best efforts on the bulletin board. If he hands in papers with handwriting that is well below his best work, show him positive samples of his handwriting, and let him know you think he can do better.

17. Do Not Use Writing Exercises as a Form of Discipline

Making students write one line over and over or copy passages from a book as a disciplinary measure may deter misbehavior, but it may also turn them off to the process of writing. This is not a tradeoff you want to make.

Find disciplinary measures that do not have undesirable academic consequences.

18. Some Miscellaneous Tips

The following additional suggestions may be helpful to you in working with a student with handwriting problems:

- Seat the left-handed student so that his arm does not hit his neighbor's arm while he is writing.

- Place a commercial tape of letters, either cursive or manuscript, on the student's desk. Cards that have manuscript letters on one side and cursive letters on the other are also available for students to keep at their desks.

- Help the student retain the visual images of letters by having him associate the shape of a letter with an object (for example, A with a teepee and h with a chair).

- Have the student practice in a group letters with similar features (for example, g, p, and y).

- Indicate where the student should begin writing by placing a green mark on the paper, and where to stop by placing a red mark.

- Have the student begin writing on the second line, with the top line serving as an upper limit for his writing.

- If the student does not leave enough space between words, teach him how to "fingerspace" to measure the appropriate space. Have him place one finger from his nonwriting hand after each word he has just written and then write the next word. With a left-handed student, for whom this is more difficult, have him use a die or a popsicle stick instead of his finger.

- If the student is receiving handwriting instruction in both a regular and special education class, talk with the other teacher to make sure you and that teacher are instructing him in compatible methods of handwriting.

FOR FURTHER INFORMATION

Hablitzel, M., and Stitzer, K. (1997). *Draw—Write—Now, Book 4: A Drawing and Handwriting Course for Kids!* Poulsbo, WA: Barker Creek Publishing Co.

Hanft, B., and Marsh, D. (1993). *Getting a Grip on Handwriting*. Bethesda, MD: American Occupational Therapy Association.

Levine, K. J. (1991). *Fine Motor Dysfunction: Therapeutic Strategies in the Classroom*. San Antonio, TX: Therapy Skill Builders. (To order, call 1-800-211-8378.)

Pendergrass, C. R. (1994). *Writing Right! Book 1: Manuscript*. Phoenix, NY: Pendergrass Publishing Co.

Pendergrass, C. R. (1994). *Writing Right! Book 2: Cursive*. Phoenix, NY: Pendergrass Publishing Co.

Rubell, B. (1995). *Big Strokes for Little Folks*. San Antonio, TX: Therapy Skill Builders. (To order, call 1-800-211-8378.)

ORGANIZATIONS

American Occupational Therapy Association
PO Box 31220
Bethesda, MD 20824-1220
1-301-652-2682

See also:
    Attention Deficit Disorder
    Cerebral Palsy
    Reading Disability
    Spelling Problem

MATH ANXIETY

Math, more than any other subject, engenders anxiety and avoidance in students. The mere mention of the "m" word is enough to send the blood pressure of some students skyrocketing. While it is normal for students to experience some insecurity about school subjects, math anxiety can be extreme, and may hamper performance. The anxious student, convinced of her inability to do math, may avoid the subject or put forth little effort, leaving significant gaps in her math development. Difficulty mounts as she confronts more advanced skills, causing further anxiety and avoidance. What begins as a mild case of math avoidance can become a severe case of math anxiety.

Students with math anxiety have confidence in only one thing related to math—their inability to do it. This belief may turn into an emotional block, causing a form of mental paralysis. The brain seems to shut down when it detects a math concept. Fear and anxiety take the place of clear thinking, and the need to avoid looking stupid before peers becomes paramount. Math anxiety can propel the student into a downward spiral. Bewildered by the math concepts, she has difficulty focusing, contributing to further difficulties in understanding. Anxiety increases and confidence declines. The student abandons her effort to understand the concept and becomes preoccupied with obtaining the right answer. The search for understanding gives way to a reliance on memorization, yet rote memorization gives the student a limited understanding of math and restricts her ability to apply these skills to various situations. A teacher tells the story of a kindergarten student who dazzled his classmates by counting to 50, only to turn to the teacher and ask, "What's a fifty?"

Unless math anxiety is confronted, it can turn into a permanent block. You can help chip away at this block by providing individualized academic support and bolstering the student's confidence. A simple "you can do it" is not sufficient, however; you must prove to the student, by exposing her to a variety of success experiences, that she is more able than she thinks in doing math. In addition, instruction should move toward a real-life approach to math—with more stress on understanding and less on memorization, more on application and less on computation, and more on student participation and less on teacher lecture.

While the causes of math anxiety are often elusive, parents play an important role in shaping a child's attitudes toward math. Many parents, recalling their own negative school experience with math, transmit their insecurities to their children with such comments as "I always hated math. To this day, I still can't figure out what the lowest common denominator is, or why we can't divide by zero." or "It looks like you've got my rotten math genes." Parents who are skilled in math may also instill fear of the subject by reacting with impatience, or even exasperation, to the child's difficulties.

The student who learns to shun math may be at a significant disadvantage later on. Math permeates every aspect of our lives, from counting jumprope turns on the playground, to figuring out batting averages, to calculating interest on a bank account, to understanding election surveys. It is also a critical skill for many careers. The math-anxious student who avoids pursuing the subject in school may limit her academic options and narrow her career choices. Indeed, the ability to think mathematically is vital to success in many careers.

GIRLS AND MATH ANXIETY

While math anxiety affects all groups of people, it is especially prevalent among girls. They are told in subtle and not-so-subtle ways that math is not for them. In school, math teachers are more likely to call on boys, wait longer for their responses, praise their answers, and ask them complex questions. Boys are typically encouraged to take higher-level math classes, while girls are steered away from them. It is not surprising, then, that as early as third grade, girls report being less confident than boys in math. At home, parents tend to engage in math activities more with their sons than with their daughters. Mothers may inadvertently pass on their own anxieties about math to their daughters with such comments as "Wait until your father gets home. I can't help you with this." or "You don't need to take another year of math. You're not going to need it." In short, girls are socialized to avoid math.

This message that "real girls don't do math" pervades our culture, and it is conveyed at an early age. As just one example of how children's attitudes are shaped from a young age, a Barbie doll was programmed to say: "Math class is tough." (Only after many complaints did the manufacturer delete it from the doll's repertoire.) The effect of these messages from various quarters is to lessen girls' confidence in their math abilities, discourage them from giving their best effort, and dissuade them from pursuing higher-level math courses. This combination of diminished confidence and lessened effort can impede math performance. In addition, girls with good math skills may intentionally avoid being seen as math whizzes for fear of being ridiculed by peers for doing well in an "unfeminine" subject. Even when girls do succeed in math, they attribute their good performance to effort rather than ability. In recognition of the significance of this problem, some school districts have gone so far as to provide math classes exclusively for girls, as a way of bolstering their confidence and encouraging their involvement.

HOW TEACHERS CAN HELP

Teachers can play a significant role in lessening the math anxiety of their students and helping them approach math with confidence. Perhaps the best antidote to math anxiety is math mastery. The more students understand the math concepts, the less anxiety they will experience. Similarly, the better prepared they are for tests, the less likely they are to become flustered or blocked during the exam. The strategies described below are thus designed to help you promote confidence in math as well as mastery of concepts.

1. Be Aware of the Messages You Convey to Students about Math

Just as parents can help to shape their children's attitudes toward math, teachers can have a similar impact on their students. If you are anxious about the subject, make sure not to convey your feelings to the students through your comments. Express confidence in their abilities, telling them that if they stick with it they will eventually catch on.

2. Be Calm and Patient

This is especially important for the math-anxious student, because the slightest sign of teacher impatience may cause her to shut down. Present instructions in a clear, calm manner, and give the student time to process them and formulate a question. If you feel yourself becoming impatient while working with a student, try backing off for a while; your impatience may only increase her anxieties and intensify her confusion. If you find that the student continues to be very anxious despite your calming efforts, take her aside and suggest that she try breathing deeply as a way of lessening her anxiety.

3. Create a Relaxed Climate in Which the Student Feels Free to Ask Questions

Students with math anxiety are often reluctant to ask questions in class for fear of appearing dumb or being taken to task by the teacher for not listening. Make it clear to your students that you want them to ask questions, and leave time at the end of class for this purpose. Tell them that there is no such thing as a dumb question and that their questions help you by indicating where you may not have been clear. Even with your encouragement, however, some students will still feel uncomfortable asking questions in class, so make yourself available to them after class or at the end of the day. Respond positively to a student's question, describing it as a "good question" or an "important point." Make sure not to allow students to ridicule a classmate's questions.

4. Promote the Student's Confidence

Students with math anxiety are almost always insecure in their abilities. They may assume they will not understand a math concept or be able to do a problem. This lack of confidence may impair their concentration and hamper their performance. Help to reshape their negative views toward math by praising their successes and highlighting what they have done well. Back up your words with evidence of their ability to be successful with math. In presenting math work, start with problems that they can complete easily and, as they master the easier problems, move on to the more difficult ones. Allow students to find alternative routes to solving problems, so they learn there is not just one right way to find the answer. Avoid continually frustrating students or exposing their difficulties in public (for example, having a student with computational difficulties add a column of figures on the board). Point out errors in a nonthreatening, nonjudgmental manner, while showing them how to do the problems correctly. As students become more confident, positive self-talk may replace negative self-talk. Instead of saying to herself, "I'm stupid in math. I'll never get this," a student may say, "I'll get this if I stick with it. I'll just go slowly and check my work." Positive self-talk sustains effort while negative self-talk impedes it.

5. Reassure the Student That Math Mistakes Are Normal and Can Even Be Helpful

Let the student know that everybody makes mistakes in math—even you. You might even bring in your scratch paper to show how you tried various possibilities before arriving at the right answer. Show the student how mistakes can be helpful by pointing to the source of the error.

6. Help the Student Make Sense of Math Concepts

Many math-anxious students approach math as a series of procedures to be memorized, not understood. When their memory fails, however, or a problem is presented that falls outside the rules they have memorized, performance falters and anxiety results. Take the mystery out of math by helping the student understand the reason behind the rule she is memorizing. Teach her the "why" as well as the "how." The better she understands a concept, the more effectively she will retain and apply it. In addition, understanding helps to relieve anxiety and fear. You may need to devote less time to math drills and more to fostering understanding and critical thinking, less time to number crunching and more to number sense. While obtaining the right answer is certainly important, so, too, is understanding why the student is using certain procedures or rules. You may also have to clarify the meaning of math terms (for example, "of," which may indicate the need to multiply, or "minus," which has many meanings).

7. Use Concrete Objects to Foster Understanding

Many students find math concepts abstract and thus hard to understand. Using objects, or what educators call manipulatives, can help them grasp and visualize these concepts in a way that words cannot. The objects may include anything that can be counted or conveys quantity or amount such as blocks, beads, coins, poker chips, or Cuisenaire rods. Sand and water can also be used to convey amount. As an example, cutting an apple in parts can help students grasp the notion of fractions in a way that worksheets can't. Of course, as the student's understanding grows, she can move from the concrete to the conceptual.

8. Make Math Relevant

"Why do we need to do this anyway?" is a common refrain heard from math students. Answer this question by showing them. Demonstrate for students how the skills they are learning are used in everyday life, how this seemingly disconnected set of facts and procedures relates to the real world. They will be more comfortable with math concepts if they understand their practical value and learn to apply them. This is especially important with higher-level mathematics, where the application of the concepts is not intuitively obvious. Encourage students to become active learners of math, rather than just passive recipients of information. Give them problems that relate to their interests and age level, and that they may encounter outside of school. You might, for example, use the weather charts from the newspaper to help them understand positive and negative numbers, have them calculate the square feet of carpeting needed to carpet their room to understand the concept of area, or have them determine their speed in the mile run in gym to understand the formula "speed equals distance divided by time." The following are other examples of practical tasks that involve the use of math skills:

- measuring how tall they are with a tape measure
- figuring out how many days until their birthdays
- determining how many books they can order from the book fair with a set amount of money
- making change at the school store
- doubling a recipe
- determining a player's batting average
- figuring out the price of an item discounted 15 percent
- calculating interest on a bank account
- figuring out how many miles to the gallon a car is getting
- determining the appropriate tip on a restaurant bill
- conducting a class survey and tallying the results
- balancing a checkbook
- making sense of election returns

9. Make Math Fun

You can use a wide variety of math games to reinforce skills and promote a positive association with math. These can be board games, card games, or games that you or the students create. Typically easy to play and requiring little time, games help to break up the classroom routine. Keep the games tension-free and relatively noncompetitive. Also, use the computer to stimulate enthusiasm for math. Many good software programs are available for students of all ages, and schools use computers to teach math more than for any other subject. Computers are well suited to teaching this subject; they indicate the source of the student's errors and instruct her on the correct practice.

10. Monitor the Student's Work Frequently

It is important that you check her work often to ensure she is not simply practicing mistakes.

11. Assess the Student's Problem Areas by Working with Her One on One

By working with the student individually, you can pinpoint trouble spots as well as gain insights into her learning style. As you work with the student, assess what seems to work and what does not. Does she need to slow down? Does she need help in identifying key words when doing word problems? Would she benefit from using manipulatives? Does she understand better when you draw a picture to illustrate the concept? Would a calculator help? Would she do better and be less overwhelmed by doing fewer problems? Review her work samples and have her talk through the problem-solving process she used in order to identify the source of the difficulties. Math difficulties may take different forms—including failure to grasp the concept, problems with computation, number reversals when reading or writing, difficulties with word problems because of a reading problem, or failure to line up the columns properly.

12. Summarize and Review Math Lessons Frequently

Reviewing material is critical in math because advanced skills often require the mastery of previously learned skills. At the end of each lesson, do an activity that sums up the key concepts learned that day. When you begin the next lesson, briefly review the lessons of the previous day. In reviewing for a test, try to review over several days, rather than just the day before the test, to avoid panic and anxiety, which impairs concentration. Keep in mind, however, that too much review can bore students, so aim for a balance between review of old skills and introduction of new ones.

13. Use Nontraditional Ways to Evaluate the Student's Math Skills

There are few things more nerve-racking for a student with math anxiety than taking a math test. While a timed math exam is an important method of assessing skills mastery, it is not the only way. The following alternative assessment methods may give a more accurate picture of the math skills of the student prone to anxiety, or lessen the chance of discouragement:

- test with little time pressure

- test with open-ended questions

- take-home test

- credit given for work that reflects understanding, even if answer is wrong

- computer-assisted assessment

- long-term assignment or project

- portfolio of math work

- structured student interview

14. Allow the Student to Use a Calculator

The calculator relieves the student of tedious calculations and allows her to focus on understanding and solving problems. While students should be expected to master math facts, those who have difficulty remembering them despite repeated practice should be allowed to use a calculator to complete problems and tests. As an alternative, you might give the student a table of math facts for reference.

15. Provide Special Paper to Compensate for Writing Difficulties

Some students have good calculation skills but err when doing problems on paper because of a failure to line up problems correctly. If a student has this difficulty, give her graph paper to help line up the numbers properly. An easier alternative is to have her turn regular lined paper sideways so that the lines are vertical.

16. Teach the Student to Verbalize the Steps of a Problem

Encourage the student to talk to herself with each step as she does it (for example, "Now I bring the number down."). The aim is to help her develop an inner voice that talks her through the problem. You may want to demonstrate for her how to solve a problem by verbalizing each step. Have the student do the next problem while you observe her approach.

17. Make a Special Effort to Encourage Girls in Math

Because girls are more vulnerable to math anxiety than boys, especially in the middle and high school years, monitor the messages you send to girls about math. Make sure that you do not sell them short by, for example, attending more to boys in math class or suggesting that girls avoid challenging math courses. Show confidence in their ability to do math, encourage them to take risks, and give them a chance to compete on a par with the boys in the class.

18. Enlist the Parents as Educational Allies

Parents can add to a child's math anxiety or help to ease it. Talk with them about the importance of being encouraging, positive, and patient in working with the child. Let them know that their negative messages about math can prompt insecurity and anxiety in the child. In helping the child with math, parents sometimes use different approaches than the teacher. If this is confusing the student, ask the parents to use only your approach, which you may have to teach them. You may want to send home activities for the parents to do with the child. Make sure that the activities are fun, and at a level the student can do successfully.

19. Offer a Program of Math Education for Families

Family Math is a non-profit organization that offers a program of math education to demystify math, and to help children and their parents see it as fun and relevant to the outside world. This program has been successful in improving attitudes toward math by having parents work with their children on applied math problems. To learn how to bring this program to your district, contact Family Math, Lawrence Hall of Science, University of California, Berkeley, CA 94720-5200 (telephone: 1-510-642-1823).

For Further Information

Arem, C. (1993). *Conquering Math Anxiety: A Self-Help Workbook*. Pacific Grove, CA: Brooks/Cole Pub.

Brush, L. R. (1984). *Encouraging Girls in Mathematics*. Lanham, MD: University Press of America.

Buxton, L. (1991). *Math Panic*. Portsmouth, NH: Heinemann.

Hello Math Reader. New York: Scholastic.
(A series of read-aloud books for students who are turned off to math.)

Tobias, S. (1995). *Overcoming Math Anxiety* (expanded rev. ed.). New York: W.W. Norton & Co.

Zaslavsky, C. (1994). *Fear of Math*. New Brunswick, NJ: Rutgers University Press.

Organizations

ERIC Clearinghouse for Science, Mathematics, and Environmental Education
1929 Kenny Road
Columbus, OH 43210-1080
1-614-292-6717

National Council of Teachers of Mathematics
Department I
1906 Association Drive
Reston, VA 22091-1593
1-703-620-9840

See also:
   The Unmotivated Student

MILD MENTAL RETARDATION

A person who is mentally retarded exhibits marked weaknesses in reasoning skills as well as in the ability to adapt to everyday life. Widely misunderstood, mental retardation is neither a disease nor a mental illness. While it is a cognitive impairment, the student who is retarded is able to learn, although she learns slowly and struggles with higher-level thinking skills. She has the same range of emotions as other students her age, and many of the same interests. While she may stand out in a regular education setting, upon leaving school she may discard the label of mentally retarded and be absorbed into the mainstream of society. She may go on to live a productive life, including holding down a job, developing enduring friendships, and participating in community activities. Her ability to develop into a contributing member of society depends in large measure on the kind of education she receives.

About one percent of all students in school are mentally retarded. (In some states, they are called "educationally retarded" or "mentally handicapped.") About 90 percent of these students have a mild form of retardation. Most are educated in public schools. Indeed, more and more, they are being educated for at least part of the day in regular classes. It is thus important for all teachers to become familiar with the characterisitics of students who are mildly retarded, as well as with effective strategies for working with them.

CHARACTERISTICS

While students with mild mental retardation make up a diverse group with a range of abilities, they have some characteristics in common. They think and learn more slowly than other students—displaying particular difficulty with abstract tasks and higher-level reasoning. Concepts that come easily to other students (for example, cause-and-effect relationships) may elude them, and they may have trouble generalizing what they learn to other situations. Speech and language skills are likely to be affected. Their sentences may be simpler than those of their peers, and their vocabulary more concrete. They may also have problems with attention, perception, and memory.

Students with mental retardation are on a slower academic timetable than other students. They may not recognize the letters of the alphabet by age

7, nor read the most basic words by age 8. While they may eventually be able to decode words relatively well, they will probably have long-term difficulty understanding what they read. Literal comprehension will be better than inferential comprehension. By the time they finish their formal education, they will probably be able to read at the third- to sixth-grade level. In some academic areas that are not conceptually demanding (for example, spelling), they may be able to keep pace with their nondisabled peers. Skills more dependent on higher-level reasoning, such as application of math skills, will be much tougher for them.

The student with mental retardation may struggle emotionally as well as academically. Usually aware of her cognitive and academic deficiencies, she may experience considerable frustration and lack confidence in her ability to be successful academically or socially. Self-esteem is often lacking. She may rely on others, particularly her teacher, to solve problems for her and give her assistance, even when she is capable of doing it on her own. Her fear of making mistakes or appearing foolish may result in a resistance to academic tasks and a reluctance to participate in class. She may experience rejection and ridicule from classmates, and as a result may withdraw from peer activities.

Her social skills may be comparable to those of a younger child. She may lack social insight and have difficulty reading social cues. She may not be aware that you are pleased or that a classmate is upset. Even when she reads the situation correctly, she may not know the proper way to respond. Part of her difficulty with social situations may stem from a difficulty in appreciating situations from another's point of view.

In some cases, a student who is mentally retarded may exhibit behavioral difficulties in school. These problems usually stem from frustration or lack of understanding of appropriate behavior. She may also act out to gain the attention of her teacher or peers. Because her language skills may be limited, it may be difficult for her to talk about her feelings in other than a basic way. Asking a question such as "What is upsetting you?" may elicit a blank stare or a simple "nothing."

ASSESSING MENTAL RETARDATION

To be classified as mentally retarded, a child must be determined to have significantly below-average intellectual ability, as measured by an individual intelligence test, and deficiencies in adaptive behavior, namely, her ability to function effectively in everyday life. This includes such skills as self-care, ability to communicate, peer interaction, and independence in her environment.

An intelligence test is given by a psychologist trained in its administration—typically a school psychologist. The two most common individual intelligence tests administered to students are the *Wechsler Intelligence Scale for Children*—3rd edition, and the *Stanford-Binet Intelligence Scale*—4th edition. These tests encompass a range of reasoning tasks tapping verbal and visual-perceptual abilities, but require little if any reading. These intelligence scales compare the performance of the student taking the test to that of many other students of the same age, yielding an intelligence quotient (IQ), which is an estimate—not a precise calculation—of learning aptitude. Scores ranging from 90 to 110 are typically considered in the average range.

An IQ score of less than 70 or 75 is usually considered within the mentally retarded range, although states vary in the criteria used to define mental retardation. Thus, a student can be considered mentally retarded in one state, but not in another. Mental retardation is often categorized by the following levels of severity, with the associated IQ range listed in parentheses: mild (55–69), moderate (40–54), severe (25–39), and profound (below 25). Schools often use the terms *educable mentally retarded*, which is comparable to mildly mentally retarded, and *trainable mentally retarded*, which is comparable to moderately mentally retarded. The vast majority of students who are mentally retarded fall into the mild, or educable, range.

Children with mental retardation are usually identified as having a disability soon after birth if the disability is severe or there are obvious signs of brain injury. Mild retardation, however, may not be apparent until the child enters school and has difficulty keeping pace with her classmates academically or socially. Teachers in early grades thus play a key role in identifying students who may be mentally retarded, as well as giving emotional and practical support to parents. Hearing this label applied to their child inevitably causes great anguish to parents, especially if they have operated on the assumption during her preschool years that she was simply a slow or delayed learner.

CAUSES

Mental retardation may be caused by events that happen before, during, or after birth. While the precise cause of mental retardation is unknown in a majority of cases, there are literally hundreds of possible causes, including genetic conditions (for example, Down syndrome), maternal substance abuse during pregnancy (for example, fetal alcohol syndrome), infection (for example, rubella), metabolic problems (for example, phenylketonuria or PKU), insufficient oxygen during birth, environmental toxins (for example, lead), severe malnutrition, and head trauma during childhood. Mental retardation may also be caused by severe lack of environmental stimulation during the early childhood years. Children who come from impoverished conditions are at high risk for mental retardation, although it is important to keep in mind that most children from low-income homes are of average intelligence.

DOWN SYNDROME

Down syndrome is one of the leading causes of mental retardation. A genetic condition generally caused by an extra chromosome, it occurs in approximately one in every 1,000 live births, which represents about 4,000 births per year in the United States. The incidence of Down syndrome is higher for women over the age of 35, although the majority of babies with Down syndrome are born to mothers who are under 35.

Children with Down syndrome have distinct physical features. While they vary in their appearance, common characteristics include a stocky physique, small stature, a short neck, small hands and feet, poor muscle tone, a flat facial profile, and slanting eyes with skin folds at the inner corners. They are also prone to physical problems. Hearing and vision impairments are common. In addition, about 40 percent of children with Down syndrome have heart defects, and 8 to 10 percent have gastrointestinal difficulties, although these problems are often correctable through surgery. Many also have a decreased resistance to infection, and are thus vulnerable to respiratory problems. As a result, they may have high rates of school absenteeism.

Students with Down syndrome exhibit a range of behaviors and abilities, although virtually all are retarded. Most have IQs in the mild-to-moderate range of mental retardation. Language and motor development are usually slow, and speech articulation may be poor. In many ways, however, children with Down syndrome are like other children. They have the same range of emotions: They are excited by expressions of friendship and hurt by acts of cruelty. Many have a cheerful and upbeat disposition, and they are typically cooperative in class. Adolescence can be especially painful for children with Down syndrome because of their different physical appearance.

Because of the recognizable physical characteristics of Down syndrome, it is usually diagnosed at birth, although the diagnosis must be confirmed by a chromosomal study. Once it is diagnosed, it is important that parents obtain educational support during infancy and the preschool years if their children are to develop to their fullest potential. Even with early intervention, children with Down syndrome are likely to require special education upon entering school.

Because of medical advances, individuals with Down syndrome are living longer than in the past. In 1910, they lived on average until the age of 9. Today, the great majority of persons with Down syndrome live until the age of 55, and many live beyond that. As adults, they are often able to hold jobs, live in group homes or even independently, sustain personal relationships, and participate actively in community activities.

EDUCATING THE STUDENT WITH MILD MENTAL RETARDATION

If a student has been determined eligible for special education—and all students with mental retardation meet the criteria for eligibility—the school district and parents must together develop a document that lays out in detail her school program. This document is called an Individualized Education Program or IEP. The program described in this document cannot begin until the parents have consented to the program. You are a member of the team that develops the IEP, and your input is critical to its development. The IEP must describe the specific placement for the student, the degree to which she will be mainstreamed, the precise goals of the program, and the related services she will receive, such as speech and language therapy, occupational therapy, and adaptive physical education.

While most students who are mildly mentally retarded attend special education classes, they are increasingly being educated in regular education settings. Federal law requires that students with educational disabilities be mainstreamed in regular education programs if their needs can be met in that setting. In special education jargon, a disabled student must be placed in the least restrictive environment. The goals of mainstreaming are to promote the self-image, confidence, and social skills of students with disabilities while fostering acceptance and understanding by nondisabled students.

In recent years, there has been a movement to include students with disabilities in regular education programs all day. Called inclusion, this approach is most successful when regular teachers are adequately prepared and a special education teacher or aide is present in the regular classroom to work with the disabled student. It requires that a support system be put in place in the form of adequate services, staff support, and instructional accommodations.

HOW TEACHERS CAN HELP

Many of the same instructional methods used with nondisabled students are effective with students with mild mental retardation, although they may need more time to master the material and frequent review to retain it. At the same time, there are many strategies that you can use in the classroom to adapt to their individual needs. Some of these strategies, described below, are appropriate for teachers in regular classes, while others are better suited for teachers in special education classes. Your attitude toward the students will be as important as any particular techniques you use. Effective instruction of students with mental retardation, including those with Down syndrome, requires a blend of patience, understanding, a belief that they can learn, and the realization that progress may be slow.

1. Help the Student Blend in with Other Students

Because the student with mental retardation may stand out in some ways in a regular class, it is important to help her fit in with her peers and give her a sense of belonging by treating her as much like her classmates as possible. Greet her as you do others when she enters in the morning, joke with her, ask her to stop talking when necessary, and gently correct her mistakes. In addition, give her the same privileges or items that you give to other students in your class (for example, a locker or cubby, a class folder, a book for keeping a journal, or an assignment book). Also, make sure to involve her in your class routines (for example, leading the class in the Pledge of Allegiance), and expect her to comply with the same rules and expectations as other students, as long as they are within her ability (for example, expect her to cover her textbooks).

2. Seat the Student in the Front of the Class

Place her desk near where you usually stand when you teach a lesson. Also, have students next to her who are willing to help her when needed, and avoid seating her next to students who are likely to be distracting. You might alternate the students who sit next to her so this helping role does not become a burden to any one student. Wherever you seat her, make sure not to separate her from classmates or group her with other students with disabilities. Encourage the student to remove all materials from her desk except for those related to the task at hand.

3. Talk to Your Class about the Student

If the parents agree, find a time to talk with the student's classmates when she is not there to help them understand her special characteristics and how they can be helpful to her. Let them know that she learns more slowly than most other children her age, but that with time she will be able to learn many of the skills of the class. Emphasize her similarities with them more than her differences, and avoid using labels or disability language that sets her apart from other students. Help them understand that she has the same feelings and sensitivities as other students, and that it is just as important to her as it is to them to fit in. Tell them about some of her interests and unusual qualities. Let them know that you expect them to involve her in activities in class and on the playground, and that teasing will not be tolerated. Suggest to them what they can say to her if she is acting inappropriately. You might also ask them for their ideas about how they can be helpful and friendly to the student. Your students may surprise you with their resourcefulness, and they may be more likely to reach out to her if they hear that other students are so inclined. Consider asking an older, respected student who has been in a class with a child who is mentally retarded to talk with your students to encourage them to be friendly and helpful to the student.

4. Adapt Instruction to the Student's Individual Needs

The student may not be able to perform at the same academic or conceptual level as her nondisabled classmates, but she can learn many of the same skills if the teaching approach is adapted to her needs. This will require flexibility, creativity, and advance planning on your part—and perhaps assistance from another staff member. Timing is also important; introduce skills when the student is capable of understanding them. Aim for a balance between giving the student sufficient help to promote success and challenging her to do as much as she can independently. The following are some ways you might adapt your instruction for a student with mental retardation:

▪ Give the student work and materials that match her ability level. Have her read high-interest, low-level books.

▪ Give the student work in the same subject as other students, but with a different goal. For example, in a project on plants, the goal for the disabled student might be to learn about the requirements for plant growth, while for the other students the goal might be to learn about photosynthesis.

▪ In teaching reading, inform the student of critical errors, namely those that alter the meaning of the passage, and ignore less important errors.

▪ Explain new terms and use consistent terminology. The student will be confused if you use different terms to refer to the same concept (for example, *times* and *multiplied by*).

▪ If the student has difficulty communicating, allow her to respond by pointing instead of talking.

▪ Give the student a different homework assignment than other students—or assign her fewer problems or pages to read.

▪ Individualize instruction through the use of computers. In this way, the student can work on the same subject as other students, but on different skills.

5. Provide Short, Simple, and Clear Directions

You may have to supplement your directions to the class with individualized instructions to the student. Make sure you have her full attention and she has good eye contact with you before giving directions. With a younger student, you may have to get down to her physical level. Maximize understanding by making the directions clear and direct and, if necessary, give one step at a time. Use vocabulary she knows. Have the student repeat the directions to you or begin the task in your presence to check her understanding. You may have to demonstrate some tasks to the student first. You might also have the student repeat directions to herself to promote retention. If she can read, consider supplementing verbal directions with written directions, with key words underlined. If you are giving complicated directions or information for parents, consider recording this information into a tape recorder the student brings to and from school.

6. Use Concrete Materials and Hands-on Experiences

A student who is retarded is better able to understand concepts if the lesson includes the use of concrete materials and hands-on experiences. This is the learning-by-doing approach. Use materials that the student can touch and manipulate (for example, Cuisenaire rods to help students understand math relationships, a yardstick to measure students and convey the concept of height, and a desk to teach about dimensions). Use your creativity to think of ways to demonstrate the concept instead of just talking about it. For example, rather than simply telling students about a scientific principle, perform a science experiment. Also, provide many examples to illustrate the concept you are teaching.

7. Present Learning Tasks in Small, Sequential Steps

Students who are mentally retarded have difficulty learning in large chunks and are better able to absorb information if it is broken down into bite-sized units. In giving directions, provide one instruction at a time. In presenting a lesson, think small; don't expect quantum leaps of understanding. Make sure the student masters one step before moving on to the next. Let her move at a pace that is comfortable for her. In the same way, help her master easier tasks before moving on to more complex ones. As she begins to understand and gain confidence, you can gradually present larger amounts of information or more difficult problems, or move at a somewhat faster pace. Similarly, give assignments in manageable sizes. For example, you might give the student a shortened vocabulary or spelling list, or give her only half the number of problems given to other students.

8. Make the Instruction Personally Meaningful to the Student

The student will be more attentive to your lessons and retain them more effectively if they relate to her interests or experiences. Make a point of finding out about the student's hobbies and interests by talking with her and her parents. Suggest books or stories for her to read on topics that you know she enjoys. Include words on her spelling or vocabulary list that are meaningful and useful to her. Use real-life situations that are relevant to her experiences to both grab her attention and foster understanding. For example, if she has a paper route, present math problems requiring her to calculate how much her customers owe her. To enhance her writing skills, have her write a paragraph describing how she cares for her pet.

9. Teach the Student Practical Life Skills

The degree to which a student's program should emphasize what are called functional or survival skills depends on the extent of her cognitive limitations and her age. With a young student, it is important to stress functional skills in the classroom (for example, making eye contact, taking turns, raising her hand, and sharing with classmates). As the student moves into secondary school, her program should focus increasingly on skills related to living and working in a community. As a regular teacher, you are limited in your ability to teach these skills, but you should look for opportunities to bring in practical applications of your lessons. For example, in presenting a lesson to your class on precipitation, you might ask the student what kinds of clothes are appropriate for different types of weather. As a special education teacher, you must teach academic skills in the context of real-life problems. In reading, go beyond basal readers and help the student learn to read street signs, the yellow pages, advertisements, bus and train schedules, menus, and the newspaper. In math, teach math facts, but also teach her how to make and receive change, tell and estimate time, read a calendar, and make sense of a bank statement. As she gets older, she will need instruction in such skills as obtaining and maintaining a job, managing personal finances, making consumer purchases, and getting around in the community. Try to find opportunities to take the student into the community to apply the skills she has learned in the classroom. Have her go food shopping with a grocery list, open up a bank account, send a package at the post office, order a meal at a restaurant, take public transportation, and fill out a job application.

10. Monitor the Student's Understanding Periodically

As you teach a lesson, check with the student frequently to make sure she is following you. Do not simply ask her whether she understands because she will probably tell you she does, either to impress you or to avoid embarrassment. Instead, find a way to assess whether she is catching on without singling her out. Use these opportunities to find out if she has questions, to provide constructive and corrective feedback, and to praise her performance.

11. Reinforce Newly Learned Skills Often

More than most other students, the student who is mentally retarded must review and practice academic skills if she is to retain them. These practice sessions should be spaced over time. Supervise the student's review to give her feedback and ensure that she is not practicing errors. You can also reinforce these skills by incorporating them into classroom activities. For example, if the student has learned how to count money, you might have her assist you in counting the lunch money.

12. Modify the Way You Assess the Student

Because the student may do poorly using traditional assessment techniques, you will probably have to adapt the way you evaluate her understanding and mastery of the topic. However you assess her, make sure it is within her ability to do well. There is little in school that is more discouraging to a student than being given a test that is well beyond her ability. The following are some ways you might modify your assessment of the student:

- Make sure she can read the test and understand the terms. If she cannot, have somebody read it to her and explain terms she does not know.

- Give her extra time to complete the test, or give her only selected questions. Consider giving her breaks during the test.

- If she has difficulty writing, give her a multiple-choice format, or give her an oral exam with questions that are appropriate to her ability and with language that she understands.

- In multiple-choice questions, do not use "all of the above" or "none of the above" as choices, and in true-false questions, do not use "always," "sometimes," and "never."

- Give her a set of questions or problems different from those given to her classmates.

- Have her demonstrate her understanding through a different format. This might be a composition, an art project, a class demonstration, a daily journal, or a portfolio of her work.

- In giving a grade, mark her on the degree to which she has achieved the goals set out for her in her IEP.

13. Reinforce Classroom Routines and Procedures with Visual Cues

Simply telling the student your rules and procedures may not suffice for her to retain them. If that is the case, give her some visual reminders by, for example, posting your classroom rules on the wall and writing the day's schedule on the board. Similarly, you might give her a written step-by-step description of how to do certain activities or a list of materials required for specific tasks. If she is unable to read, consider using pictures instead of words.

14. Prepare the Student for a Change of Routine or an Unfamiliar Situation

Students with mental retardation generally like routine and consistency. They feel more comfortable when activities take place at the same time every day. Not surprisingly, they have difficulty shifting gears and adjusting to change. When the class or school routine is altered, they can become anxious and upset. If you expect to change your classroom schedule (for example, if there is an assembly), let them know perhaps an hour in advance so it has time to sink in. New situations can also throw them for a loop, especially if it involves meeting new people. Discuss with them what they will be seeing or doing so they feel more prepared and in control.

15. Model Respectful Behavior toward the Student

Your students will look to you for cues about how to respond to the student. Foster a climate of acceptance and support by treating her in a kind and patient manner, but do not talk down to her. Speak with her in a friendly way and joke with her. Also, use language that is age-appropriate and puts her on an equal level with other students (for example, in asking a classmate to go with her to the office, you might say "I'd like the two of you to go" rather than "Take her with you").

16. Bolster the Student's Confidence and Self-Esteem

The student is probably sensitive to her deficiencies because of experiences with frustration and failure. She may have learned to distrust her abilities, and may need much emotional support as well as experience with success to become a more confident learner. Praise her for small gains as well as her final outcome. Acknowledge both academic and nonacademic successes. Let her parents know of her successes, perhaps by calling them in her presence. Find opportunities to highlight her work in the classroom. You might develop a behavior modification program to reinforce her successes, using praise, privileges, and tangible rewards as incentives. (See the chapters on the disruptive student and attention deficit disorder for a more detailed description of behavior modification strategies.) Placing emphasis on her successes does not mean ignoring her errors. It is okay to point out an important error, but make sure to show her the correct way of doing it, and avoid being judgmental. For example, it is more helpful and less discouraging to the student to say, "Kelly, you need to make sure that you capitalize the beginning of each sentence," rather than "Kelly, I had a terrible time following your paper."

17. Assign the Student Classroom Jobs She Can Do Successfully

Classroom or school jobs such as being the class messenger, reading the morning announcements, or operating the class VCR will give the student a sense of contributing to the class and also give her experience with social, verbal, or practical skills. Examples of jobs you might give her are described in the chapter on low self-esteem.

18. Structure Positive Peer Interactions

Simply placing a student with disabilities in the same class with nondisabled students will not ensure their interaction. You will probably have to play the role of social director and encourage students to reach out to the disabled student. Even encouragement may not be enough. You may have to organize activities in which the disabled student is included in activities in the classroom, during free time, on the playground, and even after school. Through these activities, the student may gain valuable social skills, and other students may learn to see her in a different light. You may have to coach the student in how to relate to her classmates by, for example, giving her ideas about how to greet other students, engage in small talk, and ask them to play a game. Consider organizing a select group of four or five students and meeting with them privately to ask them to make a special effort to involve the student in their activities. They may be more inclined to become involved with the student if they know their classmates are doing the same. Talk with the group about what kinds of activities they could do with the student, eliciting their ideas and giving some of your own based on your knowledge of the student. As one example, you might ask them to work out an arrangement so that each student phones her once a week. Encourage them to invite her to the movies, to go to an after-school activity, or to walk to school with them. The more you can build a peer support system for the student, the more she will feel a sense of belonging to the class. As she becomes more accepted by and involved with her classmates, you can pull back on your involvement.

19. Arrange Peer Involvement with the Student During Lunch and Recess

Lunch and recess can be especially difficult for the student with disabilities. Other students may go off on their own, leaving her isolated and alone. Talk with some of your students and ask them to sit with the student at lunch and invite her to join in playground games. If the student is not able or willing to participate, suggest other ways she can participate, for example, keeping score, being timekeeper, or turning the jump rope. Also, ask the supervising aide during the activity to monitor to make sure the student is not being left out of activities.

20. Provide the Student with a Classroom Buddy

The primary role of the buddy is to clarify directions and explain classwork and homework to the student. It is also an opportunity for the student with a disability to interact with her classmates. Give this job to students who are responsible and express an interest in helping the student. Alternate buddies so that no one student feels burdened by the job. Give the buddies some instruction about what to do, and what not to do. Emphasize to them the importance of explaining directions clearly to the student and confirming when she has done the work correctly. Explain that they should not do the work for her. Suggest that they praise her when she does well and encourage her when she does not. Check in with the buddy periodically to make sure she is not feeling overwhelmed and is getting her own work done. You may want to work out a similar arrangement with other students who need assistance to avoid singling out the disabled student.

21. Use Cooperative Learning

In cooperative learning, a small group of students work together in a noncompetetive manner to achieve cooperative goals, although the individual contributions may vary. These groups give the student who is disabled a chance to interact with other students, and the other students a chance to get to know her in a way they didn't previously. Divide the class into groups of from three to six students, placing the disabled student with classmates who are tolerant and considerate. Avoid placing more than one disabled student in each group. Inform the students that they must work together cooperatively, that each member is expected to contribute, and that group members must support one another. Structure the responsibilities in the group so the student with disabilities is assigned a specific task that is within her ability and also gives her a feeling of contributing to the group's final product.

22. Stop Teasing Immediately

While it is important for the student who is mentally retarded to learn to stand up for herself, she may not have the skills to cope adequately with peer ridicule. Talk with the offending students to elicit their understanding of how teasing is hurtful. If they persist, contact their parents or take disciplinary action. In addition, find time to teach the student steps she can take and things she can say when someone teases her.

23. Discipline the Student When She Knowingly Misbehaves

Students should not be exempt from discipline because they have a disability. They need to know when their behavior is inappropriate (they may not always know) and to understand that there are limits to their actions. A student with limited mental abilities can learn to behave appropriately from your response as well as the resulting consequences. In disciplining her, tell her clearly and concretely what she did wrong and what she needs to do differently next time. Of course, make sure to praise her when she acts appropriately. You may want to use behavior modification strategies to spur positive behaviors and deter negative behaviors with students who are retarded. These strategies are described in detail in the chapters on attention deficit disorder and the disruptive student.

24. Be Alert for Possible Hearing and Vision Problems

Children with Down syndrome are especially vulnerable to hearing and vision impairments. These problems may emerge after students begin school and, if undetected, can contribute to academic and behavior problems. The chapters on hearing and visual impairment provide lists of signs suggesting possible difficulties. Alert parents if you observe concerns in these areas so they can have their children examined.

25. Work Collaboratively with the Special Education Teacher

If a special education teacher is assigned to work with a disabled student in your classroom, bear in mind that this person is not your assistant, but rather your colleague. The special education teacher has expertise in how to teach the student and what materials to use. Together, you form a teaching team. Meet with this teacher before the student enters your class to clarify each of your responsibilities (for example, how to adapt instruction, what materials to use, how to discipline the student, what the special education teacher's role is with other students, and who will grade the student). It is important that the special education teacher work with other students in your class so the disabled student is not singled out. If the student's special education teacher is not working with you in the classroom, you may still want to consult with her or him to get ideas for working with the student in a regular class, as well as suggestions for materials. Also, consider getting help from other school specialists who know the student (for example, the speech-language pathologist, occupational therapist, or vision consultant).

26. Request a Classroom Aide

You may require an aide in your classroom because of the demands the student places on your time. Talk with the school team (of which you are a member) that developed the student's Individualized Education Program and suggest that an aide be placed in your class. A classroom aide (also called an educational assistant) may be assigned full- or part-time to a particular student—or to more than one student. If an aide is assigned, clarify your expectations, including the aide's response to misbehavior and involvement with other students. Monitor to make sure the student does not become too dependent on the aide and the aide does not restrict the student's contact with her peers. Be positive and encouraging of the aide's efforts, but do not abdicate your teaching responsibility. A classroom aide is there to support your instructional decisions.

27. Establish a Communication System with the Parents

You can enhance the parents' support of the child's education by keeping them informed of what she needs to do or bring to school, as well as what is happening in the classroom. It is also important that parents have an easy way of informing you about questions, concerns, and relevant information.

Have the student carry a notebook back and forth that you and her parents can use to record information. Make sure to check it daily.

28. Arrange for the Student to Participate in the Special Olympics

Open to children who are mentally retarded and at least 8 years old, the Special Olympics allows these children to shine in a wide variety of physical activities, from bowling to volleyball. Talk with your school's director of special education to find out the procedure for enrolling a student in the Special Olympics, or call the sports director of your state's Special Olympics program. Also, encourage the parents to sign the child up for community sports, but keep in mind that she is likely to respond better to such individual sports as bowling, swimming, or hiking than to team sports.

For Further Information

Cunningham, C. (1996). *Understanding Down Syndrome: An Introduction for Parents.* Cambridge, MA: Brookline Books.

Gable, R. A., and Warren, S F. (eds.). (1993). *Strategies for Teaching Students With Mild to Severe Mental Retardation.* Baltimore: Paul H. Brookes Publishing Co.

Oelwein, P. (1995). *Teaching Reading to Children With Down Syndrome: A Guide for Parents and Teachers.* Rockville, MD: Woodbine House.

Shalom, D. B. (1984). *Special Kids Make Special Friends.* Bellmore, NY: Association for Children With Down Syndrome. (This book is intended to teach young children about Down syndrome, and can be obtained by calling 1-516-221-4700.)

Smith, R. (ed.). (1993). *Children With Mental Retardation: A Parents' Guide.* Bethesda, MD: Woodbine House.

Trainer, M. (1991). *Differences in Common: Straight Talk on Mental Retardation, Down Syndrome, and Life.* Rockville, MD: Woodbine House.

Organizations

The Arc (formerly the Association for Retarded Citizens of the United States)
500 East Border Street, Suite 300
Arlington, TX 76010
1-800-433-5255

American Association on Mental Retardation
444 North Capitol Street NW, Suite 846
Washington, DC 20001
1-800-424-3688

Division on Mental Retardation and Developmental Disabilities
The Council for Exceptional Children
1920 Association Drive
Reston, VA 20191
1-703-620-3660

National Down Syndrome Congress
1605 Chantilly Drive, Suite 250
Atlanta, GA 30324
1-800-232-6372

National Down Syndrome Society
666 Broadway, Suite 810
New York, NY 10012
1-800-221-4602

Special Olympics
1701 K Street NW, Suite 203
Washington, DC 20006
1-202-628-3630

See also:
  Hearing Impairment
  Low Self-Esteem
  Reading Disability
  Speech and Language Problems
  The Unmotivated Student
  Visual Impairment

READING DISABILITY

Reading is the single most important skill that students learn in school. It unlocks the door to a world of knowledge and is the gateway to the learning of other subjects. If students cannot read effectively, they will probably encounter difficulty with social studies, science, and even math. Judging by recent test results, many students fall into this category. The National Assessment of Educational Progress, a federally funded program that monitors the academic skills of American schoolchildren, found in its 1994 assessment of reading that 40 percent of students in fourth grade read below what was defined as a "basic" level of reading proficiency for that grade. This study is one of many that underscores the challenges that schools face in teaching children to read. Given the critical importance of reading to success in school and later life, it is essential that teachers identify these struggling readers and provide appropriate help as soon as possible.

THE ABC'S OF READING INSTRUCTION

Reading is a complex task involving two abstract skills: decoding, the ability to convert written symbols into words, and comprehension, the ability to gain meaning from these words. Both skills are essential to reading. The student who has difficulty with decoding will also have difficulty with comprehension. Being able to decode words without understanding their meaning is also problematic; this is not reading, but rather word calling. Reading instruction must thus focus on the student's ability both to identify words and to gain meaning from those words.

The debate about the best way to teach reading has gone on for decades, and continues with fervor today. Some teachers believe the stress should be on phonics—namely, teaching students to sound out letters and blend these sounds into meaningful words. Learning these skills, which most students complete by the end of second grade, allows them to break words into parts when reading or put them together when writing. Students who understand the rules of phonics can figure out most unfamiliar words with relative ease. Other teachers stress a sight-word approach (sometimes called the whole-word or look-say method) in which students memorize whole words as well

as their meaning. The whole-language approach to reading, which empha-
sizes the meaning of words rather than their sounds and the use of real literature rather than basal readers, has established a solid footing on the
academic terrain. Underlying this approach is the principle that reading
is a language activity closely connected with speaking and writing, so enhancing students' language skills promotes reading comprehension. Teachers
using a pure whole-language approach provide little direct instruction in
phonics.

While each school of reading has fervent adherents, there are few purists
in the classroom. In fact, most teachers employ eclectic reading programs in
which they make use of all three approaches. The issue, then, for most teachers is not which approach to use, but rather which to emphasize. Whatever
approach you favor, make sure to provide your students with a good ground-
ing in phonics, especially during the first two years of reading instruction.
Extensive research has documented the importance of phonics in learning
how to read.

Students cannot read competently just using the rules of phonics, however. While there are 166 rules of phonics, there are also 45 exceptions. To
read and write words that do not follow the rules of phonics (for example,
phone, night, who, and said), students must retain their visual image or use
context clues to figure them out. An effective reading program must therefore
teach students to sound out words that conform to the rules of phonics and
memorize the images of those that do not. Because students have different
learning styles, no one approach to reading is right for every child. Some
learn better memorizing sight words, while others are more successful learning the sounds of letters and blending them together. Ideally, the reading program should be adapted to students' learning styles and provide them with a
variety of reading strategies, including phonics, the sight-word approach,
structural analysis (root words, prefixes, suffixes, and endings), word families, and context clues.

READING DISABILITIES

It is estimated by reading experts that 10 to 15 percent of schoolchildren have
reading disabilities. In a typical classroom, there will probably be from two to
four students who are having difficulty "breaking the code." A student with
a reading disability—which is often referred to as dyslexia—usually has av-

erage or above-average intelligence. His reading level, however, falls well short of what you would predict based on his thinking ability. He typically has trouble hearing the sounds of spoken words, called phonemes, and putting these sounds together to make words. (The word *pan* has three phonemes: /p/, /a/, and /n/.) He may reverse letters when reading (for example, he may read a *d* as a *b*), transpose letters (for example, he may read *sacred* as *scared*), or omit letters (for example, he may read *boring* as *bring*). Keep in mind that letter reversals are common in kindergarten and first grade, and should not be of significant concern unless they persist into second grade.

The process of reading requires that words be identified rapidly, automatically, and accurately. The student who reads slowly and inaccurately, as many with reading disabilities do, is likely to have problems comprehending. If the process of decoding is not effortless, the student's energy and attention will be focused on sounding out words at the expense of gaining meaning. His reading problem will begin to affect his performance in other subjects, particularly in secondary school, where the reading and writing demands increase. If there is little evidence of progress in reading, his frustration will mount and motivation will wane. He may come to associate reading with drudgery and perceive books as something to be avoided. It is essential that teachers intervene to try to break this cycle of failure.

HOW TEACHERS CAN HELP

While it is beyond the scope of this book to offer a comprehensive approach to reading instruction (see the references at the end of this chapter), the following strategies may be useful to regular and special education teachers in working with students with reading problems. You may also find some of these ideas useful as general classroom strategies. As you develop a plan for assisting a struggling reader, keep in mind that the goal is to teach him not just to be an effective reader but also to be a confident and enthusiastic reader.

1. Provide a Variety of Language-Related Activities

The ability to use and understand language is critical to the development of reading. By fostering students' expressive and receptive language skills, you can lay the groundwork for the emergence of reading. Help your students see that words are all around them—in books, in catalogs, on labels, on signs, on birthday cards, on T-shirts—and that the printed word has many important uses. Expand their vocabulary—an essential component of comprehension—by talking with them as much as possible, both in a group and an individual context. Encourage them to share their experiences or ideas, and ask them thought-provoking questions. Write down their made-up stories and read them back to them. Teach young students nursery rhymes, rhyming games, and alphabet songs.

2. Have a Wide Range of Reading Materials in Your Classroom

Establish a class library with a range of materials at different reading levels and on various subjects, including fiction and nonfiction books, magazines, newspapers, tapes of books (and headsets), and even catalogs. If your students have created their own books, make these part of the library as well. You might organize the books by genre or by author. If you have access to a computer in your classroom, consider setting up a database of the reading materials (or, better yet, have students do it). Establish a reading corner with a rocking chair or beanbag chair.

3. Determine Whether the Student Can't or Won't Read

A reluctant reader is not always an incapable reader. Find out if he is able to read by giving him an informal reading inventory (obtain this from the school's reading specialist) or doing your own assessment. For a young elementary student, see if he can recognize the letters of the alphabet and identify the corresponding sounds. Also evaluate whether he can rhyme words (for example, ask him to name words that rhyme with the word *ball*). Assess his ability to blend by giving him three sounds (for example, /b/, /a/, and /t/) to see if he can put them together to make the correct word. Have him read for you privately a selection that students at his grade level can read with relative ease. Note the fluency of his reading and the frequency of errors. Assess not only his decoding skills, but also his ability to comprehend. Ask him to read silently a story appropriate to his grade level, and have him tell you what happened. Pose a few questions to evaluate his grasp of the main idea and the supporting details, and his ability to make inferences. Also, take note of his enthusiasm for reading. Does he shy away from reading, or does he eagerly seek out books? If you are uncertain of his reading ability after your informal assessment, ask the school's reading specialist or the remedial reading teacher to work with him and give you his or her opinion.

4. Give the Student Material He Can Read Successfully

With a likely history of frustration, a student with reading problems is at risk for being turned off to reading and losing confidence. The key to preventing this is to tailor instruction, and the accompanying reading materials, to his reading development rather than his chronological development, to *where* he is rather than *how old* he is. Find materials he can read comfortably. In selecting or suggesting reading materials, consider their length, the difficulty level of the vocabulary, the complexity of the syntax, and the use of headings and pictures to enhance understanding. Make sure the student has exposure to almost all of the letter combinations in the story and is able to decode the great majority of the words. As a general rule, a student should be able to read with relative ease at least 90 percent of the words if a book is to be considered at a comfortable level for him. If he is struggling to decode many of the words, he will quickly become frustrated and may resort to guessing. Giving him books that he can read without much trouble, and encouraging him to reread them, will also help him become a more fluent reader.

5. Use Reading Materials That Relate to the Student's Interests or Experiences

It is not enough to give a student materials he can read. It is also important to give him materials he wants to read. Supplement basal readers with children's classics or current children's books of high quality. Suggest books or stories that tap his interests or are personally meaningful. If his reading is below grade level, ask the school librarian to find high-interest, low-level materials so he can read comfortably in areas of his interest. An older student may respond positively to reading the newspaper or materials that are useful to him (for example, the driver's manual or the Boy Scout handbook).

6. Use Large-Sized Books

With large pictures and words as well as predictable word patterns, these Big Books are an effective way to promote reading with young elementary students. Read the story with enthusiasm to your students, using a pointer to indicate the word you are reading. Read it a few more times over the next week or so, and encourage them to join in and read with you if they are able. You may be able to obtain the same book in a regular size for your students to read on their own, or to each other. They might even take it home to read to their parents. Tapes of the books may also be available for students to listen to as they follow along in the regular-sized book.

7. Use a Multisensory Approach

An especially useful tool with young struggling readers is to give them activities that use more than one sense. If you have a student who is having trouble learning the alphabet, you might have him engage in tactile activities to help him retain the visual images of the letters. For example, he might draw letters in finger paint or trace them in a shoe box filled with sand, salt, or shaving cream. Or he might write the letters in the air or on the back of a classmate. Tell him to say the name of the letter every time he makes it. In this way, he is seeing, hearing, and touching the letters. The Fernald method, also called the VAKT method, is a commonly used multisensory approach to reading instruction in which the student traces a word, written in large letters, while saying it. He does this several times until he can write the word accurately and effortlessly on his own. The words that he traces come from his own experiences, and are thus personally meaningful. Another method for reinforcing letter sounds and syllables involves using rhythmic activities, for example, having the student clap for each syllable of a word. You can also use blocks or cards to help the student learn to sound out words. Have each block represent a letter or sound, and use these blocks to construct words and pull them apart. Magnetic letters can also be used to form words and sentences. These activities demonstrate in a concrete way that words are made of parts, and that reading is a matter of blending these parts together to make words.

8. Teach the Student to Visualize What He Reads

Having the student imagine what he is reading helps words and passages become firmly planted in his mind's eye and fosters retention of what he has read. This approach is particularly effective with students with reading problems. Have the beginning reader picture the individual words he is reading. This may help him connect the word with the object so he can retain the printed word more easily. With regard to sentences or paragraphs, it is not sufficient to simply tell the student to visualize the event he has read about. Model how to do this by describing aloud the scene you are visualizing based on a passage you have read. Of course, some passages simply do not lend themselves to visual imagery.

9. Provide Phonics Instruction in the Context of Reading

It is widely accepted that students will have difficulty learning to read if they do not have a firm grasp of phonics. Do not rely on the students' naturally learning phonics through exposure to a variety of reading materials. While some students figure out the rules of phonics on their own, many others do not. These other students need direct instruction in phonics. Students with auditory perception problems for whom phonics will be difficult need exposure to these skills as well, although they will also need instruction in other reading strategies. In teaching a student phonics, assess his level of understanding. With some students, you may have to start at the beginning—learning the letters of the alphabet and the accompanying sounds. As you move on to teaching the student how to blend sounds to make words, use a variety of steps, including explaining the skill, modeling it, having him practice it as you give feedback, asking for other examples, and then giving him experience with the skill in actual text. It is critical that you teach sounds and blends in the context of meaningful words, sentences, and stories rather than as isolated activities. Give the student a concrete cue word with the sound or blend (for example, "b as in ball" or "pl as in play"). Give him stories that include words with the letter combinations he has just learned so he can practice reading these sounds in the context of literature. You might do this by identifying the sounds in the story the student is going to read, giving him lessons in those sounds, and then having him read and reread the story. In this way, students come to see phonics as a useful reading tool rather than an isolated exercise or a series of rules.

10. Teach the Student to Recognize High-Frequency Words by Sight

Reading can be slow and laborious if the student must decode every word he reads. Fluency and comprehension can be increased if he learns to recognize instantly the most commonly used reading words (for example, *and, you, the, it, has*). An excellent source for these words is *Fry's Instant Word List*, which is readily found in many reading texts. The first 100 words of this list make up about 50 percent of the words a student will encounter in most reading selections. Learning these words will also help reading become a less abstract task for the student. You can help etch these words into the student's memory for instant recognition by using the sight-word method. Some teachers use a "word wall" to teach sight words. This involves placing on a large bulletin board five commonly used words every week in alphabetical order, and reviewing the meaning of each. Keep these words posted throughout the year. Choose five for the student to practice daily so that with time he learns to read the words on the word wall automatically through repeated practice.

11. Provide Alternatives to Traditional Oral Reading Activities

Round-robin reading, in which students take turns reading in class, can be anxiety-provoking and embarrassing for the student with reading problems, and boring for his classmates. Listening to a reader falter and stumble can be painful for reader and listener alike, yet oral reading can be a useful way to promote fluency, share information, convey the joys of reading, and give students a chance to read their own work. You can lessen a student's anxiety about oral reading by having him practice silently or assigning him passages to read in advance so he can rehearse with his parents. If you have time, have him practice with you so you can coach him in pronunciation, expression, and volume. Establish a general classroom rule that students are not to correct the reader or laugh at mistakes. You should ignore most mistakes unless they significantly change the meaning of the text. If the student remains resistant to reading in front of the class, even after being given the chance to practice, do not force him to read orally. Keep in mind that a student's ability to read silently and understand what he reads is much more important than his ability to read orally. An alternative to oral reading before the class is to pair students up, preferably matching struggling readers with competent readers, and have them read alternating paragraphs or pages to each other. You might give them specific questions to answer. Choral reading is another way you can have students read aloud without the risk of anxiety or embarrassment. If you work with the student individually, you might build in oral reading in the following way: Read a story orally to him, have him read the story with you one or more times, and then have him read it out loud on his own. Even though you may de-emphasize oral reading by students, you should continue to read to them. This is an effective way to model fluency and expression, and to generate interest in a story. Prior to or while you are reading the story, ask a question to spur their attention and interest (for example, "What do you think is going to happen next?").

12. Have the Student Listen to Books on Tape

Make tapes of stories for the student to listen to, or arrange for him to obtain books on tape. An organization called Recording for the Blind &

Dyslexic (see Organizations at the end of this chapter) lends tapes of a wide variety of books, including textbooks, to individuals with "print disabilities." The student can use these tapes in various ways. He can simply listen to the book on tape, or he can listen to the tape as he follows along in the book. Or he can read aloud as he listens to the tape and follows along in the book. Suggest that the younger student move his finger under the words as he follows along. Allow him to listen to the tape of a story several times, after which he may be able to read it on his own. If you do the recording, use high-quality tapes and make sure to cue the listener when to turn the page. Adapt the pace of your reading to the reading ability of the student. You might have parent volunteers or older students make the tapes. This "talking books" approach has been very successful in promoting the skills of students with reading disabilities, as well as in building their confidence.

13. Personalize Reading Instruction

An effective way to motivate the discouraged reader is to make the reading instruction personally meaningful. In this way, reading becomes more interesting and less threatening. A simple way to do this is to use his name and interests as well as school events in his reading selections. You might also personalize the reading by suggesting before he reads the story that he consider how he might handle a particular situation in the story. The language experience approach to reading makes use of events in students' lives. Use this approach with a young elementary student by having him describe to you a personal experience. You may have to elicit from him an experience by asking about his interests or activities, or you may suggest he talk about a school experience such as a field trip. Write down his description on a large tablet or a piece of paper. You might use the computer to record his story. This story can then be used as a reading lesson by reading the story to him, having him read it with you, and then having him read it alone. Point to the words as you and he read them. Have the student reread the story frequently until he has mastered it. There are many variations to this approach. For example, when the student has mastered the words of the story, he can write them on 3″ by 5″ cards and create a word bank.

14. Model Comprehension Strategies

Good readers have a natural understanding of how to gain meaning from a text. Poor readers often need assistance. You will more than likely have to teach them specific strategies for comprehending what they read. Present these strategies in the context of passages they are reading rather than as isolated exercises. An effective way of doing this is to model the process of understanding a text by thinking aloud how you make sense of a specific reading passage and then guiding students as they go through the same process with different passages. Some key comprehension strategies are described below:

- *Using Text Structure:* Students can gain meaning by using the information contained in the book's organization, including the title, subtitle, table of contents, chapter questions, pictures, captions, bold print, and introductory and summary paragraphs.

- *Making Predictions:* When students predict what might happen in a story, it enhances their focus on the text and promotes understanding.

- *Asking Questions:* By asking themselves questions about the text (for example, why did this character act the way he did?), students learn to read with a specific purpose in mind. To help organize their thinking when reading a story, suggest that they ask themselves two key questions: (1) What is the basic problem or conflict? and (2) How do the characters resolve the problem?

- *Self-Monitoring:* When students become aware that they are confused by what they are reading, they must compensate by slowing down their reading rate, rereading for clarification, and looking up words in the dictionary. They must also learn to recognize inconsistencies in the text and resolve them.

- *Summarizing Information:* Students benefit from pausing to consider the main points of what they are reading.

- *Reading Out Loud:* Students may understand a confusing section better by reading it out loud. Seeing and hearing what they are reading may also focus their attention on the material.

15. Provide Reading Aids to Facilitate Understanding

The following are some prereading supports you can provide to make the content of the story or reading assignment more accessible to students:

- Teach students how to decode words of the story that you expect will give them trouble.

■ Summarize the story for students before they read it silently.

■ Provide background information to help students make sense of the assignment and connect it to previously learned information. You might show a related filmstrip or indicate on a map or globe where the story is taking place.

■ Provide students with an outline of the reading material or a written summary highlighting key information.

■ Give students a list of key vocabulary words from the text that may be unfamiliar to them. Define the terms briefly, using language they can understand, and note the pages on which they occur.

■ Underline key terms or concepts, and make notes in the margins explaining their meaning in language the students understand. If this is not feasible, you might reproduce the material and make notes on the copy or insert in the book a sheet with notes.

■ Distribute a time line to help students understand the sequence of events.

■ Draw a simple diagram to help students understand confusing information. For example, if they are reading a chapter in their science text about energy, draw a branching diagram on the board illustrating the different sources of energy and examples of each.

■ Provide students with a semantic map, a visual representation of how concepts in the reading material relate to one another. You might do this on the board or give them a handout. Construct the map by placing a term in a circle and drawing lines from it to other related terms. After students get the idea, give them partially completed maps to finish. With time and frequent exposure to this strategy, you might encourage them to develop their own maps. The resulting web may be used as a guide for students when they are reading the passage, or as a study guide. As an example of this technique, if your students are reading a chapter on the Civil War, you might have an item on the semantic map for battles, which is connected to the names of the various battles, which are in turn connected to the generals involved in those battles.

16. Conference with the Student

You can help the student become a more critical reader by discussing with him, one-on-one, a book he has read. Your role is not to tell him what to think, but rather to ask questions that focus his attention on important aspects of the book and to respond with encouragement to his comments. Offer specific comprehension strategies, when warranted. Begin by asking him such nonthreatening questions that elicit basic information as the following:

- "What is the story about?"
- "Who are the main characters?"
- "Where does the story take place?"

Gradually move to questions appropriate to his age that promote comprehension and higher-level thinking such as the following:

- "Which character did you like the most?"
- "What do you think this expression means?"
- "How do you think (name of character) felt when . . . ?"
- "Do you think the story was realistic?"
- "If you were the author, how would you have ended the book?"
- "If the story were to continue, what do you think might happen?"

17. Provide Accommodations to the Student

Consider making some of the following classroom adjustments for the student with a reading disability:

- Shorten the length of his reading assignments.
- If he has trouble reading your writing on the board, encourage him to tape your lectures.
- Ask a responsible and willing classmate to sit next to him and, if necessary, read to him what he cannot read on his own.
- Allow him to take oral instead of written tests.

- Give him additional time to complete tests. A student with a documented reading disability can also take the Scholastic Assessment Test (SAT) untimed.

- Allow him to take tests in another room (for example, a special education class) and request that the supervising teacher read him questions, if necessary.

18. Schedule Uninterrupted Reading Daily

You might set aside time daily for your students to read a book of their choice. If you do, join them. This period does not have to be long—perhaps 10 to 20 minutes, depending on the age of your students. This may even be done on a schoolwide basis. Allow students who have difficulty reading silently for a sustained period to listen to a tape of a story while they follow along in the book.

19. Foster Enthusiasm for Reading

Partially because of the focus on standardized test scores, students may spend considerable time learning to read, but not much time actually reading. When this happens, they may come to see reading as a tedious, joyless activity. Research indicates that many students do very little reading. One study found that 90 percent of fifth graders read four minutes or less a day outside of school. Children who choose not to read are denying themselves a wealth of important information and a rich source of enjoyment. As Mark Twain said, "The man who does not read books has no advantage over the man who cannot read them." The following are some ways that you can motivate your students to read:

- Put posters on the wall that show celebrities reading.

- Talk with enthusiasm about books you have read.

- Read part of a book to the class to whet their appetite.

- Take your students to the school library. You or the librarian may suggest books to them, but let them make the final decision (with some rare exceptions). Don't make an issue of it if they select books that they have read before or that are very easy for them. The key is not to stifle their enthusiasm for reading.

- Stimulate interest in a book by showing the movie. After the students have finished reading the book, have them compare the two versions.

- Have your students engage in enjoyable activities related to books. This might include acting out parts of the story, doing a creative writing task (for example, describing a different ending to the book), doing an art project (for example, creating an illustrated advertisement for the book), or making a special food connected to the story.

- Organize students into cooperative learning groups of no more than seven students of mixed reading ability to talk about books they are reading.

20. Make Use of the Computer

While a computer cannot replace a teacher, it embodies many of the characteristics of an effective reading teacher: It gives a student undivided attention; it can motivate even the most discouraged youngster; it individualizes instruction; it teaches skills in steps; it has unlimited patience and can repeat a task or question endlessly; it provides immediate feedback; it minimizes failure and frustration; and it can measure the student's progress and identify areas of mastery and nonmastery. Computer programs can be particularly helpful in improving vocabulary and structural analysis skills (for example, root words, prefixes, and suffixes). Many reading programs for the computer employ a multisensory approach with auditory and visual feedback.

21. Teach the Student How to Use the Dictionary

This is an important skill for students to learn, and one that is easy to teach. Give the student a dictionary, and show him how the words are listed in alphabetical order. Open to any page and teach him how the guide words work at the top of the page. Also, explain the pronunciation key to an older student. Show him that if he opens to the middle of the dictionary, he will probably come to words beginning with the letters *l* or *m*. Ask him which way he would turn to look up a word beginning with another letter. Give him some practice looking up words.

22. Arrange for the Student to Read to Younger Children

This is a valuable way of enhancing the student's self-confidence. It also gives him a rationale for reading books that are below his grade level, but appropriate for his reading level.

23. Obtain Extra Help for the Student

The student may qualify for special reading help through your school's remedial reading or Reading Recovery program. Students often qualify for these programs based on standardized test scores. If the student is not in the program but is struggling with reading, check his test score to see if a mistake was made. If his score does not qualify him, ask the principal if he or she will make an exception and admit him to the program. If the student has been receiving remedial reading for a substantial period and continues to lag well behind his classmates in reading, consider referring him for evaluation to determine if he warrants special education.

24. Coordinate with Other Teachers Providing Reading Instruction

Students can be confused when they are being taught to read by more than one teacher, especially if they are using different instructional approaches. Talk with the other teacher to make sure the two of you are not working at cross-purposes. If the student is attending a special reading program, ask the special teacher what skills he is working on and how you can reinforce them in your classroom. The same is true if he is receiving outside tutoring. Try to make contact with the tutor to make sure his or her instruction dovetails with what you are doing in the classroom.

25. Encourage Parent Support of Reading

There may be no more important step you can take to improve your students' reading skills than getting parents to support your reading goals. You will have various opportunities to convey your message to parents—parent-teacher conferences, back-to-school night, occasional calls home—but you may want to take the additional step of sending a letter to parents explaining specifically how they can foster their children's reading development. You might include the following in your letter:

- Let parents know that their job is not to teach their children to read; that is your job. While they can certainly assist their children if they run into a problem, their primary role is to help their children enjoy and feel confident about reading. There is nothing wrong with their playing letter or word games with their children, but they should avoid giving them reading exercises or drills. Persisting with reading tasks that children do not enjoy can engender frustration and, ultimately, resistance to reading.

■ The single most important thing parents can do to promote a child's reading is to read to him from an early age. This will help him feel comfortable and confident around books and associate reading with warmth and security. Encourage parents to ask their children questions about the stories—not yes or no questions, but rather questions designed to provoke thought and conversation.

■ Suggest they have the child read to them. This gives him a chance to practice, and also provides them with a good opportunity to praise the child for his reading. Tell them to let the small errors go. For errors that alter the meaning of the sentence, suggest that they supply the correct word or help him sound it out without turning it into a reading lesson.

■ The best present parents can give to a child is a love of reading. While they should not force the child to read, they can foster an enthusiasm for reading by providing a comfortable, quiet place for him to read; allowing him to stay up 15 or 30 minutes later at night if he spends the time reading; giving him reading materials keyed to his interests; having him join a book club; helping him get started with a long book by reading the beginning pages or chapter to him; and having him make a paper chain or mobile listing the books he has read.

FOR FURTHER INFORMATION

Clark, D. B., and Uhry, J. K. (1995). *Dyslexia: Theory and Practice of Remedial Instruction* (2d ed.). Timonium, MD: York Press.

Cunningham, P. M. (1995). *Phonics They Use: Words for Reading and Writing* (2d ed.). New York: HarperCollins College Publishers.

Duffy, G. G. (ed.). (1990). *Reading in the Middle School* (2d ed.). Newark, DE: International Reading Association.

Linksman, R. (1995). *Solving Your Child's Reading Problems*. Secaucus, NJ: Carol Publishing.

Miller, W. H. (1993). *Complete Reading Disabilities Handbook*. West Nyack, NY: The Center for Applied Research in Education.

Tierney, R. J., and Readence, J. E. (1994). *Reading Strategies and Practices: A Compendium*. (4th ed.). Needham Heights, MA: Allyn & Bacon.

Organizations

Center for the Study of Reading
Room 158 CRC
51 Gerty Drive
Champaign, IL 61820
1-217-333-2552

Division for Learning Disabilities
The Council for Exceptional Children
1920 Association Drive
Reston, VA 20191
1-888-232-7733
1-703-620-3660

The International Dyslexia Association
8600 LaSalle Road
Chester Building, Suite 382
Baltimore, MD 21286-2044
1-800-222-3123

International Reading Association
800 Barksdale Road
P. O. Box 8139
Newark, DE 19714-8139
1-800-336-7323

Learning Disabilities Association
4156 Library Road
Pittsburgh, PA 15234
1-888-300-6710
1-412-341-1515

Recording for the Blind & Dyslexic
20 Roszel Road
Princeton, NJ 08540
1-800-221-4792
1-609-452-0606

See also:
  Hearing Impairment
  Mild Mental Retardation
  Speech and Language Problems
  Spelling Problem
  The Unmotivated Student
  Visual Impairment

Speech and Language Problems

Learning to communicate—to understand the expressed thoughts of others and to convey one's own thoughts—is an essential part of education. Students are engaged in communication virtually all day, whether through listening, speaking, writing, or reading. It is critical that teachers promote their students' language skills and provide help for those who exhibit difficulties. Communication includes both speech and language, and the two are distinct. Speech is the oral form of communication, while language comprises not only the words one says but also an agreed-upon set of rules for combining these words to convey information or ideas.

Upon entering first grade, a student should be able to follow basic directions, speak in full sentences, express her needs, ask and answer questions, and convey information. Her speech should be mostly intelligible, although students are normally still learning to produce speech sounds through the age of 8. For many students, however, speech and language do not develop normally. They may be delayed in reaching certain milestones, or they may exhibit disorders in their speech or language development. Most of these students attend regular classes.

TYPES OF COMMUNICATION PROBLEMS

A child has a communication disorder when she has significant difficulty understanding, formulating, or expressing a message. These disorders, which can range from mild to severe, include problems of speech or language and affect an estimated 5 percent of schoolchildren. A speech disorder, the most common type of communication problem, can affect the student's articulation, fluency, or voice.

An articulation problem is a difficulty forming sounds, syllables, or words. The child's speech may sound garbled and hard to understand. The listener is likely to be distracted from what she says by how she says it. Errors of articulation, which are normal at an early age, most often affect the pronunciation of consonants. The following are the most common types of articulation errors:

- *Omission:* A sound is omitted. For example, *hen* is pronounced *en* or *milk* is pronounced *mik*. Because children learn to say blends later than other sounds, omissions often take the form of leaving out the second sound of a blend (for example, saying *gape* for *grape*).

- *Substitution:* A sound the student can make is substituted for one she cannot make. For example, *ribbon* is pronounced *wibbon* or *third* is pronounced *fird*.

- *Distortion:* The word is pronounced inaccurately, although it sounds like the intended word (for example, saying *shore* for *sore*).

A child with a fluency disorder experiences a disruption in the flow or rhythm of her speech. This disorder is discussed in the chapter entitled Stuttering. A voice disorder may take the form of a difficulty with the pitch, intensity, or quality of a person's voice. A child with a voice disorder may sound hoarse, gravelly, nasal, or breathy. The most common source of a voice disorder with children is the presence of vocal nodules, which may be caused by frequent yelling. In its most extreme form, the child with nodules can lose her voice. If nodules are a problem, it may be necessary to keep the student from yelling. Check with the speech-language pathologist if one of your students has voice nodules, to determine if there are any classroom restrictions.

Language problems can be receptive or expressive in nature. A receptive language problem involves difficulty in understanding what others say. The student with this problem has trouble processing what she hears, even though her hearing acuity may be fine. This problem is discussed in depth in the chapter entitled Auditory Processing Problem. A student with an expressive language problem has trouble expressing her thoughts so the meaning is clear to the listener. She may be able to articulate words clearly, but her statements may be confusing, and she may have trouble finding the correct words. This problem may be especially evident beginning in fourth grade, when the student is expected to discuss more abstract concepts and engage in more complex discussions.

There are three main components to expressive language:

- *Semantics:* Grasping the meaning of words and being able to retrieve the correct word when needed.

- *Syntax:* Understanding how to place words in the correct order so they make a coherent phrase or sentence. For example, the student with poor syntax might say "Choose you me?" rather than "Can you choose me?"

■ *Pragmatics:* Learning how to use language appropriately in social situations, such as entering or initiating a conversation, taking turns when speaking, maintaining the conversation, expressing an opinion, asking for information, and adjusting your language according to the listener.

A student with an expressive language problem may exhibit some of the following characteristics:

■ is hesitant to participate in class, ask a question, or initiate a conversation

■ prefers to use gestures rather than words

■ has trouble finding the correct word for an object or event (called word retrieval or word finding)

■ has a limited vocabulary, and uses the same group of words for different situations

■ uses incorrect verb tense, or omits verbs entirely

■ has difficulty with subject-verb agreement

■ has problems putting words into correct sequence when speaking

■ speaks in short, simple sentences without expanding on ideas

■ has trouble relating an experience or story in the proper sequence

■ uses vague words such as "stuff" or "thing," and makes indirect, ambiguous statements

■ switches topics without using a transition phrase or sentence

■ fails to adapt language to the needs of the listener

CAUSES

Children learn to talk by listening to the speech of others and then trying out what they hear. With time, they develop an understanding of the rules of the language. As with many types of learning, children vary in the rate at which they learn the sounds and rules of a language. Certain factors can interfere with their progress, notably a problem with hearing. If a child has hearing difficulties or a history of chronic ear infections during the critical early years, she may not learn certain speech sounds when most children do, affecting her articulation at least temporarily.

A communication disorder may be the primary problem, or it may be secondary to other problems, including brain injury, mental retardation, autism, and cerebral palsy. Children with cerebral palsy often exhibit a speech problem called dysarthria, a neurological condition affecting the speech muscles and causing slow and slurred speech. In addition, physical abnormalities such as a cleft lip or palate or poorly aligned teeth may interfere with speech production and give rise to articulation problems.

Children can also have speech and language problems for nonphysical reasons; they may have been exposed to faulty or insufficient learning. Parents who have speech problems serve as poor role models, and may contribute to a child's articulation difficulties. Some children have limited language experiences during the critical preschool years. They may have little verbal interaction with their parents and thus limited opportunities to practice using language to communicate.

SCHOOL IMPACT

Because reading and writing are inherently language activities, communication problems can affect academic performance. The student who has difficulties understanding and using language may have trouble in almost every phase of school, but most notably in reading, writing, and spelling. Phonics may pose special problems for children with articulation disorders. A student who struggles to produce sounds and blend them together to make words will probably also struggle to sound out words in an effort to read. Indeed, by one estimate, students with speech or language difficulties are six times more likely to have trouble with reading. The pressures do not ease for these students upon entering secondary school, where teachers use more advanced vocabulary and more complex sentence structure.

Speech and language problems can also affect a student's emotional status, her self-esteem, and her relationship with peers. She may experience a range of emotions, including anxiety, frustration, and anger. Speech problems may elicit ridicule from peers, while language problems may give rise to puzzled stares. Self-conscious about her speech and fearful of embarrassment, the student with articulation difficulties may avoid participating in class or asking questions of the teacher. She may become withdrawn and isolated from her peers, which can be as significant a problem as the speech impairment. Behavior problems may also surface in school. In an effort to cover up her speech difficulties, or out of frustration with her inability to speak like her peers or express her feelings adequately, she may act out in class. If so, it is important that you not only respond to her misbehavior but also give her appropriate help with her speech.

SPEECH AND LANGUAGE THERAPY

Because of the potential impact of a speech or language problem on the student's social and emotional development, it is important that she receive help as early as possible, in some cases even before kindergarten. Some communication problems are subtle and may escape detection until after the student begins school, which makes it critical for the teacher to recognize problems and obtain help at the earliest possible time. This help may take the form of speech or language therapy provided in school by a speech-language pathologist. The majority of speech disorders that do not have a physical or neurological basis can be treated successfully.

As a teacher, you have an excellent vantage point from which to observe a child's language development and thus play a key role in identifying possible problems. If you have concerns about the communication abilities of one of your students, consider referring her for evaluation to the speech-language pathologist. Examine the above characteristics of speech and language problems and then ask yourself the following questions in deciding whether to make this referral:

- Is the student's speech or language development behind that of her peers?
- Is her speech hard to understand?
- Is she reluctant to speak in class?
- Is she upset and frustrated by the communication problem?
- Is she being teased by classmates?

■ Has the problem persisted for a long period without showing signs of getting better?

In considering a referral, keep in mind that some speech problems are normal during the early elementary years (for example, a frontal lisp such as saying *thaw* for *saw* where a child's front teeth are missing). Similarly, it is not unusual or reason for concern if a student has difficulty producing the sounds of the letters *j, l, r, s, v,* or *z* by the time she enters school. In addition, the blends *ch, sh,* and *th* are typically not mastered until the age of 5. If a student is unable to make specific sounds by the age of 6 or 7, talk with the speech-language pathologist; a child should be able to say almost all sounds of the English language correctly by the age of 6 or 7. Keep in mind that boys are more likely to have speech problems than girls and are slower to develop speech sounds. Also, note that a student with articulation problems resulting from speaking a dialect or English as a second language should not be considered to have a disorder.

The speech and language evaluation will include an assessment of the child's oral muscles required for speech, her ability to pronounce a variety of sounds, the intelligibility of her speech, and her receptive and expressive language skills. The pathologist will conduct formal testing in a one-on-one setting and, in addition, may observe the student in your class to assess how she uses language in casual conversation. The school nurse may also screen her hearing to determine if there is evidence of a hearing loss that may be affecting her speech. The pathologist may conclude from this evaluation that the student is a late bloomer and the problem is developmental, suggesting that with time it will correct itself as many do by the time a child reaches 8 or 9. On the other hand, the pathologist may conclude that speech or language therapy is warranted.

The therapy will focus on the weaknesses identified by the evaluation. If the student has articulation problems, the pathologist will teach her how to say specific sounds correctly, including how to position her tongue and mouth. The therapy will also include having her practice sounds through exercises and drills. If the student has problems in language usage, she will learn and practice rules in which she is deficient (for example, verb tense). The therapy may be given individually or in a group, and may occur one or more times per week. The speech-language pathologist may observe the student in your class to determine if the speech gains made in therapy are generalizing to the classroom.

HOW TEACHERS CAN HELP

The student who receives speech therapy will spend much more time with you than with the speech-language pathologist. You thus play an essential role in promoting her speech and language development. Your role, however, is not to remediate her specific problem, but rather to give her experience and confidence in interacting with you and her classmates. Many speech and language problems are not physical in origin, so they can be improved through practice and experience. You can use the following strategies in the classroom to foster speech and language development:

1. Reassure the Student Privately about Her Speech

If the student has a significant articulation problem, take her aside and in a calm, supportive manner let her know that her speech difficulties are not a problem for you and that if she has difficulty pronouncing some words, you and the class will be patient with her. Let the student know that many students get tangled up in their words. Ask her if she has any particular concerns or questions about your class that you can help with. Talking about her speech problem openly may help to defuse any anxiety she is experiencing. Keep this discussion brief; don't belabor the point. There is no need to discuss this issue again with the student unless you see signs of distress.

2. Do Not Draw Attention to the Student's Articulation Errors

In responding to the student, focus more on what she has said than how she has said it. If she mispronounces a word, do not correct her, supply the word for her, or have her imitate your pronunciation. Commenting on her speech is likely to discourage her from talking in class. Respond to the content of what she has said. If you did not understand her, do not act as if you did. Instead, you might say something like "I didn't catch all of that, but I really want to know what you said. Try saying it in another way." Or tell her your understanding of what she said, and ask her if that is correct.

3. Emphasize Correct Language Expression without Correcting the Student

When a student mispronounces a word, rather than stopping the lesson to point out her error, restate the word with the correct pronunciation in the context of a sentence. For example, if she says, "I really love aminals," you might respond, "I know how much you love animals," placing mild empha-sis on the correct pronunciation. Similarly, if the student uses incorrect gram-mar, echo the student's statement using the correct grammar, perhaps expanding on her statement to reinforce the concept. For example, if while reading a story to the class, the student comments on a picture by saying, "Look, the boy's hat blow off," you might say "You're right, his hat blew off. The girl's hat also blew off. They blew off because of the wind."

4. Model Effective Language Expression

A student with a language disorder may speak in short, simple sentences and have difficulty expanding on what she says. Model for the student how to elaborate on her thoughts. If she says, "The book was exciting," you might say, "Yes, the book was exciting. The part that I liked best was when the lost dog was able to find her way home, even though she was far away. How do you think dogs are able to do that?" Other ways to model good language skills are to describe what you are doing or thinking, called self-talk, and to describe what other students are doing, called parallel talk. This not only shows the student how to use language for descriptive purposes, but also draws her attention to salient factors of the activity. In engaging in self-talk and parallel talk, use language skills that are slightly more complex than those the student uses so that she is challenged without being confused. There is no need to have the student repeat what you said.

5. Find Opportunities to Talk with the Student Informally

Engaging in conversation is one of the best ways for students to improve their language skills. It also enhances their comfort in verbal interaction. Find a few minutes every day before or after school or during recess to talk with the student about things she is interested in, whether a favorite movie, a special interest, a game she likes to play, or a family activity. Encourage her to speak so she is doing at least as much talking as you. Ask her open-ended questions rather than yes or no questions, and show interest in her responses. Be patient in waiting for her answers. If she approaches you to talk and you are busy, make a note to see her later.

6. Teach the Student the Basics of Classroom Communication

While the rules of social communication may come naturally to most students, the student with language difficulties may need direct instruction. Even such basic skills as maintaining eye contact, taking turns, not interrupting or yelling out, and raising your hand may elude her. The following are some examples of situations that the student may find awkward and need help with:

- greeting and saying good-bye to classmates
- asking to join in a game
- making a request of the teacher
- asking or answering a question in class
- staying with a topic
- using a transition statement to change a topic, such as "That reminds me"
- telling a classmate to stop teasing her
- apologizing to a classmate whom she bumped into by accident
- resolving a conflict with a classmate

Consider using role play to teach these skills, offering the student suggestions about what to say, and what not to say. Help her understand that her language should change depending on the situation and the listener. Take advantage of natural situations to teach the student. For example, if she tells you that a student is bothering her, encourage her to tell the student to stop. Also, create these situations by, for example, asking the student to give a message to another teacher or encouraging her to ask others to play a game with her. Give her some ideas on what to say as well as feedback on how she does, making sure to find something positive to highlight.

7. Promote Class Participation

A student who has speech or language problems has a built-in tendency to interact less, perhaps out of a desire to protect herself or avoid awkward situations. Resist this tendency by making a conscious effort to involve her in class discussions. Provide a nonthreatening, unpressured climate in which the student is not afraid of your or classmates' responses if she does speak up. Encourage her participation by calling on her to answer a question you are certain she knows, or tell her ahead of time you will call on her so she can prepare a response. (Call on her early to lessen the anxiety.) Do not interrupt her while she is talking, listen attentively, and respond enthusiastically to her comments and questions. If she gives a one-word answer, ask her to tell you more or put it in a sentence, and praise her when she does. If she mumbles, tell her that what she is saying is important and she must say it more clearly. One way to monitor who is participating in class is to keep a seating chart on your desk and place checks next to the names of students who have contributed.

8. Integrate Expressive Language Activities into Your Academic Program

You have a wealth of opportunities to promote language expression in the classroom. Indeed, every time you speak or listen to your students, you are giving lessons in expressive language. Try the following classroom activities to give students practice in language skills:

- Have students tell you from their seats their date of birth and birthplace.

- Have students interview a classmate and then talk about the student to the class.

- Have students talk to the class about what they would change about school to make it more fun.

- Have students describe their ideas for inventions.

- Have students give sales pitches.

- Have students explain a game or describe a new toy.

- Have students describe their idea of a perfect day.

- Have students ask questions of the teacher in preparation for a test.

- Have students record jokes or riddles on tape, which you might place in a class listening center after reviewing them.

- Have students serve as co-leaders with you during class discussions.

- Have each student describe to a partner, who is separated from the student by a barrier, how to build an object she has built using blocks. Allow the partner to ask questions of the student who did the original design. Have them switch roles. Design your own version of this exercise in communication.

- Have students discuss a book, current event, or topic of your or the students' choosing in a small-group setting. Monitor the discussion to make sure they stick to the topic and everybody has a chance to participate.

■ Have a student in your class begin talking about a topic you have identified. After a minute or two, switch to another student, who must pick up where the first student left off. Continue with other students until the topic is exhausted. Suggest another topic, or have students choose the topic so that everybody has a chance to talk.

■ Have students describe in sentence form clues to a common object for classmates to guess.

■ Have students participate in parent-teacher conferences and elicit their views or reactions.

9. Orchestrate Successful Classroom Presentations

Skilled at avoiding public speaking situations, and often protected from them by sympathetic teachers, the student with a speech or language disorder often has little experience speaking in front of her peers. If she panics at the prospect of giving a class presentation, adjust your expectations to give her courage to take up the challenge. Let her know that you will work with her to make the experience more comfortable. Give her a topic that she is interested in, and rehearse with her until she feels comfortable, giving her honest feedback as well as praise. Also, ask her parents to practice with her. Be flexible about the length of her presentation. Allow her (and other students) to use notes. If she is uncomfortable standing in front of the class, let her make the presentation from her seat. If you cannot persuade her to do the presentation, don't push the issue, but also don't excuse her from the assignment. Instead, allow her to make the presentation to you in private or tape the presentation at home. As a last resort, let her do a written report.

10. Provide the Student with Extended Wait Time

A student with language problems may need more time to organize her ideas and formulate a response. She may also have trouble retrieving the right words, and her speech may be slow and labored. As a result, she may take more time than usual to answer a question. If this is a problem with one of your students, allow her more time to answer by extending your wait time after asking her a question, and avoid showing impatience. If she has difficulty answering, instead of moving on to another student, try giving her a clue to prompt an answer or restating the question in yes or no form. If she has trouble coming up with a specific word, give her the initial sound or suggest the category; if she still can't come up with it, supply the word.

11. Stimulate Higher-Level Language Development

In discussing a topic or story with the student, ask questions that stimulate good language usage but are within her ability level. Begin by asking for factual information, and gradually move to higher-level questions. Avoid yes or no questions. For example, in talking about a story, ask what it was about, but also find out what she liked best about the story or how it might have ended differently. Ask her about the meaning of difficult vocabulary in the story as well as examples of how the vocabulary might be used. Rephrase your questions if she has difficulty answering them.

12. Develop Nonverbal Signals to Alert the Student about Her Speech

If a student tends to speak too loudly or softly in class, work out with her in advance a subtle signal to let her know that she should either raise or lower her voice. This signal might be as simple as touching your ear or raising or lowering your hand when it is extended horizontally. You might also work out a signal to indicate to the student if she is speaking too quickly or mumbling. Do not use a signal to alert her about speech errors. Ignore them.

13. Talk with Your Class about How to Respond to the Student

If the student has a severe speech problem, ask her parents for permission to talk to the class briefly when the child is not in the classroom. Help the students understand that her speech problem is a result of difficulty in making sounds and is not related to how smart she is. Emphasize that speech problems can be very frustrating, and encourage their sensitivity in responding to her. Let them know they should not say anything to her about her speech or try to teach her how to pronounce words. Suggest that they listen calmly and patiently when she talks. Tell them it is okay to ask her to repeat what she said or to say it in a different way if they did not understand the first time. Make it clear that teasing her, or any student, is not acceptable and will not be tolerated. Encourage them to involve the student in activities in and out of school.

14. Encourage Social Interaction with Classmates

An important way that children learn and practice language is talking with their peers. If they have problems with speech or language, they may be tentative about interacting with their classmates, and their classmates may hesitate to interact with them. As a result, they may miss out on opportunities to learn such skills as initiating a conversation, sharing experiences, and asking other students to do things with them. Find ways for the student who has a language problem and is isolated from her peers to become involved in activities with classmates that require verbal interaction. Children talk with each other most during unstructured times (for example, recess and snack time), so make sure your students have downtime when there are no formal activities. You might encourage classmates to initiate conversations with the student, ask her to join in an activity with them, or invite her to sit with them during lunch. Ask them to respond positively and naturally when the student speaks with them. Also, ask the lunchroom and playground aides to try to get her involved with other students. In addition, suggest to the parents that they get the child involved in community activities that she is likely to do well in and enjoy.

15. Use Cooperative Learning

Having students work cooperatively in small groups is an effective way to foster verbal interaction among peers, but these group activities must be planned carefully. To enhance the experience for a student with a language disorder, select carefully the classmates she will work with, choosing students who are verbally competent but not dominating. Try to choose a topic or activity that interests the student. You may need to talk privately with the other students in the group to encourage them to draw out the student by asking for her views and responding positively to her efforts.

16. Intervene Immediately if the Student Is Being Ridiculed

The student with a speech impediment may be teased by her classmates and is sometimes the butt of jokes. If so, take the students who are doing the teasing aside, and help them understand how upsetting and hurtful ridicule can be. Ask them if they have ever been teased and how it felt. If they continue to ridicule the student after your discussion, take firmer steps, perhaps phoning their parents or keeping them in for detention.

17. Support the Student's Self-Esteem

A student with speech or language problems may feel different from her peers and have little social confidence. Find ways to enhance her self-esteem by giving her opportunities to shine in the classroom and spotlighting her talents and accomplishments. Of course, also look for opportunities to praise her, whether for a good oral report, an outstanding art project, or a kind act toward a classmate. If public praise is uncomfortable for her, do it privately. Try highlighting her language successes without interrupting the flow of conversation by noting the usefulness of the information. For example, if the student has explained to the class how to do a math problem, you might say, "Did everybody catch that? If you did, you should have a good idea of how to do this kind of problem."

18. Consult with the Speech-Language Pathologist

Your school's pathologist can suggest accommodations in your class for a student with speech or language problems. If the pathologist is not familiar with the student, ask him or her to observe in your class, offering specific questions to keep in mind during the observation. If the student is receiving speech or language therapy, find out about the student's weaknesses from the pathologist, and ask how you can foster her language development in the classroom without singling her out. Remember, however, that your job is not to remediate these deficiencies or provide the student with speech exercises, but rather to give her opportunities to practice and apply the skills she is learning in therapy in a natural setting—and to help her feel more comfortable interacting with others. The therapist may give you specific concerns to watch for. For example, if a student has a voice disorder, the speech-language pathologist may want you to monitor her speech to make sure she does not aggravate the problem by yelling—or you may need to pay attention to the student's use of verb tenses or pronouns.

FOR FURTHER INFORMATION

Hamaguchi, P. (1995). *Childhood Speech, Language, and Listening Problems: What Every Parent Should Know*. New York: John Wiley and Sons.

McCormick, L.; Schiefelbusch, R. L.; and Loeb, D. F. (1996). *Supporting Children With Communication Difficulties in Inclusive Settings*. Paramus, NJ: Prentice Hall.

Oyer, H. J.; Crowe, B.; and Haas, W. H. (1993). *Speech, Language, and Hearing Disorders: A Guide for the Teacher* (2d ed.). Needham Heights, MA: Allyn & Bacon.

Ratner, V. L., and Harris, L. (1994). *Understanding Language Disorders: The Impact on Learning*. Eau Claire, WI: Thinking Publications.

Wallach, G. P., and Butler, K. G. (eds.). (1994). *Language Learning Disabilities in School-Age Children and Adolescents*. New York: Merrill.

ORGANIZATIONS

American Speech-Language-Hearing Association
10801 Rockville Pike
Rockville, MD 20852
1-800-638-8255

Division for Children With Communication Disorders
c/o The Council for Exceptional Children
1920 Association Drive
Reston, VA 20191
1-703-620-3660

See also:
  Auditory Processing Problem
  Cerebral Palsy
  The ESL Student
  Hearing Impairment
  Low Self-Esteem
  The Shy Student
  Stuttering

SPELLING PROBLEMS

Learning to spell is a daunting challenge for many students. Because English has its origins in Latin, French, German, and other languages, it contains many words that are spelled differently from how they sound. Indeed, about one of every five words in the English language does not follow the rules of phonics. Learning these irregular words can exasperate the best of students.

Some English words are pronounced very similarly but spelled differently (for example, *where* and *wear*). Some letter combinations can be pronounced a number of ways (for example, the *ea* in *read, break, head,* and *dearth*). And some words with foreign roots are spelled differently from the way they sound (for example, *lieutenant*). George Bernard Shaw illustrated the complexity of English spelling by observing that *fish* could be spelled *ghoti* by taking the *gh* from *enough,* the *o* from *women,* and the *ti* from *nation.* It is not surprising, then, that so many children find spelling a difficult and confusing subject.

Spelling continues to occupy a prominent place in the nation's classrooms. The electronic speller and the computer spell checker may have made life easier for problem spellers, but it has not lessened the importance of spelling instruction. Teachers understand that frequent misspellings can give rise to negative consequences for children and adults—including poor grades on written reports, failure to obtain job interviews, and low ratings on job performance.

The teaching of spelling has not changed much over the years. Because of the need to memorize the spelling of many words, particularly those that defy the rules of phonics, spelling instruction requires drill and practice. While many teachers continue the time-honored practice of giving weekly tests, the true measure of a student's spelling ability is not how he does on these weekly tests, but rather how well he spells in his writing assignments. Many students do well on their weekly tests, but misspell the same words they have spelled correctly on the tests on their other assignments.

DIFFICULTIES WITH SPELLING

To be a good speller, a student must be able to hear and reproduce in writing the sounds of words that are spelled phonetically, and to visualize the words that are not. Students with a poor visual memory have a hard time retaining the visual images of words, and tend to be poor spellers. Spelling problems may also result from difficulty in hearing the differences in sounds, or auditory discrimination. A child who cannot hear the difference between, say, *hat* and *hit*, will have difficulty spelling words phonetically. If you suspect that one of your students is not hearing sounds accurately, suggest to his parents that they consider obtaining an evaluation of his hearing by an audiologist.

Students with learning disabilities often struggle with spelling. Indeed, a child who is a poor reader will almost always have trouble spelling. But the reverse is not always true; a poor speller may be a very capable reader. A student who has difficulty spelling is no less intelligent than other students, on average, nor is he necessarily a poor writer. Many well-known writers, such as F. Scott Fitzgerald and Ernest Hemingway, were notoriously bad spellers.

HOW TEACHERS CAN HELP

While spelling is a key component of good writing, teachers need not devote a large block of time to the subject. Indeed, experts recommend that, even with students who are problem spellers, 15 to 20 minutes per day of spelling instruction is sufficient. But simply giving a spelling test to students every Friday on words they have studied during the week will not ensure that all your students will become good spellers. Spelling instruction must be provided, and it must be purposeful and stimulating to make optimal use of the time. While most teachers receive little training in how to teach spelling, many have developed effective strategies for working with students who have difficulty spelling. These strategies, described below, will also be useful with your other students.

1. Don't Dwell on Spelling Errors During the Early Elementary Years

Placing too much emphasis on spelling mistakes at an early age can inhibit the child's desire to write. Many educators thus believe that misspellings should not be corrected in the writings of young students. Spelling, like language, is developmental, so the "creative" spelling of most children will eventually be replaced by accurate spelling. *Bl* will eventually become *bal*, which will eventually become *ball*. Of course, as the student moves into later elementary grades, you will want to begin correcting his spelling mistakes. If you are using this approach to spelling, it is important to inform parents of the rationale for this method, and to reassure them that you will be providing spelling instruction.

2. Be Patient and Encouraging

The problem speller may experience much frustration and anxiety from his difficulty, especially if other subjects come easily to him. Reassure him that good spellers are no smarter than poor spellers (which is true), and be encouraging of his efforts and his successes. Rewarding him for his performance by giving him stickers or other tangible items may motivate him to want to do well. You may also show him concrete evidence of his improvement by graphing his progress in spelling or having him keep a notebook with words that he has mastered. He might also put 3″ by 5″ cards with words he can spell in a box or on a ring. This way, he can see evidence of his progress.

3. Help the Student Understand the Importance of Correct Spelling

Some students may not grasp the value of good spelling. Find opportunities to remind the student that incorrect spelling can impede understanding of what he writes. Give him some examples of consequences of poor spelling, including lowered marks on school assignments, negative perceptions of the writer's ability, and poor job evaluations.

4. Encourage Reading

The student who reads well and often is likely to spell well. In the process of reading, the child encounters the same words repeatedly, reinforcing their visual images in his mind.

5. Have the Student Develop an Individualized Spelling List

While many teachers use the same spelling words for all students, you may want to have problem spellers (and perhaps other students as well) develop their own lists each week, derived partially from words that have meaning to them. When spelling words are drawn from topics of interest or relevance to the student (for example, the name of his dog, his favorite game, or activities associatied with an upcoming holiday), he may be more motivated to learn them. The spelling list might also include words that he has misspelled in his own personal writing, vocabulary from school subjects such as science or social studies, and frequently used words (see item 6). Review the words he has placed on his list to ensure that he has spelled them correctly. Suggest that he highlight or color-code the troublesome letter combinations and group words together that have similar spelling patterns. Because students will have different lists, you should consider having students test each other to save time. Words that are not spelled correctly on the test should remain on the following week's list.

6. Teach the Student How to Spell Frequently Used Words

It is said that about half of the written English language is composed of the 100 most frequently used words. Give the student a list of the most common words, and have him check off each word as he masters its spelling, or incorporate some of these words into each week's list. Many teacher texts have lists of commonly used words (for example, *The Quick-Word Handbook*, published by Curriculum Associates).

7. Have Students Study Only Those Words They Misspell

While many teachers follow the traditional practice of pretest-study-test, resulting in a 20-word spelling test on Friday, you may find it a more efficient use of your students' time to have them study and take the test only on the words missed on the pretest. If your student is having difficulty handling a 20-word weekly list, consider instead giving him three or four words a day to learn.

8. Have the Student Practice His Spelling Words by Writing Them

Spelling is primarily a visual task, and students should use visually oriented study methods. Having students write the words promotes spelling better than having them spell the words orally. In addition, they need to see the words to judge whether they are correct. Also, reinforce the visual image by writing down the words when students request correct spellings, and by playing spelling games that require students to write the words (see item 17).

Make sure that the study technique you suggest to your students includes a writing component. You may find the following method of study, or a variation, helpful to your students: Have the student look at the word, say it, cover it up, spell it orally, write it from memory, and check the spelling. Repeat this sequence until he masters the word. You might also have the student, particularly a young student, trace the word prior to writing it from memory. Whatever technique you decide upon, make sure to demonstrate it to the students. Avoid having them write their spelling words over and over; the value is lost after a few repetitions.

9. Analyze the Student's Errors for Patterns of Mistakes

It is more important to see where the student is making his mistakes than to tally how many mistakes he has made. Identify patterns in his spelling errors (for example, the failure to understand a spelling rule) and correct them as soon as possible, before they become habits. Also, note other examples of the spelling to reinforce the pattern. For example, if the student has difficulty with the *ea* sound in the word *bean*, give other words with the *ea* sound such as *lean, clean,* and *mean.*

10. Reproduce the Student's Error and Then Present the Correct Spelling

While this may seem to go against your teaching instincts, studies have shown that this is an effective way of improving the spelling of children with learning disabilities. Rather than just noting misspelled words, you might write the incorrect and correct spellings while saying, "You spelled this word incorrectly. It is not spelled b-e-l-e-i-v-e. The correct spelling is b-e-l-i-e-v-e." This is especially effective with irregular words. Try to point out the student's error in private.

11. Teach the Student about Word Families and Word Patterns

Give words to the student that form the basis for a word family, and have him generate other words containing the base word (for example, *play, played, player, playful*). Similarly, teach him words with the same spelling pattern as the original word (for example, *tough, rough,* and *enough*). In this way, the student learns how knowing one word can help him spell other words in the same family or with the same pattern.

12. Teach Spelling Rules—Selectively

Teaching spelling rules should be only one of your approaches because of the many irregularities not covered by rules. Students will retain only a few spelling rules, so be careful about bombarding them. Simply telling students a rule is not always effective, because they will probably forget it. Rules are better retained if they learn them through a process of discovery and then are asked to explain them. For example, in teaching students how to spell words in the past tense, you might give some examples of verbs in both the present and past tenses and then ask, "What happens to a verb that ends in *e* when *-ed* is added to it?" Ask students to find examples of this rule in passages that they read. Remember to teach them exceptions to the rule.

13. Give the Student Memory Aids

You might make up your own, but remember to be selective and not overwhelm the student. The following examples of aids may help your students remember spelling patterns:

- *I* before *e* except after *c*, or when sounded like *a*, as in n*ei*ghbor or w*ei*gh.

- *Here* is in the words *where* and *there*.

- I am a *fri*end to the *end*.

- You get re*lief* when you *lie* down.

- *Q* is always followed by *u*.

- *Sp* is always followed by a vowel, or by *l, h,* or *r.*

14. Help the Student Hear the Sounds in Words

Students typically try to spell unfamiliar words by listening to their sounds and spelling them phonetically. As you read a story to your students, ask them to tell you words with a specific sound while you write the words on the board and underline the letter or letters that convey the sound. Have the students think of other words with this sound. Say the word while emphasizing the particular sound. Remember that while it is important for students to learn how to sound out words, phonics should not be the exclusive approach to spelling instruction because of the many irregular words in our language.

15. Use a Multisensory Approach

Reinforcing the visual image of the word through sight and touch helps the student retain the word. Have the student write the word in large print and then trace the letters with his finger as he pronounces them. Repeat this process until he can trace the word from memory.

16. Do Not Spend Much Time Teaching the Meaning of Spelling Words or Dividing Them into Syllables

While it is useful for students to learn the meaning of their spelling words, research suggests that this does not improve their ability to spell them. Studies also show little or no benefit, in terms of spelling, from breaking the words into syllables.

17. Make Spelling Fun with Word Games

Because many students find spelling tedious, teachers must find ways to motivate them to focus on the subject. Many teachers do this through word games such as hangman, wordsearch, Scrabble for Juniors, Speak & Spell, Wheel of Fortune, Spill & Spell, and Boggle. You can modify the rules to make the game more rewarding and less pressured. You might also have students make words from other words by rearranging the letters (for example, *dear* and *read*), or scramble the letters of words from their spelling list and challenge them to find the original words. Another idea is to ask students to identify words relating to a topic your class is studying, in which you have removed the vowels. Give them the number of missing vowels and the meaning of the word as clues; for example, hrt + 2 = body organ (heart) or y + 2 = a part of the face (eye).

18. Encourage Good Spelling Practices with Your Comments

Use your questions or comments to students to teach or reinforce spelling strategies. For example, you might say:

- "I like the way you checked your paper for spelling errors."
- "I'm impressed by how you will try to sound out words that you have not heard before."
- "Can you figure out the root word?"
- "Can you think of other words with the same spelling pattern?"
- "Can you think of a memory aid that can help you here?"

19. Provide the Student Access to Spelling References

Teach the student how to use the dictionary and spelling references, but do not expect him to look up every misspelled word—especially if he is prone to spelling errors—or he will quickly become turned off to writing. In addition, if he doesn't know how to spell the word, he may not be able to look it up! It is certainly acceptable to tell the student how to spell a word on occasion. Some spelling references that you may want to have on hand are *50,000 Words Divided and Spelled* by Harry Sharp; *Webster's Instant Word Guide,* which list words in alphabetical order and helps children find correct spellings quickly; and *How to Spell It: A Dictionary of Commonly Misspelled Words* by Harriet Wittles and Joan Greisman.

20. Require the Student to Proof His Work for Spelling Errors

If you find spelling errors on a student's paper, put check marks in the margin and have him find and correct the mistakes. For the younger student, suggest that he correct spelling mistakes by circling the incorrect letters, writing the correct letters above the incorrect ones, and then writing the word correctly above or below the misspelled word, or on a separate piece of paper.

21. Make Use of Technology

For many problem spellers, the way to spell relief is technology, most notably the spell checker and the electronic speller. While these tools help students check and correct spelling, they do not lessen the need for spelling instruction. A spell checker in a word processing program highlights and even corrects spelling errors. The electronic speller solves the dilemma of a student's having to look up in the dictionary a word that he cannot spell. To use this device, he types in the word the way he thinks it is spelled and the electronic speller shows him the likely correct spelling. Computer spelling programs that teach spelling in a way that is lively and interesting are also available.

FOR FURTHER INFORMATION

Bolton, F., and Snowball, D. (1993). *Ideas for Spelling.* Portsmouth, NH: Heinemann.

Dixon, R. C. (1993). *The Surefire Way to Better Spelling.* New York: St. Martin's Press.

Gentry, J. R., and Gillet, J. W. (1993). *Teaching Kids to Spell.* Portsmouth, NH: Heinemann.

Loomer, B. M., and Strege, M. G. (1990). *Useful Spelling: Levels 2–8.* Mount Vernon, IA: Useful Learning.

Stowe, C. (1996). *Spelling Smart!* West Nyack, NY: The Center for Applied Research in Education.

See also:
    Auditory Processing Problem
    Hearing Impairment
    Reading Disability

THE UNMOTIVATED STUDENT

Perhaps the most common problem that teachers face in the classroom is lack of motivation. While motivational difficulties occur with students of all grade levels, this problem often emerges during late elementary or middle school. The zest for learning that students felt in kindergarten or first grade may lessen as the work becomes more demanding and their academic standing more apparent. They may come to see school as a place of drudgery and begin to take detours during the learning process. The student who is unmotivated in elementary or middle school may be at risk for dropping out in high school. By then, his lack of interest in school may be deeply entrenched and resistant to change. It is thus critical that schools address motivational problems as soon as they emerge by helping students perceive school as a place where they can be successful, and schoolwork as interesting, relevant, and meaningful.

UNDERSTANDING MOTIVATION

To be motivated means to be willing to put forth effort to achieve a specific goal. Educators make a distinction between intrinsic and extrinsic motivation. A student who is intrinsically motivated performs a task because of the satisfaction he gains from the activity, the pride he derives from accomplishment, and the joy he gets from learning. In contrast, a student who is extrinsically motivated performs a task because of the rewards it offers him, such as parent and teacher approval, good grades, and entry into a good college. It is, of course, preferable that students be intrinsically motivated—that they enjoy learning for its own sake—but this is often not the case. Many teachers thus find it necessary to motivate students extrinsically in the hope that, as they invest energy in the task, they will discover aspects that are inherently rewarding.

Lack of motivation is not always easy to define, but teachers have no trouble recognizing it. They see the student whose attitude toward school screams, "I don't care." He is highly motivated when it comes to schoolwork—motivated to avoid it. He invests more energy eluding challenges than tackling them. His test scores may suggest high potential, but his classroom performance conveys something very different. Seemingly satisfied with work well below his potential, he may do just enough to get by. He may start a task half-heartedly and give up at the first sign of trouble. When given an assignment, he may shrug his shoulders and complain, "Why do we have to do this?" or "This is stupid." He may fail to turn in work or, if he does, he may do it with little care or thought.

Motivation can vary depending on the setting and situation. A child may be a reluctant learner when it comes to reading, but pursue math with enthusiasm. Another child may be inattentive and uninterested during a teacher's explanation of a science principle, but be absorbed watching a science experiment demonstrating that same principle. It is thus misleading to describe a student simply as motivated or unmotivated. Children are usually motivated by something. It just may not have anything to do with school. Or they may be unmotivated in one subject, but not another—or by one teaching approach, but not another. The task for the teacher is to find out what does motivate him, namely, to identify the settings, situations, and conditions that he responds to and that can be used to ignite his interest.

FACTORS THAT INFLUENCE MOTIVATION

While unmotivated students may behave similarly in class, the sources of their resistance to schoolwork may be very different. There are a myriad of reasons why students may be unmotivated, including the following:

- *Fear of Failure:* The student may fear making mistakes and appearing foolish in the eyes of his peers. He may conclude it is safer not to try than to try and risk embarrassment. He may aim low, putting forth effort only when he is certain of success.

- *Lack of Meaning:* The student may believe that schoolwork is not important for him to know or relevant to his life.

- *Emotional Distress:* The student may be unable to focus in class because he is anxious or upset, perhaps relating to problems at home. Low motivation may also reflect a problem with depression.

- *Learning Disability:* The student may have greater difficulty mastering the material than his peers and may give up in frustration.

- *Lack of Challenge:* The student may be bored with schoolwork for good reason—it is well below his ability. It is not uncommon for gifted students to display problems of low motivation. They may exert effort only in areas they find challenging or personally satisfying.

- *Desire for Attention:* The student may be trying to gain the teacher's attention and support through the appearance of being helpless.

- *Peer Concern:* Fearing that his popularity will suffer if he appears smart, the student may choose being "cool" over being competent.

- *Low Expectations:* The student's apathy toward school may stem from the low academic expectations conveyed to him by his parents and the lack of their encouragement and support of his school performance.

- *Expression of Anger:* The student may be angry with his parents because of the pressure they have placed on him to excel in school, and his non-performance may be his way of striking back.

What many unmotivated students share in common is a belief that they are not able to succeed with academic tasks. They may perceive that academic success results more from ability than from effort. Similarly, they may attribute academic failure to low ability rather than minimal effort or use of faulty strategies. Believing that they have little academic ability, they anticipate that their efforts will be futile. They lack a feeling of what is called self-efficacy. As a result, they shy away from tackling difficult tasks and give in easily to frustration. If they do succeed, they may write it off as a fluke, attributing it to luck, the ease of the task, or perhaps teacher charity. Their perceptions may thus have more to do with their academic success than their abilities. With these students, the task for the teacher is to help change their belief system—no small matter—so they come to see effort and learning strategies as the key ingredients to academic success.

HOW TEACHERS CAN HELP

Motivating the uninterested student is a challenge teachers face almost every day. This challenge can be especially daunting with a student who has a long history of not performing, and whose low motivation is deeply embedded. In figuring out how to light a motivational fire within this student, it is important to assess why he is not putting forth effort. Is he demoralized by previous failures? Is he confused about what to do? Is he anxious about his performance? Is he unable to concentrate because of concerns about family problems? Is he experiencing learning difficulties? Does he find the lessons irrelevant and uninteresting? To answer these questions, try to identify any patterns with the student by checking his school records, observing him in different school situations, and talking with his parents and previous teachers. This information may give you some ideas for motivating him. You may find some of the following strategies helpful, but keep in mind that students vary in what gets them going: What motivates one student will not necessarily motivate another. Some of the strategies described below are appropriate for use with individual students, while others are suitable for use with the entire class.

1. Talk with the Student Privately

Ask the student to help you understand his seeming lack of interest in schoolwork. If he has difficulty responding, suggest that he think out loud. Listen for responses signaling low self-confidence ("There's no way I'm going to understand this stuff") or lack of interest ("I'm never going to need to know this") or anxiety ("I get upset the moment I walk into math class"). If this is not productive, offer some possible reasons based on your observations of him in the classroom, and ask him if you are on the right track. Elicit his suggestions about what you might do differently in the classroom to increase his effort. You might have him write out for you a list of three specific reasons why he is doing poorly in school as well as three ideas for making the situation better. Develop a written improvement plan with the student, incorporating both your suggestions and his, and get his commitment to this plan. Meet with him briefly every day to review how he is doing and whether he is following through on what he agreed to do. Focus on what he has done well, praising him for his efforts as well as his successes. Also, find time to talk with him about nonschool matters, so he feels you care about him as a person. Ask about his interests and activities outside of school.

2. Provide a Warm, Accepting Climate

Foster a supportive environment by treating all students with respect and understanding. Unmotivated students will be more likely to participate if they believe that your class is a safe setting in which to take risks. They need to feel that their responses will be accepted and their errors will not result in ridicule. Encourage them to ask questions and make comments, and respond positively to their contributions without any trace of criticism or sarcasm. Make sure you do not talk so much that there is little opportunity for them to participate in class. Show concern if a student has difficulty, reacting in a calm, patient manner. If he seems self-conscious about making mistakes, convey to him privately that mistakes are a normal and natural part of learning, perhaps offering the slogan: "We all make mistakes; that's why they put erasers on pencils."

3. Stay Close to the Student

Students who are near you are more likely to be on task. Take advantage of this by seating the student close to where you usually stand while teaching a lesson. As students are doing seatwork, circulate among them, making sure to spend time near those who are frequently off task.

4. Introduce the Lesson with Enthusiasm

The way you introduce a lesson to students will affect their level of interest in the topic and their understanding of its importance. Be positive in your presentation. Your enthusiasm may be contagious. Conversely, if students perceive that you find the topic uninteresting or unimportant, you can be sure they will follow your lead. Begin by stating precisely what they will be learning and the purpose for learning it. Talk about why this topic is meaningful, offering a reason that will grab their attention. In teaching the metric system, for example, mention various familiar objects that are measured in metric units such as bottles of soda, camera lenses, and skis; ask students for other examples. You might explain how learning a particular skill is necessary to do another (for example, multiplication facts are needed to do division). You might also spark their interest by emphasizing the enjoyment or intriguing nature of the task. You might say, for example, "This is one of my favorite topics" or "I think you're going to find this different from anything you've ever done." You can also increase their attention to and understanding of a lesson, film, or reading passage by telling them specifically what you want them to focus on.

5. Give Clear Directions and Feedback

Students' failure to complete assignments, either in school or at home, may reflect their confusion about what to do. Provide directions to students that are clear, concise, and explicit, and make sure you have their attention prior to directing them. Do not give directions while handing out papers.

With complicated assignments, do an example for them. Ask your students if they have any questions about what to do. You might ask a student who tends to confuse easily to repeat the directions to you, or check to make sure he is doing the task correctly. If the students are doing the assignment in class, monitor the performance of at-risk students and, if necessary, provide constructive and encouraging feedback. Consult the chapter on the disorganized student for additional strategies to increase homework completion—in particular the use of a daily assignment sheet signed by you and the parents.

6. Orchestrate the Student's Success

Some students fail to put forth effort because they lack confidence that they will be successful. If a student has a history of academic frustration, take steps to break this cycle of failure. Give him work and materials that he is capable of completing successfully, but that will still give him a feeling of satisfaction. Finishing a task will provide a sense of accomplishment. Structure assignments so that the first part is relatively easy—to give him some experience with success. Plan his classroom contributions in advance to maximize his chances for success. For example, you may want to have the student rehearse a math problem at home with his parents before presenting it to the class—or you may want to let him know at the beginning of class that you will be asking him a particular question so he can think about a response. As he experiences success, he is likely to become more confident and more willing to take risks. If he struggles with a task, emphasize what he has done well while gently correcting his mistakes. Help him to see mistakes as a natural stepping stone to mastery. You may also want to de-emphasize with a low-performing student the formal evaluation process. He may be more likely to take on challenges if he knows he isn't being graded on his performance.

7. Highlight the Student's Talents

An unmotivated student is often a demoralized student. He may perceive school as a place of failure and frustration. Try to alter his perceptions by finding opportunities for him to excel in his areas of strength, demonstrate his talents to the class, or talk to his classmates about one of his hobbies. Be sure to get the student's okay before you display his work in the classroom.

8. Vary Your Teaching Style

Students may become bored by your use of the same instructional approach day in and day out. This is particularly true if your lessons include a steady diet of material to be memorized. Nothing will stifle interest as quickly as mindless recitation of facts. Grab your students' attention by varying your presentation style and incorporating novel approaches. While some lessons will of necessity emphasize the learning of facts, also present lessons that challenge your students' thinking ability and call for them to use their imagination and creativity. Encourage them to ask questions and offer their own ideas. Respond positively to their contributions. Make use of a variety of teaching formats such as lecture and discussion, hands-on activities, cooperative learning, class debates, role playing, related art projects, computer work, student presentations, guest speakers, and field trips. If you do group work in your class, be sure to vary the composition of the groups. In particular, avoid consistent grouping of students by ability, which saps the motivation of students always placed in low-ability groups. Just as you should vary your instructional approaches, you should also vary the types of assignments you give to your students.

9. Relate Instruction to the Students' Interests

Making your lessons personally meaningful to your students requires that you learn about their interests and personal experiences. You can do this by observing the students, having private chats with them, and talking with their parents. Also, consider asking the students to complete an interest inventory to find out how they like to spend their free time. You might keep a notebook with a page for each student, noting their interests and talents, academic strengths and weaknesses, and areas of special sensitivity. Find ways to incorporate their interests into your lessons and assignments. Simply using a student's name in a math problem or story can spark his interest. (With the merge feature on word processing programs, you can easily create math word problems or language arts exercises that include the names of your students.) If you know the student has a paper route, you might give the class math problems requiring them to calculate how much a child earns delivering papers under various conditions. If the student is a Girl Scout, use the example of selling cookies to generate math problems. If you are doing a transportation unit and you know the student builds model airplanes, have him bring in some models to show the class. In addition, suggest books for the student to read that are related to his interests or experiences. Also, use his interests to get him more involved in class activities. If he is talented at art, you might have him help you design your bulletin boards. If he excels on the computer, have him become the class troubleshooter.

10. Relate Instruction to the Real World

Students who are unmotivated often ask, "Why do I have to know this?" It is a fair question. Try to give them some answers by helping them see how the lessons of the classroom can be applied to life outside the classroom. Don't just do this when they ask. Get in the habit of giving your lessons a real-world focus. In studying different shapes, have students point out examples of shapes in the classroom. Show how being able to count change is useful when trying to determine if you were given the correct change by a cashier. Demonstrate how knowing percentages can be used to figure out interest on your bank account. Look for opportunities to use newly learned skills for practical purposes (for example, using division to figure out the cost per student of a class trip). Also, use materials that are connected with everyday life. Supplement texts with articles from newspapers or magazines. Have students write for information from companies, travel bureaus, or even famous people. Plan field trips that show how the lessons they are learning work in real life. If you are teaching students how a law is made, take them to the state legislature. If you are doing a unit on the environment, plan a trip to a recycling center. You can also help close the gap between school and the real world with your assignments. If your students are studying the McCarthy era, have them interview their grandparents, or other family members, about what it was like to live during that time. In teaching about plant life, have your students make a leaf collection. For older students, present contemporary problems (for example, how to curb teenage smoking) that are related to topics they are studying, and have them use their knowledge to formulate potential solutions.

11. Invite Guest Speakers to Your Class

People from the community can help your students understand how the lessons of school life can be applied to the realities of everyday life. Do not invite only professional people to speak to your class; a person who works in a factory can help explain the importance of computer technology in manufacturing, while an auto mechanic can discuss how an engine powers a car. Have students complete a brief questionnaire at the beginning of the year describing their parents' occupations so you have a potential bank of guest speakers.

12. Provide Hands-on Activities

Students who are in the dark when listening to classroom lectures may suddenly light up when given an opportunity to experience the topic directly. Hands-on activities can be used in virtually any subject. For example, you might have students act out parts of a play that they are reading in English class, carry out an experiment to illustrate a science principle, do a cooking project to help them understand different types of measurement or the use of fractions, or conduct a debate about a controversial historical issue. These activities not only spur students' interests, but also help them retain concepts.

13. Challenge the Student

Student motivation suffers when the task is either too easy or too hard. If a student feels a task is too easy, he may race through it, gaining little satisfaction from his performance; if he feels it is too hard, he may give up quickly, perceiving that he has little chance of success. Give him work at an optimal level of difficulty—challenging yet achievable. The task should demand some thought from the student, but be able to be done successfully with moderate effort. In selecting work for the student, keep in mind that students often feel challenged by assignments that are thought-provoking, and unchallenged by assignments that require rote memorization. Monitor his progress, and adjust the difficulty level, if necessary. Giving your students tasks that match their abilities may present problems if you have a range of skill levels in your class. The following strategies may ease the process of adapting instruction: computer-based instruction, parent volunteers, peer tutors, and cooperative learning.

14. Make Learning Fun for the Student, and Spark His Curiosity

Activities that are fun can also be instructive. The following are some ways you can grab your students' attention and pique their interest:

- Begin class by offering a question, dilemma, or "brain teaser" for students to think about that is related to the topic you are teaching. Encourage class discussion, posing questions to stimulate their thinking, but not being too quick to answer their questions. Ask them to back up their point of view.

- Present a topic in the form of a mystery, and ask students to try to solve the mystery with their questions.

- Tell stories that make important educational points.

- Inject humor into the class.

- Use music to supplement your lessons (for example, use songs from the Depression to illustrate people's concerns at that time).

- Act unpredictably (for example, dress in a costume from a historical period that the class is studying).

- Use games for such mundane learning tasks as memorizing spelling words or math facts (for example, see how many math facts students can do on paper in three minutes).

- Make up crossword puzzles to teach vocabulary words (or have students compose them).

Keep in mind that the purpose of these activities is to teach a concept or make an educational point, so your students should be clear on the connection between the activity and the concept you are trying to convey. If the activity is too unrelated to the topic, they may not perceive this connection.

15. Present Tasks in Manageable Doses

Some students may resist tackling academic tasks because they perceive them as overwhelming and undoable. If so, break the task into small, bite-sized parts, and make certain they are within the student's ability. Present one step at a time, making sure he masters each step before moving to the next. Let him determine the pace of instruction. As he gains skill and confidence, you can gradually present larger amounts of information or more difficult problems, or move at a somewhat faster pace. You might approach homework the same way. For example, if the student struggles with math and resists doing assignments, you might give him half the problems of the other students, selecting problems you are confident he can do.

16. Allow the Advanced but Bored Student to Bypass Topics He Has Mastered

Academically advanced students may feel frustrated by the slow pace of teaching and the tedious nature of assignments. They may be bored to tears learning about topics they already know. Their boredom may manifest itself in the form of inattentiveness, incomplete assignments, and nonparticipation in class discussions. Consider allowing the student to skip topics that he can show he has mastered. You might evaluate his proficiency in the topic by giving him a pretest, unit test, end-of-year test, or a test you have designed for this purpose. If he demonstrates mastery of the topic to your satisfaction, excuse him from the tests and assignments connected with the topic, and give him more advanced work in that area, perhaps offering him a choice of projects. See the chapter entitled The Gifted Student for a more detailed discussion of how to adapt instruction for advanced students.

17. Allow the Student Some Control over What and How He Learns

Uninterested students often respond positively when given some ownership of the learning process. They are more likely to be attentive and exert effort when they have had input into instructional decisions. This does not mean ceding authority to students or giving them complete freedom, but rather allowing them some choice in what and how they learn. The following are some ways you can involve them in educational decisions:

- Hold a class meeting periodically to ask for their suggestions about how the class might be run differently, and be willing to accept those that make sense to you.

- Allow students to select which seats they sit in. Reserve the right, however, to assign seats if problems emerge.

- Allow students to choose the sequence of daily activities.

- Allow students to select from a menu of assignments (see item 18).

- Allow students to choose from a variety of rewards for achieving preestablished goals.

- Allow students to evaluate their own work (see item 20).

- Allow students to choose the book the class will read from a selection you have provided.

- Allow students to choose the topic they will do a paper on, or the book they will read for a book report. Monitor their choices to make sure their selections are realistic.

- Allow students to set specific, short-term goals for themselves (for example, how many problems they will get right on math assignments). These goals may serve as incentives for students to try to match or exceed them. Make sure the goals they establish are realistic, since students often overestimate what they can do.

18. Give the Students a Choice of Assignments

In an effort to give students more control of the learning process, you might allow them a say in their assignments. Consider giving them a choice of three or four assignments, each of which fosters an understanding of the topic. For example, you might allow students to do a book report on the topic you are studying, make an oral presentation, or do a related art project. Allow them to do a project that is not on your list, if it meets with your approval (see item 19). Through this assignment menu, you empower students while still retaining control of the work they do. Of course, you still reserve the right to require them to do certain critical assignments.

19. Allow the Student to Do an Independent Project

The student who is unenthusiastic about a classroom assignment may be excited by the opportunity to do a project in his area of interest. Indeed, the apathetic student can quickly become focused and hard-working when given the chance to work on something that sparks his interest. Even elementary students can do independent projects. As an example, if the student is artistic, you might allow him to demonstrate his understanding of a social studies topic by making a diorama or creating a collage. The project may be in place of or in addition to the regular assignment, depending on whether you consider the assignment critical for the student to do. Allow the student to work on the project during free time or recess, or after school. You may have to assist him in coming up with a topic as well as useful resources. You might connect him with an adult in the school or community who is involved in the subject of the project. Allow the student control over many aspects of the project as long as he is making realistic choices. Refrain from taking over; the key is not to stifle his enthusiasm. Talk with him about how he will communicate the results of his project, perhaps through a presentation to the class or a school display. If he has an interest in science, encourage him to do a project for the science fair, perhaps suggesting some topics.

20. Have the Student Evaluate Himself

Another way that a student can be actively involved in his educational program is to evaluate his own performance and monitor his progress. This may increase his investment of energy in schoolwork and decrease his reliance on the evaluation of others. For example, you might have him evaluate a project he completed, giving an overall evaluation as well as identifying specific strengths and weaknesses. He might also score his own assignments, using an answer sheet that you provide to him, and then correct his mistakes. In addition, you might have the student keep track of his progress in certain subjects by recording his performance daily or weekly (for example, his scores on weekly spelling tests). Show him how to graph his performance, or allow him to devise his own charting system. Suggest that he write a specific short-term goal on the chart based on his previous performance. For example, if he has been getting grades in the 60's on spelling tests, his goal might be to improve by five points each week until he is getting a score of at least 80 each week. The graph will provide visible evidence of his progress (or lack of progress) and serve as an incentive to improve. The student might graph other aspects of school performance (for example, grades on homework assignments, percentage of homework assignments handed in weekly, or number of times he answered a question in class each day).

21. Have the Student Tutor a Child in a Lower Grade

The student who is inattentive to his own work may surprise you by being very attentive and capable when working with another student. Teaching a younger child may give him a feeling of competence and spark some interest in completing his own work. Give him a sense of importance by asking for his ideas about the child's strengths and weaknesses as well as the best way of working with him.

22. Emphasize the Importance of Effort as a Building Block of Success

Many students who lack motivation have concluded that no amount of effort will bring about success. Believing that they have little ability, they may feel there is no point in trying. They may make such comments as "I'll never get this stuff. I'm no good in math." Help to change their thinking by stressing the value of effort in conjunction with the use of the correct strategies. You might say, "A lot of students find this difficult, but if you work hard and use the strategies we talked about, I'm sure you'll see progress." Consider reading to early elementary students the book *The Little Engine That Could*, to demonstrate the value of a belief in oneself and persistence. Placing too much emphasis on the final product—on test scores, on grades, on awards—will be discouraging, especially to the low-achieving student. Instead, applaud displays of effort as well as signs of progress ("John, your effort has really paid off. Look how much you've improved from last mark-

ing period."). Attribute a student's difficulties to lack of effort, lack of information, or a faulty strategy rather than to poor ability. If you are successful
in changing the student's mind-set, he will be more willing to invest effort,
more confident that with effort he will succeed, and more determined to
persist in the face of difficulty.

23. Focus on the Student's Progress Rather than on His Performance Relative to That of Others

When students are evaluated against their classmates, there are always
winners and losers. A student who is a consistent loser—who always falls
short when measured against his peers—will eventually become so demoralized that he will probably just shut down in school. If this is the case with one
of your students, evaluate him based on his improvement in a particular area,
or his mastery of a specific goal rather than his performance relative to that of
classmates. Similarly, base classroom rewards on his progress rather than his
relative performance. For example, if you issue certificates for outstanding
performance, you might give one to a student who has improved his math test
scores on four consecutive tests, even though he began with a 65. Also, display in your classroom the work of students who have put forth considerable
effort or made significant improvement rather than just the most outstanding
work. Portfolio assessment, in which you evaluate representative samples of a
student's work during the year and consider his progress, is a useful and increasingly popular way of assessing his performance without comparing him
with his peers. You might even incorporate self-evaluation into the portfolio
assessment by having the student comment on his own work.

24. Show Confidence in the Student, and Provide Support When He Struggles

Unmotivated students typically have little faith in their academic abilities. By expressing confidence in a student's ability to be successful, you can
give him the courage to take risks. It is not enough, however, to simply convey your confidence in him. You must also structure learning activities so he
experiences success (see item 6). If he does not, make sure to avoid criticizing him or drawing attention to his performance. Help him understand that
setbacks normally occur in the process of learning. Make sure you do not signal that you are giving up on him, because he will then be quick to give up
on himself. Focus on what he has done well, but if you think his performance

can be improved, say so. Tell him in private the specific areas of weakness, and suggest ways they can be improved. In an indirect way, you are saying to him that you believe he can do better. Sympathizing with a student who has done poorly may convey the opposite impression—namely, that you believe that he has little ability. Offer help to the student when it is clearly needed, but be careful about providing too much help, or he may grow dependent on your assistance. When he does succeed with your assistance, find a way to give him credit for the success.

25. Use Rewards Judiciously

Rewarding students for their effort or performance is an effective way to increase their work output. The incentive might be a note home to parents, a classroom privilege, a homework-free pass for an evening, or a tangible reward such as stickers, markers, or candy. You might consider developing a behavior modification program to improve specific behaviors. For one student, it may be completing homework, for another it may be participating in class, for still another it may be finishing seatwork within the allotted time. Behavior modification strategies are described in the chapters on attention deficit disorder and the disruptive student. Reward the unmotivated student for evidence of effort or progress—not just for completed performance or outstanding achievement. For example, you might reward him for completing two of the three assignments you gave the previous day if he has a history of rarely doing assignments. With time, you can increase the standard he must meet to obtain the reward. In using an incentive program, keep in mind that while rewards can spur a student's effort, they are not as effective in bringing about a permanent change in his work habits or a lasting commitment to learning. Indeed, in some cases, students who are accustomed to tangible incentives may lose interest in a task if they are not rewarded. In addition, students who receive rewards are less likely to take risks when doing an academic task, or to appreciate the value of what they are studying. They may pursue a strategy of exerting the least effort necessary to gain the biggest reward. Thus, if you employ a system of rewards, use it in conjunction with strategies discussed in this chapter to promote intrinsic motivation. Rewarding the student may be an effective catalyst to get the student started, but you also must nurture his curiosity and desire for excellence to help sustain his interest. In short, use rewards as a last resort to increase a student's motivation.

26. Use Praise Selectively

While it is certainly important to recognize a student for his effort or performance, students are expert at discerning sincere feedback from empty praise. Selective praise that conveys genuine appreciation for a student's work will mean much more to him than vague or exaggerated compliments. He may even interpret your excessive praise to mean that you think he has little ability. Tell him specifically what you like about his performance, and praise him for small steps forward. If he feels awkward being acknowledged publicly, let him know in private, or send him a note.

27. Consider Whether the Student Has a Learning Disability

A student's resistance to schoolwork may mask a learning problem. He may feel frustrated, even hopeless, about meeting with success, so he may decide he can better preserve his self-esteem by not trying than by trying and failing. If you see evidence of a learning disability, talk with your principal about initiating a referral for evaluation.

FOR FURTHER INFORMATION

Brophy, J. E. (1997). *Motivating Students to Learn*. New York: McGraw-Hill.

Clemmons, J.; Laase, L.; Cooper, D.; Areglado, N.; and Dill, M. (1993). *Portfolios in the Classroom: A Teacher's Sourcebook*. New York: Scholastic, Inc.

Hartman, D. (1987). *Motivating the Unmotivated: A Practical Guide for Parents and Teachers to Help Them Help Teenagers Through the Tough Years*. Lakeland, FL: Valley Hill Publishing Company.

Mandel, H. P., and Marcus, S. I. (1996). *Could Do Better: Why Children Underachieve and What to Do About It*. New York: John Wiley & Sons.

Raffini, J. P. (1994). *Winners Without Losers: Structures and Strategies for Increasing Student Motivation to Learn*. Boston: Allyn & Bacon.

Wlodkowski, R. J., and Jaynes, J. H. (1990). *Eager to Learn: Helping Children Become Motivated and Love Learning*. San Francisco: Jossey-Bass.

See also:
   The Disorganized Student
   The Disruptive Student
   The Gifted Student
   Low Self-Esteem
   The Perfectionist Student

BEHAVIORAL PROBLEMS

This section discusses ten common behavioral problems that students often exhibit in school. Some of these problems involve behaviors that are disruptive to the class (for example, the aggressive student) while others involve behaviors that are not disruptive but still reason for concern (for example, the shy student or the student with low self-esteem). While you will want to respond promptly to any problems that are interfering with your instruction or your students' concentration, it is also important that you give attention to problems that are not disruptive but still troublesome for the students exhibiting them.

Studies show and teachers know that students make greater academic progress in a classroom with few disciplinary problems. As a result, it is critical that you find ways to minimize these disruptions. Try to respond early to these behaviors before they become entrenched and difficult to change. In deciding which measures to use, give preference to positive over negative strategies. Bear in mind that your goal is not just to stop students from misbehaving, but also to foster self-control. The purpose of discipline is to teach appropriate behavior rather than to punish.

Low self-esteem underlies many behavior problems. While you cannot give your students self-esteem, you can create a climate that nurtures it through a continual process of encouragement. This demands much more than simply the awarding of gold stars or points. It requires that you provide an accepting atmosphere in which students feel valued and supported—in short, a setting where students feel respected.

THE AGGRESSIVE STUDENT

Bullying is one of the most pervasive problems that schools face. Studies show that 15 to 20 percent of all students are victimized by bullies at some point in their school career. Bullying, which is unprovoked and repeated physical or psychological abuse of a usually weak or vulnerable student by another student, may range from mild teasing to a physical attack. Bullies may torment their classmates by shunning, ridiculing, taunting, intimidating, or assaulting them. They may extort lunch money from them, trip them while on line, prevent them from getting off the bus, jostle them in the hallway, or hit them in the locker room. Bullying can surface as early as preschool and continue through secondary school, although it tends to taper off as students move through school.

Bullying can have serious consequences for the physical and emotional welfare of students. According to a survey of schoolchildren, about 10 percent of students are afraid during much of the school day. Being victimized by bullies can be one of the most painful experiences of childhood and can leave lasting psychological scars. Its impact also extends beyond the victim. It can engender a climate of fear and anxiety in school that creates disharmony among students and distracts them from their schoolwork.

Despite the widespread and serious nature of this problem, schools do not always give bullying the attention it deserves. Staff may take the view that "boys will be boys" and that students have to learn to defend themselves. Putting up with bullies may be seen as a necessary rite of passage, but being tormented and intimidated is neither a normal part of growing up nor a character-building experience. While some schools may not take action in response to reports of bullying, others may not act because they are unaware of the behavior. Surveys indicate that students often fail to report bullying to school staff because they are not confident that the school will take their concerns seriously or take steps to curb the problem. Students may also avoid reporting bullying because of shame about what happened or fear of retaliation.

While children must learn to resolve conflicts with their peers, this does not mean that they should be left to fend for themselves in the face of bullies. Some students are simply unequipped to deal with intimidation from often bigger and stronger students. Schools have an obligation to ensure that students and teachers are provided with a safe and secure environment. Students need assurance that adults are in charge, have firm rules against bullying, and are willing and able to enforce them.

THE PSYCHOLOGY OF THE BULLY

What kinds of students become bullies? Mostly boys, bullies are typically bigger and stronger than their classmates and may have a history of aggression toward peers dating back to kindergarten or first grade. While they are generally of average intelligence, their school performance is often below average. They tend to be rejected by their classmates and to have difficulties forming friendships. Their quickness to anger may be fueled by their social misperceptions, as they are often quick to perceive hostility where none is present. They can be very reactive to social slights, and may lash out at classmates with little provocation.

Bullies may pick on their classmates to gain a sense of power and control over them and boost their status and influence with peers. The aggressive behavior of some students may be an effort to compensate for their feelings of inadequacy. Others may use it as a way of venting frustration with problems at home (for example, parental conflict, divorce, or financial difficulties) or problems in school (for example, learning problems or peer rejection). They usually choose as targets peers who are weak, unpopular, and unlikely to resist, and they generally show little sympathy for their victims. They may zero in on children who stand out in some way, such as the teacher's pet, the child with a speech defect, the slow learner, or the ESL student. Contrary to popular belief, however, the appearance of a student (for example, clothing, weight, or wearing of glasses) does not usually make it more likely that he will be victimized.

Children are not born bullies. They learn from an early age that the way to get what they want is through force. They may be taught to respond to challenges with confrontation and to express themselves with their fists rather than words. Their education in aggression usually begins at home, where their parents may model aggressive behavior as a way of solving problems. The bully at school is often a victim of this aggression at home. His parents may discipline him by using a combination of angry outbursts and corporal punishment. He may be the recipient of abuse from a parent or witness another family member being abused. The message this child receives is that might makes right. Indeed, his parents may support his displays of aggression toward peers by their failure to disapprove of his behavior or their outright endorsement of it. They may also fail to teach him more appropriate ways of behaving, so he may lack the social skills to resolve conflicts through cooperative means.

Children also learn aggressive behavior from the media—notably television. The amount of violence they are exposed to on television is simply astounding. By the age of 14, a child will have seen as many as 11,000 murders on television. Even the average cartoon has 26 violent incidents. Children may see television characters who get their way, settle disputes, and acquire things by using force without suffering any consequences. The lesson they learn is that aggression pays off. Research indicates that children who see violence frequently on television may become less sensitive to the pain and suffering of others and may view aggression as an acceptable way of solving problems. The National Institute of Mental Health concluded in an extensive study that children who watch violent TV shows are more likely to be aggressive in dealing with others.

While most bullies are boys, girls may also engage in aggressive or abusive behavior toward their classmates. Their methods are likely to differ from those of boys, however. While boys are more likely to physically intimidate their peers, girls who bully tend to use words rather than their fists, although there is evidence that girls—especially those from ages 12 to 16—are increasingly resorting to physical tactics to intimidate their peers.

The class bully often faces problems as an adult. His aggressive behavior in childhood may be a harbinger of professional, social, and legal problems to come. Bullies are more likely than their peers to drop out of school, have difficulty holding onto jobs, have problems sustaining relationships, be abusive of their spouses, and have aggressive children. One study that followed individuals over a 22-year period found that children who were aggressive to their peers at age 8 were five times more likely than their nonaggressive peers to have a criminal record (usually antisocial offenses) by the age of 30. A particularly alarming pattern is that aggressive children often grow up to be harsh, punitive parents who give rise to children who become bullies themselves. In short, children of bullies often become bullies themselves. The challenge for those working with aggressive children and their families is to find a way to break this cycle.

UNDERSTANDING THE VICTIM

The victims of bullying tend to be shy, sensitive, insecure youngsters with low self-esteem. Often overprotected by their parents, they may lack independence and assertiveness. They are usually physically weaker than their tormentors, and thus have difficulty defending themselves. In addition, few classmates may rally to their defense because of their tendency to be isolated from peers. While most victims usually do not respond to aggression from classmates, some can be hot-tempered and may vent their frustration by retaliating against the bully or picking on younger students.

Students may react to being bullied by dissolving in tears or withdrawing. Academic performance may decline as a result of difficulty focusing on schoolwork. They may go through school in a constant state of fear, avoiding unsupervised areas and activities where bullying is likely to occur. They may dread walking the halls, entering the rest room, going to the playground, or changing for gym in the locker room—all areas where bullying may take place. They may change their route to school in an effort to avoid meeting up with their tormentors. In extreme cases, victims of bullying may resist coming to school. According to one study, 8 percent of students who avoid coming to school do so because of fear for their safety. They may even develop stomachaches or headaches from the pressures of being bullied.

HOW TEACHERS CAN HELP

Because patterns of aggressive behavior can be established in elementary school, it is important that schools intervene early when students exhibit this behavior. Your job in working with aggressive students is to help make your classroom bully-proof by furthering two goals: (1) to make it clear to your students that bullying behavior will not be tolerated; and (2) to help students develop more appropriate ways of interacting and settling disputes with their peers. The strategies listed below further these two goals:

1. Foster a Climate of Cooperation and Caring

Reinforce acts of kindness in your class, and communicate values of cooperation and tolerance. You might give out courtesy awards to younger students for such actions as helping a classmate with an assignment, comforting someone who is upset, inviting a new student to join in a game, or coming to the defense of a child who is being bullied. Praise students when you observe them resolving a conflict peacefully. Also, incorporate into your lessons activities that promote understanding of those who are different, and consider using cooperative learning projects in which students must work together to attain success. Keep in mind that the most effective way to foster a caring attitude in your classroom is to model this behavior yourself by relating in a warm, sympathetic way to your students.

2. Mediate Student Disputes

Where students cannot settle a conflict and it does not involve bullying, get them together to try to resolve it. Let them know your job is not to assign blame but rather to help them work out their differences. Tell them that each student will have a chance to speak and that interruptions and name-calling are not allowed. Begin by having each offer his version of what happened. Listen attentively and ask questions to clarify their views as well as their goals. Suggest that they switch roles and state the problem from the other's point of view. Ask them for ideas about how to solve the problem. If they cannot come up with a solution they both agree with, offer some ideas, such as negotiating their differences, changing the activity, or developing new rules. Stay the course until they agree upon a solution. At the end, make sure to ask them what they would do differently next time.

3. Teach Your Students Conflict-Resolution Skills

Help them learn to solve problems themselves without resorting to arguing or aggression. Spell out the basics of talking things out: honesty; no interrupting, blaming, or put-downs; using "I" messages to convey feelings; and considering the other's point of view. Your students may even be able to use these skills to mediate disputes among their classmates. Educational programs are available that teach children to serve as neutral third parties who listen to their peers and calmly offer suggestions for resolving conflicts without adult involvement (see the references at the end of this chapter). You might even recruit students with a history of being aggressive to settle disputes. They may gain a sense of importance from this role and take it seriously. Designate an area of your class as the "peace corner" where students go to settle conflicts.

4. Communicate a No-Bullying Rule

Make it clear that you will not tolerate students' taunting or intimidating others. Post your rules prominently in the classroom, and make sure that "No bullying" is among them. Describe for the students what you mean by bullying, and let them know that there will be consequences for students who engage in these behaviors. Make sure to follow through when these behaviors occur, so students know you mean business.

5. Reach out to the Aggressive Student

Aggressive students typically distrust teachers and perceive them in an adversarial manner. Make a special effort to connect with an aggressive student in your class by listening attentively to what he says and showing respect for his thoughts and concerns. Find a few minutes every day to talk with him about his interests and hobbies.

6. Survey Your Class about Bullying

Reports from students suggest that many school staff are either unresponsive to complaints of bullying or unaware of its occurrence. Find out what is happening in your class or school by asking students to complete a survey anonymously. Ask for specifics about when and where they have been bullied or witnessed incidents of bullying. Also, find out which school areas students use and which they avoid. These responses may suggest areas that require greater monitoring.

7. Talk with Your Class about Bullying

Help your students understand how making fun of others can be hurtful. Ask them to talk about times they have been teased or bullied and to describe how it felt. Volunteer experiences of your own. Also, get your students' thoughts about why they think other students engage in bullying and teasing. The reasons they offer may deter some students from acting in this way. You might even role-play by having students assume the roles of bully, victim, and witness; then talk about how they felt and what they might have said or done differently. At the end of the discussion, let your students know that you are available to discuss any specific concerns they have privately. Tell them the best time to do this. Meet again with the class if bullying continues to be a problem.

8. Empower the Silent Majority to Take Action

Because teachers are not always present when bullying takes place, you must encourage other students to help resolve the problem, or at least bring it to your attention. These students who in the past may have stood by silently as they witnessed their classmates being tormented play a critical role in reducing bullying behavior. It is not enough, however, to encourage them to become involved. They need guidance in what steps to take, including telling the aggressive student to stop what he is doing, showing support for the victim, trying to mediate the dispute by offering potential solutions, and if necessary obtaining adult assistance.

9. Coach Students in How to Respond to Teasing or Taunting

In a nutshell, you want to teach students to be assertive without being aggressive. Being assertive means stating what you feel without making demands of another or confronting him. Standing up to a bully without escalating the conflict can be a challenge. If a student is making offensive comments, suggest that the student who is the target try ignoring them. If the student persists with his ridicule, the student being teased should tell him in a direct and brief way to stop it by using an "I" message and then walking away. For example, he might say: "I don't like what you're saying, and I want you to stop." As an alternative, he might ask the bully to restate what he said so that the comment loses its power. The offending student may refuse or say it less emphatically. The idea is to deflect the taunting of the bully without provoking him or appearing upset. If these strategies do not work and the bully continues, the student should get help from an adult. Have the student practice these techniques by role-playing. In some cases, you might encourage the student to cope with the problem by avoiding it—perhaps taking a different route to school or staying close to the teacher or aide. You might also suggest that the student counter the negative comments with positive self-talk (for example, "When Matthew calls me stupid, it's because he wants other kids to think he's cool. But he's the one with the problem, not me. My grades are a lot better than his anyway.").

10. Supervise Unstructured Activities Closely

Bullying often takes place in relatively unsupervised areas such as the bus stop, rest room, locker room, hallway, cafeteria, or playground. As a result, students who fear being bullied may try to avoid these settings. Schools must make sure there is sufficient monitoring in these areas, with an adult visible to students at most times. Teachers standing in doorways during the passing of classes may help to curb problems in the hallway. If you become aware of bullying taking place in specific parts of the school, talk to the principal about increasing supervision in those areas, perhaps by using parent volunteers. If you have a concern about a specific case of bullying, alert the aides in the areas outside the classroom to monitor the situation closely.

11. Provide a Student Prone to Angry Outbursts with a Cooling-off Area

Suggest to the student that, when he feels himself getting angry, he leave the room and go to a prearranged spot in the school where he can calm down. This might involve going to the bathroom or water fountain, sitting in the office, or visiting his guidance counselor. If necessary, teach him some internal cues that may signal to him that he is getting angry. You might also set up a timeout area in your classroom where a student can be sent after an aggressive act to reflect on what happened and calm down. After he calms down, he may return to the group.

12. Be Alert for Signs That a Student Is Being Victimized

Possible indicators of bullying include a student's avoidance of such school areas as the playground, withdrawal from peers, unusual fearfulness or anxiety, difficulty focusing in class, and a decline in grades. Obvious signs of a problem, such as torn clothing or bruises, should be followed up with the student, to find out what happened.

13. Decide Whether to Intervene

Because students cannot be (and should not be) shielded from all conflicts with peers, they must develop the skills and confidence to solve some problems on their own. The challenge is deciding when to let students resolve a problem themselves and when to intervene. Where one student is bullying or taunting another and there is a clear imbalance of power, you must step in. On the other hand, where students are having a dispute and they are verbal, generally caring, and willing to consider the other's point of view, allow them to work it out themselves. Also, children who are friends are likely to be motivated to settle their differences. You may be surprised at the ability of students to come up with creative solutions in the absence of adults. Indeed, the presence of adults may inhibit their ability to resolve conflicts.

14. Take Reports about Bullying Seriously and Act Quickly

Investigate all reports of bullying. Keep in mind that the incident may appear minor to you but loom large to the student. Do not automatically dismiss the incident with a "boys will be boys" attitude or tell the victim of a bully that he must fight his own battles. Assess the student's degree of distress, and factor in your knowledge of his reactions in determining whether to respond. Be especially attentive to those shy students who come to you. If you become aware that a student is being emotionally or physically harassed, take immediate action to ensure his safety and security. Make sure he knows that what happened to him was wrong and that you will try to make sure it does not happen again. The longer the abuse goes on, the greater the emotional impact on the student. Putting an immediate end to this behavior is important not only to protect the student but also to send a message to your other students that you will not tolerate this behavior and will do what is necessary to ensure that your classroom is a safe haven.

15. Respond Calmly but Firmly to the Student

In trying to restrain a student who is being aggressive, use the least force necessary to protect yourself as well as other students. Respond to him in a way that helps him become more reasonable and willing to hear what you have to say. Pay attention to your verbal as well as your nonverbal language. Even if the student is screaming or threatening you, remain calm without giving in to him. Allow him to say what he is upset about without interrupting him; acknowledge his feelings. Avoid crossing your arms, pointing your finger, or making threats—all of which will provoke his anger and stiffen his resistance. If there is something you want him to do, tell him in a calm, firm, but slow-paced manner. If he refuses, use the "broken-record" technique; continue repeating what you want him to do without raising your voice. Allow him to feel some control by giving him a clearly stated choice with consequences and letting him determine which course to follow. For example, if the student's behavior requires that he be removed from the classroom, you might say: "You have a choice. You can walk with the aide to the office, or you can go with me."

16. Do Not Bully the Bully

While you may be inclined to punish a bully severely, consider that this may only fuel his anger and make him more determined to continue his aggressive behavior without regard for the school consequences. In a similar vein, it is inappropriate to use corporal punishment (still in use in many schools across the country) to teach a student not to be aggressive to other students. The message of corporal punishment—that one can control behavior through physical force—is precisely the lesson that the bully needs to unlearn.

17. Discipline the Student in a Way That Deters Future Aggression

In disciplining a student who is acting aggressively, keep in mind that your goal is to deter his aggressive behavior rather than to humiliate or embarrass him. Consider excluding him from places or activities in which he has had difficulties. For example, if he is constantly bullying students during recess, he might be barred from the playground for a defined period. If he is taunting students on the bus, he might lose the privilege of riding the bus for a set period of time, as long as this does not create undue hardship for the parents. If he is shoving other students in the hallway, he might be escorted from class to class by a school aide. If he is continuously ridiculing the student next to him, his desk might be moved next to yours. You might also design a behavior modification system in which he loses a specific amount of recess time for every act of verbal abuse.

18. Assign the Student Tasks That Involve Helping Others

Bullies often have little sympathy for their victims. Consider assigning them—as a consequence for their behavior—the school equivalent of community service. Experiencing the rewards of helping others may prompt changes in the way they relate to their peers. Examples of these tasks include helping students with homework in an after-school program, organizing a game for students in a lower grade during recess, coming in before school to help the teacher put up a bulletin board, recording acts of kindness by students to help determine who receives school courtesy awards, helping the principal monitor younger students in the lunchroom, or making a poster for the classroom stating the teacher's rules, including "No bullying."

19. Try to Connect with the Student Rather than Control Him

Once the student has calmed down, take him aside and talk with him in a nonthreatening manner. Listen to him attentively without condoning or reinforcing his behaviors. Try to find out what triggered his behavior. It may be that he wrongly perceived hostility from the other student. If so, offer other possible explanations for the student's behavior. Talk with the aggressive student about how his behavior will cause classmates to avoid him out of fear, and make him unpopular. Ask him how else he might have responded, while offering some suggestions of your own. Suggest responses that allow him to save face in the eyes of his peers, while not disparaging or hurting the other student. Consider having him call his parents in your presence to explain what he has done. You might also bring in the student he offended to tell how he felt. Encourage the student who was in the wrong to tell the victim that this will not happen again. Ask him how he might feel if an older or bigger student did the same thing to him.

20. Help the Student Appreciate That He Can Win with Other Students by Maintaining Control

Aggressive students may feel a strong need to get the best of other students, which to them may mean physically or verbally dominating them. Redefine for an aggressive student in your class the meaning of winning with other students. Tell him that, when he loses control and lashes out at a classmate, he has been manipulated into acting in a way that makes him look foolish to his peers. Suggest that the way to win with students who trigger his anger is not to allow himself to be manipulated into losing his cool, and the way to impress peers is to keep his temper in check in the face of bothersome students.

21. Contact Parents to Seek Their Support

Where a student exhibits a pattern of aggressive behavior, set up a meeting with his parents to inform them of his behavior and gain their support for your approach to the problem. After discussing your course of action with them, bring the student in and let him know of the plan. Make sure the student sees that you and the parents are in agreement. Try to get the parents to endorse the plan in the child's presence.

22. Attend to The Victim Even after the Bullying Is Halted

While most victims tend to be shy and unassertive, some are provocative and annoying to their classmates. In either case, the victim of bullying may be isolated from other students. If so, make an effort to connect him with his peers through group activities, and help him develop friends by pairing him with students who are likely to be accepting. He may need help with social skills in terms of becoming more assertive and learning what to say and how to say it. A provocative student will also need help in learning what *not* to say. If the student has low self-esteem, as many victims do, help find areas where he can be successful, and highlight these to his classmates.

23. Refer an Aggressive Student to the Guidance Counselor

The bully may warrant more than just discipline—especially if his aggressive behavior is a long-standing pattern. If so, ask the guidance counselor to meet with him. The counselor will want to look beneath his behavior to understand what prompted him to act this way. His behavior may be an effort to gain status with his peers, or it may reflect a learning problem, low self-esteem, or distress about family matters. He may need guidance in solving social problems and finding alternatives to using force or coercion. He may also need help in interpreting the behavior of his peers. Bullies are quick to perceive hostile intent with classmates when none is intended. The counselor might help him understand other explanations for a student's actions and encourage him to carefully consider his social perceptions before acting on them. The counselor might also role-play with the student, asking him to take on the roles of both bully and victim, so that he can experience how it feels to be bullied and consider alternative responses to being aggressive.

24. Encourage Aggressive Students to Play Team Sports

Playing sports provides a constructive outlet for their energy and aggression. It also helps teach them discipline and self-control. In addition, their coaches may serve as positive role models and wield considerable influence with them. Don't hesitate to use this influence to help curb their aggressive behavior.

For Further Information

National School Safety Center. (1989). *Set Straight on Bullies*. Westlake Village, CA. (Publisher's address is listed under Organizations.)

Bodine, R.; Crawford, D.; and Schrumpf, F. (1994). *Creating the Peaceable School: A Comprehensive Program for Teaching Conflict Resolution*. Champaign, IL: Research Press.

Doyle, T. (1991). *Why Is Everybody Always Picking on Me? A Guide to Handling Bullies*. Middlebury, VT: Atrium Society Publications.

Garrity, C.; Jens, K.; Porter, W.; Sager, N.; and Short-Cammilli, C. (1994). *Bully-Proofing Your School: A Comprehensive Approach for Elementary Schools*. Longmont, CO: Sopris West.

Girard, K., and Koch, S. (1996). *Conflict Resolution in the Schools: A Manual for Educators*. San Francisco: Jossey-Bass.

Pepler, D. J., and Rubin, K. H. (eds.). (1991). *The Development and Treatment of Childhood Aggression*. Hillsdale, NJ: Lawrence Erlbaum Associates.

Rhode, G.; Jenson, W. R.; and Reavis, H. K. (1992). *The Tough Kid Book: Practical Classroom Management Strategies*. Longmont, CO: Sopris West.

ORGANIZATIONS

National Institute for Dispute Resolution
Conflict Resolution Education Network
1726 M Street, NW, Suite 500
Washington, DC 20036
1-202-466-4764

National School Safety Center
4165 Thousand Oaks Boulevard, Suite 290
Westlake Village, CA 91362
1-805-373-9977

See also:
    Attention Deficit Disorder
    The Disruptive Student
    The ESL Student
    Low Self-Esteem
    The School-Phobic Student
    The Shy Student

ATTENTION DEFICIT DISORDER

Matthew has exasperated almost every teacher he has had. He is in almost constant motion. If he isn't roaming around the room, he is sitting restlessly in his seat, fidgeting. He defines the words "space cadet." His attention is easily diverted, and he is often at a loss about what to do. He struggles to understand directions, often relying on other students to keep him on track. Even when he knows what to do, he has trouble settling down and doing the work. He is usually the last to finish an assignment, if he finishes it at all. Basic tasks elude him: keeping his desk neat, remembering to bring papers home, even bringing a pencil to school.

If you have not had a student like Matthew, you probably will. Matthew has attention deficit disorder (ADD—often referred to also as ADHD, or attention deficit-hyperactivity disorder), a problem typically characterized by inattention, impulsivity and a high activity level. More common with boys than girls, attention deficit disorder is said to affect 3 to 5 percent of schoolchildren, so on average the typical classroom will have one child with ADD. These students are able to learn, but their difficulties in focusing and their tendency to become frustrated and give up easily hinder their academic performance. Organizational and learning problems often accompany the inattention and impulsivity. About one third of students with attention deficit disorder exhibit a learning disability. If unrecognized and unattended to, attention deficit disorder can lead to significant social and emotional difficulties.

Of course, these problems can also be found in children who do not have attention deficit disorder. Many children have trouble paying attention in class at one time or another but do not have attention deficit disorder. Children may have trouble focusing in school when they are anxious, distressed, not feeling well, or simply bored. Attention problems can also reflect hearing or vision difficulties. Identifying the source of a child's problem provides important clues about how to respond to him.

There is no litmus test for identifying attention deficit disorder. No one procedure or test can definitively identify the presence or absence of ADD. An accurate diagnosis requires the careful integration of information from different persons and sources. The teacher plays a key role in this process.

Because the behaviors of ADD often surface in a setting where a child is expected to pay attention, sit for long periods, and work in a sustained manner, the teacher is often the first person to spot the signs of ADD. While it is inappropriate for a teacher to offer a diagnosis of ADD, you should alert the school's principal and evaluation team of your concerns. A diagnosis of attention deficit disorder requires a multidisciplinary approach, in which your observations are considered in conjunction with parent information, psychological and educational testing, and a thorough medical evaluation. You may be asked to complete a behavior checklist to assist in the evaluation process.

A central purpose of the school's evaluation is to assess the child's need for special education. The United States Department of Education has issued a ruling that children with attention deficit disorder may qualify for special education solely based on their attention deficit when the problem hinders learning. There must be evidence, however, that the ADD has significantly impaired the student's academic performance. While many students with attention deficit disorder can be taught in regular classes, others may need a small-group setting to learn effectively. Some students with ADD are able to perform adequately in a regular classroom with the assistance of a classroom aide or special education teacher who is available to help them.

MEDICATION: THE TEACHER'S ROLE

Many students with attention deficit disorder are given medication to help them focus and attend in school. The most common medications prescribed for this purpose are Ritalin, Dexedrine, and Cylert. While these medications are central nervous system stimulants, they have the seemingly paradoxical effect of calming the student and lessening his impulsivity. Some medications such as Ritalin are of the short-acting variety; the student will take medication before he goes to school and again around noon. Others such as Cylert are longer acting; a morning dosage will typically last all day. If a student takes medication during the day, the parent will be required to provide medical authorization before the school nurse can dispense the medication to the student.

While there is considerable controversy about whether too many schoolchildren are being given medication to help them focus in school, there is little question that the medication has had positive effects with many children. Those students for whom the medication has been effective may show a marked increase in on-task behavior, a decrease in activity level, an improvement in the quality and neatness of work, and a generally calmer demeanor. As a result, they are more productive in class and less likely to have problems with their peers or disrupt the class.

Some students have side effects from these medications which you should be watching for. In school, you may see a child on medication manifesting lethargy, reduced appetite, and on rare occasions the development of tics. Children on medication sometimes exhibit a glassy-eyed look. If you see any of these side effects, it is important that you contact the parent so that a decision can be made with the child's physician whether to adjust or change the medication.

While medication may enable some children to perform better in school, keep in mind that medication does not teach and does not impart knowledge to children. It only makes them more available for learning because they are better able to focus. If a child had learning deficits before the medication was started, he will still have learning deficits after he takes the medication. In addition, while medication may lessen some of the behavioral problems, it is unlikely to eliminate them. In almost all cases where medication is helpful to the student, you will still have to make some accommodations in the classroom.

The proper dosage of medication will vary with each child, and there is typically a trial period to determine the optimal dosage. The physician usually begins with a small dosage and increases it only if minimal change is noted. If the student does not seem to be responding to the medication or is experiencing side effects, the physician may prescribe a differrent medication. This process of trying to determine the optimal medication and dosage may take several weeks.

You play a very important role in this process inasmuch as it is the student's classroom behavior that the parent and doctor will use to gauge the effect of the medication. The effects of the medication are likely to be more evident in school than at home, so your observations are crucial. The doctor may ask you to complete a form or checklist to assess the behavioral changes as well as signs of any side effects. The Conners' Teacher Rating Scale is a popular form used by physicians. A shortened version of this scale is often used and takes just minutes to complete. You are asked to rate ten behaviors related to ADD on a four-point scale. The information from this scale is particularly helpful if you complete it both before and after the medication is begun. It is thus important that you be informed when the child is starting on the medication and that you observe carefully his behavior during the initial period of medication. It will be helpful to jot down some notes about his behavior during this time.

> *A note of caution for teachers:* While you may believe that a particular child will benefit from medication, it is not your role to recommend medication. This is a strictly medical issue; you should encourage a parent to discuss it with the child's physician.

BEHAVIOR MANAGEMENT STRATEGIES

A child with attention deficit disorder may present significant management problems for the classroom teacher. He can present a real challenge to your disciplinary methods and, if not managed successfully, can disrupt the structure of your classroom. Many teachers have found behavior modification strategies helpful in managing the student.

In a nutshell, behavior modification attempts to change a student's behaviors by altering the responses that follow these behaviors. The simplest application of behavior modification principles is to praise the student when he is displaying appropriate behavior. While virtually all teachers use praise to encourage their students, ADD students have a particular need for a pat on the back. Many have experienced failure and frustration during their years in school and are lacking confidence and self-esteem. Many children with ADD have learned to distrust their abilities by second grade. The challenge for the teacher, especially with a large class, is to "catch the child being good" and then praise the child promptly and genuinely. As a way of reminding yourself to check on the student and praise him if warranted, place a visual reminder at a place you look at frequently (for example, a smiley face near the class clock or on your lesson plan book). Where a child is exhibiting mostly inappropriate behaviors, you will have to find some positive behavior to reinforce, even if those behaviors are minor and routine for your other students (for example, "Jessica, I like the way you sat quietly during the announcements.").

Praise and encouragement certainly constitute a valuable tool for teachers, but that one tool is insufficient to manage the behaviors of many ADD students. You may wish to provide reinforcement in a more tangible form. You can be as creative as you wish in finding ways to reward students for appropriate behavior. You may want to set up a systematic plan for rewarding the student with points, chips, checks, or even smiley faces, which the student can then exchange for tangible rewards or privileges (for example, stickers, baseball cards, markers, line leader, class messenger, or teacher assistant).

Keep these points in mind as you set up this plan, making sure that you have the student's involvement and input in the process. Choose two or three behaviors that are most troublesome for that student, describe them clearly and concretely for the student, and state them in positive form (for example, "finish morning seatwork" or "raise hand before answering question"). A chart with this information is kept on the student's desk or in his notebook. With the student's input, choose some rewards that he desires and set the "exchange rate." Set up a schedule for when you will reward the points and exchange them for rewards, keeping in mind your time constraints. You may want to assign points, for example, at midmorning, before lunch, and at the end of the day. Gradually, you can extend the intervals between rewards. At the end of the day or week, the student can add up his points or chips and select his reward from a prearranged menu. While this takes some time to establish initially, once it gets going it requires minimal time—although you may have to make some adjustments along the way. One point is certain, however: Failure to manage the behaviors successfully will require much more teacher time and energy than implementing a plan that lessens the behaviors.

Some behaviors may call for an undesirable consequence for the student. Often, a simple reprimand is warranted. Reprimands are most effective when delivered calmly, firmly, and immediately after the misbehavior. When a student displays inappropriate behaviors that call for stronger action (for example, having a tantrum, kicking a student, or constantly yelling out), you may want to withdraw some rewards or privileges. This may be done in conjunction with the behavioral reward system described above; in this case, you take away points or chips promptly when inappropriate behaviors are exhibited. Some teachers give to students cards entitling them to class privileges (for example, recess) and take them back one at a time if the student exhibits a significant behavioral problem. Make sure you go over the possible consequences with the student ahead of time.

Under some circumstances, you may want to use a procedure called "timeout," in which the student is excluded from participation in class activities as a result of inappropriate behavior. For example, you may have a student sit in a designated place for a limited time right after he has misbehaved (some teachers call it the "thinking chair"). If you have set up a reward system, you may not allow him to earn points during a specific time interval. If the child is isolated from the class, it is important that it not be in a location that is enjoyable.

The use of undesirable consequences such as timeout or withdrawal of privileges is most effective if you respond in a relatively neutral but consistent manner. Avoid displays of emotion and keep talking to a minimum, other than a statement of the rule and the resulting consequence. Do not engage in lawyerlike discussions of fairness. While students with ADD often need much repetition before they learn, they should eventually catch on to the pattern, respond to consequences, and internalize the desired behaviors.

HOW TEACHERS CAN HELP

You may find the following additional strategies helpful. Some of these are applicable to all students, while others are more specific to the problems presented by ADD students. In addition, some of these strategies may be feasible to implement in a regular classroom, and others may be more appropriate in a special education class with fewer students.

1. Structure the Classroom So That Expectations Are Clearly Understood, Rules Are Plainly Stated, and Routines Are Predictable

Students with attention deficit disorder have difficulty providing their own structure, and often need structure and organization imposed externally. ADD students do much better in a climate of certainty, clarity, and consistency. They need to know what they are expected to do, what is allowed, and what is prohibited. It is helpful to post the class rules prominently in the room. Limit the rules to a manageable number, perhaps three to four for younger elementary children and four to five for older elementary children. State the rules plainly and in positive form (for example, "raise hand before speaking" rather than "no calling out").

Begin the day by helping the students get organized and previewing the day's activities and schedule. Post a daily schedule as well as a monthly calendar indicating special events. Go over the schedule for the day and highlight any special activities and changes in the routine. ADD students often do not adjust well to change or make transitions easily, so you want to alert them in advance. You may want to put the work for the day on the board and perhaps even post the ADD student's personal schedule on his desk on a 4″ by 6″ card, including reminders about class behavior and tasks to be completed. You may want to number the tasks in priority order and suggest times when he is to work on the tasks.

2. Place the Student in a Location with Minimal Distractions

Placing the ADD student's desk near you so you can monitor him usually helps keep him from drifting off—but not always. If other students are frequently coming up to you to get help and ask questions, being seated near you may be one of the more distracting spots in the room. Choose a place where you can monitor the student closely and help him stay focused but where the distractions are minimal. Avoid placing him near the pencil sharpener, or with views of the hallway or outside—spots sure to lure him away from his work. You may find that he is able to focus best seated near the middle of the class, surrounded by quiet, hard-working students. Avoid having the desks close together to minimize physical interaction among the students. Try to reduce the visual and auditory distractions in the classroom to a bare minimum. While displays on the walls certainly make the classroom more inviting, displays that catch your attention at every turn can be distracting. Also, make sure there are no visual distractions in the line of sight from the student to you.

3. Give Directions in a Manner That Promotes Understanding and Retention

In trying to gain the student's full attention, use his name and make sure his eyes are focused on you. Keep the directions short and simple, and avoid giving a long string of commands at one time. Emphasize through tone and volume essential information. If necessary, write them down in addition to giving them orally. Have the student repeat them to you to ensure understanding. He may appear to be attending but be miles away.

4. Develop a System to Monitor the Student and Keep Him on Track

Because ADD students are prone to confusion and drifting off, you must keep track of how they are progressing. Make frequent eye contact with the student. Work out with him a private signal that you can use to convey to him that he must pay attention or get back to work—something as simple as scratching your head or raising your eyebrows. Similarly, develop a signal that he (and other students) can use to indicate that he needs your help. For example, you might have him stick a pencil with a little "help" flag in a piece of clay in the corner of the desk. If feasible, ask him to signal you after he completes an assignment, so you can check it over.

5. Help the Student Get Organized

Many students—but especially ADD students—need help organizing themselves. Managing school materials can be particularly troublesome for students with attention deficit disorder. Make sure that their desks are cleared of unnecessary items before they begin working. Consider creating a storage box for the disorganized student that is near his desk, with color-coded folders for each subject. Suggest that the folder and spiral notebook be the same color as the textbook for each subject. Older elementary and secondary students will benefit from having a three-ring binder divided by subjects, with a pocket folder for papers to be completed, one for papers already completed, and one for papers to give to parents. The notebook should have an assignment sheet that is easily accessible, with a place to note upcoming tests and long-term projects. At the end of the day, spend a few minutes with the student to make sure he is bringing home all the materials he needs and has recorded the assignments accurately. You may want to give this responsibility to a classroom aide or special education teacher. Also, consider pairing the disorganized student with a conscientious student who can help keep him organized. Older ADD students are likely to need help—perhaps in a special education setting—learning such study skills as outlining, underlining, and studying for tests.

6. Keep Work Periods Short

Students with ADD have trouble working for long periods of time. You will find that these students are much more productive if you have them work for two 25-minute sessions rather than one 50-minute session.

7. Break Down Tasks into Manageable Parts

You may also find that the student is overwhelmed by a large task. He may feel that he won't be able to finish it, so his response may be to give up easily or not even attempt it. Try breaking the task into smaller, more doable pieces so that he feels more in control and more confident of success. In a similar vein, do not give him all the class assignments at once; rather, give them to him one or two at a time.

8. Grab the Student's Attention through Novel Presentation

Capture your students' attention by varying the presentation. This is especially helpful with tedious or repetitive tasks. For example, you might write key words in a different color on the board, underline them, or write them in all capitals. When preparing worksheets, change fonts or the size of the type to grab their attention, or use colored type. Students who make careless math mistakes may benefit from having the math signs circled or highlighted in color.

9. Find Ways for the Student to Communicate without the Need for Handwriting

Many ADD students find the task of handwriting difficult and arduous. If so, try to find alternative ways for him to communicate what he knows. Many students who resist handwriting are comfortable composing on a computer, which can be used as early as first or second grade. If you find that a student knows more than he is able to convey on a written test, consider giving him an oral test instead. Allow older students who have trouble taking notes in class to tape the lessons or photocopy the notes of classmates. This is not to say you should bypass teaching handwriting to the student, but be careful about placing too much emphasis on neat writing with ADD students, and avoid excessive recopying of papers unless you are confident they raced through a paper and can do much better.

10. Allow the Student to Release Excess Energy

It is difficult for many ADD students to sit for long periods of time. Allow these students some time to take breaks and move around. This may be accomplished with a trip to the bathroom (although watch for abuse of this privilege), serving as a messenger to another classroom, helping erase the board, or simply standing and stretching. You may also incorporate physical activity into academic tasks (for example, having students go up to the board to do problems). ADD students respond particularly well to tasks they learn by doing.

11. Present Tasks That Reflect the Student's Interest and Promote His Confidence

For many ADD students, school is synonomous with drudgery. More than likely, their school days have been filled with frustration as they have struggled to keep pace with their peers. Confidence and self-esteem are probably lacking. ADD students will be more engaged and attentive if the task taps areas of competence. Identify any skills and talents they may have and arrange tasks that allow them to demonstrate their skills in the presence of their classmates. Similarly, use their interests to motivate them (for example, having them learn percentages by figuring out batting averages). Find ways of making learning fun, using your sense of humor and playfulness to offset the tediousness and repetition that they may associate with schoolwork.

12. Coach the Student in Social Skills

Students with attention deficit disorder often have difficulties getting along with their peers. Simply put, their behaviors may turn other students off. They may cut in line, talk too much, call out an answer, interrupt conversations, or intrude in games. They may have trouble making and keeping friends. While these problems are not easily resolved, you can help a child ease these problems and raise his understanding of what happened and where he can improve. When incidents with other children happen, take the student aside and help him look at what happened by asking some pointed questions: Why do you think she reacted that way? How do you think she felt? What could you have done or said differently? Give the student some tips about how to handle various situations (for example, count to three silently before acting, wait for the other child to finish talking before you talk, look at the person you are talking to, and ask the other child what he wants to do). In these ways, you can help the student become more observant of his behavior, more aware of alternative ways of acting, and less impulsive in responding. And, of course, make sure to lavish praise on the student when you see him demonstrating good social skills.

13. Tailor Homework So the Emphasis Is on Quality Rather than Quantity

If you find that the student is having trouble completing seatwork and is taking much longer than average to do homework, consider reducing the length of his assignments. Rather than give him twenty problems, give him ten or fifteen. Place the emphasis on understanding and accuracy rather than completion of the full-length assignment. You may find that he can master the concepts with a shorter assignment. Otherwise, you run the risk of his being frustrated and overwhelmed. If so, you may find that he is racing through the work and producing sloppy or careless work. Or he may conveniently forget to bring the assignment home or "lose" it between home and school. Similarly, you may want to tailor test requirements, either allowing him more time to take the test or letting him take the test in a special education setting.

14. Seek Assistance from School Staff

Asking for help is not a sign of defeat but an acknowledgment that you are dealing with a real challenge. First, consult with the student's previous teacher. Find out how that teacher handled him, identifying what worked and what did not. The school psychologist may be able to assist you in developing a behavior management program that is appropriate for the child and workable to implement. Also, talk with the principal to inform him or her of the student's difficulties, and find out if the student can be sent to the office when his behavior is very disruptive to the class. A school aide may be available to assist in your class during the student's most difficult times. Many students who are eligible for special education remain in the regular classroom but have aides or special education teachers come into the class to work with them. Last, check with the student himself. You may be pleasantly surprised to find that he can give you some worthwhile insights about ways in which he learns best.

15. Work with Parents to Support Your Efforts

Your best resource may be the student's parents. Meet with them early in the year to apprise them of their child's difficulties and strategies you are using in the classroom. You may want to keep in touch with the parents on a daily or weekly basis, using a sheet that the student takes home. It is important that the student see this as a *progress* report—not as a *disciplinary* report. This report can be adapted to the needs of the child. If, for example, the student is not bringing in homework consistently, this form can be used by the student to record his homework. You then review it at the end of the day for accuracy and initial it. The parent is expected to initial it nightly as well. The student then returns with the form the next day to begin the process anew. The form should have a place for you and the parents to make comments; it ensures that parents know what the assignments are and can make certain homework is completed. You may also want to develop a home-school program with the parents, in which you rate the student's performance in a few areas (for example, completing seatwork, staying in his seat, and staying on task), and the parent can set up a reward or incentive system based on his ratings.

For Further Information

Dowdy, C. A.; Patton, J. R.; Smith, T.E.C.; and Polloway, E. (1997). *Attention-Deficit/ Hyperactivity Disorder in the Classroom: A Practical Guide for Teachers.* Austin, TX: Pro-Ed.

Fowler, M. (1992). *CH.A.D.D.Educators Manual: Attention Deficit Disorders.* Plantation, FL: Children and Adults With Attention Deficit Disorders.

Gordon, S. B., and Asher, M. J. (1994). *Meeting the ADD Challenge: A Practical Guide for Teachers.* Champaign, IL: Research Press.

Rief, S. (1993). *How to Reach and Teach ADD/ADHD Children.* West Nyack, NY: Center for Applied Research in Education.

Organizations

National ADDA (Attention Deficit Disorders Association)
1788 Second Street, Suite 200
Highland Park, IL 60035
1-847-432-ADDA (to leave a message)
Fax: 1-847-432-5874
E-mail: mail@add.org
Website: www.add.org

Children & Adults with Attention-Deficit/Hyperactivity Disorder (CHADD)
8181 Professional Place, Suite 201
Landover, MD 20785
1-301-306-7070
Website: www.chadd.org

The Attention Deficit Resource Center
1344 Johnson Ferry Road, Suite 14
Marietta, GA 30068

See also:
   Auditory Processing Problem
   The Disorganized Student
   The Disruptive Student
   Handwriting Problem
   Low Self-Esteem

AUTISM

Autism, a lifelong neurological disorder, has been called "the ultimate learning disability" because of its impact on a person's ability to communicate, to relate with others, and to reason. Usually apparent by the age of 3, autism occurs in approximately one of every 2,000 children. It is found about four times more often in boys than in girls. A child's chance of developing autism is not affected by his family's economic circumstances or educational level.

While the precise cause of autism has not been identified, research suggests that abnormal brain development and heredity can play a role in causing this disorder. It is clear, however, that autism is not the result of environmental or psychological factors. It used to be thought that autism was caused by parents who were cold, unloving, and inattentive. This theory was prevalent until the mid 1970s, but we now know it to be invalid. Autism is not an emotional or mental disorder.

CHARACTERISTICS OF THE AUTISTIC CHILD

Autism may take very different forms and may range from mild to severe. In its most severe form, the child with autism exhibits significant social, cognitive, and language deficiencies and needs much help with basic living skills. Intelligence, language skills, and behavior may vary greatly so that two children diagnosed as autistic may act and communicate very differently. While a majority of children with autism test within the mentally retarded range, a small minority (about 5 percent) are of average intelligence or above. Some may not speak at all, while others have only mild language delays. Some display significant problems of inattention and a high activity level, while others tend to be passive and underactive.

The following are the most common characteristics of autism:

- *Social Difficulties:* The autistic child typically has problems relating to people. Eye contact is often poor, and he may stare into space, seemingly lost in his own thoughts and oblivious to what is happening around him. He may shy away from others and withdraw into himself, showing little interest in making friends. A friendly comment or a warm smile may elicit little response. He may not even look up when his name is called. The child's social difficulties may stem in part from his inability to grasp the basic rules of social behavior. He may interrupt a person who is talking because he cannot tell when that person is finished speaking. He may have difficulty understanding what someone has said because he cannot interpret the facial expressions and gestures. In addition, he may be so self-absorbed that he has difficulty seeing another's point of view or understanding the other person's motivations. As an example, an autistic child who is asked to show a picture to his class may not turn the picture around because he may not appreciate that the point of view of others is different from his own.

- *Language Problems:* A delay in the ability to both express and understand language is a prominent feature of children with autism. Their language skills may range from having no functional language (about half of children with autism), to using repetitive phrases, to being able to discuss a few concrete topics. If the child is not speaking by the age of 5, he is unlikely ever to develop functional speech, although he may develop ways of communicating non-verbally. For those with language skills, their speech may be stilted and concrete, and accompanied by a flat tone and little body language. Some speak in a whisper, while others speak in a singsong manner or talk backward. They may also exhibit unusual speech patterns, including pronoun reversal (using "you" instead of "I") and echolalia (repeating what others say without necessarily understanding the meaning). In addition, they may have difficulty formulating meaningful statements of their own. Their speech is usually geared to obtaining something rather than engaging in conversation. Starting or holding a conversation is not something they do with ease. Even understanding what others say can be a challenge for autistic children. They may have difficulty making sense of long, complicated verbal messages. Sarcasm, jokes, idiomatic expressions, and metaphors elude them.

- *Unusual Repetitive Behaviors:* The autistic child may exhibit repetitive, random behaviors such as spinning, rocking, arm flapping, or finger flicking. He may become distressed if prevented from engaging in these acts of self-stimulation. In extreme cases, he may display self-injurious behaviors such as handbiting or headbanging. Objects may fascinate him, particularly those that move or spin. He may spend long periods of time spinning the wheels of a toy car, playing with a rubber band, or arranging and rearranging a line of blocks.

■ *Resistance to Change:* Keeping things the same is important to the autistic child. He may wear the same clothes, eat the same foods, and engage in the same activities. Trying new things or meeting new people may hold little appeal for him. He can become easily upset when his daily routine is changed or his surroundings are altered. A new arrangement of desks or a change in the classroom schedule may throw him for a loop. The movie, *Rain Man,* which told the story of an autistic man named Raymond, depicted this well. Raymond insisted on seeing his favorite television show every day and had to have the salt and pepper shakers lined up the same way at every meal.

■ *Extreme Reactions to Sensory Information:* The autistic child may be un usually sensitive to physical sensations such as loud noises or bright lights. Even smells and textures may disturb him. Children with autism are likely to differ in their sensitivities. Some may be very sensitive to touch (called tactile defensiveness), and may become upset if someone puts an arm on their shoulder or accidentally bumps into them. Routine sounds may not be so routine to the autistic child and may actually hurt; the sound of a school bus may sound to the autistic child like a plane taking off. He may react to sounds by putting his hands over his ears, by screaming or throwing a tantrum, or by withdrawing. His sensitivity to sounds may interfere with his ability to understand oral messages effectively.

Some children who are autistic display unusual or "savant" skills. As impressive as these skills may be, they often have little practical value. Some autistic children may display a photographic memory—having the ability to remember entire train schedules—or draw with incredible accuracy a picture of an object they had seen only briefly. Some may exhibit musical talent in the form of having perfect pitch or being able to play a melody after hearing it only once. Some have even befuddled psychologists with their ability to identify the day of the week corresponding with a particular date in history. At the same time, the child with savant skills may have very poor conceptual understanding. The same child who can do complicated math problems in his head may have difficulty grasping the meaning of "in" and "out" or understanding cause and effect. As a general rule, children with autism are strong in tasks requiring rote memory and spatial abilities and weak in tasks requiring higher-level thinking and understanding of language.

Adolescence can be an especially difficult time for children with autism. About one of five children with autism begins to have seizures during the teen years. In addition, behavior problems can emerge or get worse during this period.

DIAGNOSING AND TREATING AUTISM

While research points to neurological problems as a probable cause of autism, this disorder cannot be detected through medical or laboratory tests. Rather, autism is identified by observing the child's behavior, language, and social skills, and by conducting a comprehensive interview with the parents. Because autism shares characteristics with a variety of other conditions, the diagnosis is difficult and best done by a multidisciplinary team that should include, at a minimum, a pediatrician, neurologist, psychologist, and speech-language therapist. A child with autism can be mistaken for one having mental retardation, a behavior disorder, Tourette syndrome, or a hearing problem. A behavior rating scale such as the Childhood Autism Rating Scale may aid in the diagnosis.

You may have a student who is said to be "autisticlike" or to have "autistic tendencies." This means that the child exhibits only some of the characteristics associated with autism, notably the difficulty in relating to people. Sometimes autistic children are described as having a pervasive developmental disorder (PDD). This is a general term for a lifelong disorder affecting a child's communication and interpersonal abilities, with autism being the most common form of PDD. Asperger syndrome is another type of PDD. Children with this disorder are higher-functioning than autistic children but share some of the same characteristics, including interpersonal difficulties, concrete thinking, resistance to change, and obsession with one or two topics. They are typically not socially withdrawn and self-absorbed in the way that autistic children are.

The care of autistic children has changed dramatically since the condition was first described in 1943. While there is no cure for autism, many approaches have been used in school with varying degrees of success, including special education, behavior modification, speech and language therapy, social skill development, and vocational education. These approaches have helped many autistic individuals learn to compensate for and cope with their disorder and become more independent and productive persons. Some children with autism may take medication such as Ritalin to deal with an attention deficit or hyperactivity. Some experts have advocated the use of food supplements and dietary restrictions to treat autism, but there is no definitive evidence that these approaches are helpful.

As children with autism grow up, they are less likely to be institutionalized than in years past and more likely to live in a variety of community living arrangements, ranging from highly structured residential facilities to group homes to independent households. While their autistic behaviors may decrease as they get older, they are likely to retain some features of autism throughout their lives. Some may need the support of professionals or family throughout their lives, and may continue to live at home with their parents. A small minority, however, may grow up to lead relatively independent lives, graduate from college, obtain a job, and marry. An autistic child who develops functional speech by the age of 5 has the best chance of becoming an independent and productive adult.

EDUCATING THE AUTISTIC CHILD

Children with autism will almost always need some degree of special education. They should qualify for special education based on their condition, although the formal classification of disability will vary with the state. In some states, the autistic child will be classified as "autistic," in others as "neurologically impaired," and in still others as "emotionally disturbed." The particular label applied to the child is less important than the kind of educational program he receives—and when he receives it. As with most childhood disorders, early intervention with children who are autistic is crucial. If they qualify for special education, they should be able to receive special education services from the age of 3 (and possibly sooner, depending on the state's policies).

When an autistic child reaches kindergarten age, the school and parents must decide what kind of educational program is appropriate to the child's needs. While many autistic children are best educated in special schools for autistic children, others are educated in regular schools, with varying degrees of mainstreaming in regular classes. Many of those in regular schools attend special classes, while some attend regular classes for much of the day. The degree to which the child can attend and adjust to regular classes depends largely on his intellectual ability and his communication skills.

Whatever setting the student is placed in, the use of behavior modification will be important for teachers to improve the student's behavior and develop his communication skills. The chapter on attention deficit disorder discusses at length the use of behavior modification strategies with students. These same strategies apply to children with autism, although it is important to note that children with autism are more responsive to tangible reinforcers (for example, poker chips that can be exchanged for toys) than social reinforcers (for example, smiles, hugs, or compliments).

While the educational program should vary with the particular needs of the student and his ability level, most programs for autistic children should include instruction in skills they will need to function in society and that will increase their independence. Thus, teachers may instruct students in such skills as crossing the street, taking a bus, making a purchase, using the library, and making a telephone call.

HOW TEACHERS CAN HELP

Teaching the child with autism is a formidable challenge because of his unusual characteristics. The methods that are effective with children with other disabilities are often ineffective with autistic children. For example, while many children with autism are mentally retarded, the approaches typically used with retarded children such as group activities and a highly stimulating educational setting are not appropriate for children with autism. Fortunately, there are many strategies that teachers have found effective in dealing with the unusual combination of problems presented by autistic children. These are described below.

1. Work Closely with the Student's Parents

It is especially important when teaching autistic children that you develop a close working relationship with the child's parents. They will have a wealth of information about their child that is important for you to know—namely his strengths and weaknesses, his special sensitivities, and strategies that work with him and those that don't. In addition, many of the skills that you teach in class must be practiced and reinforced at home, so you must talk regularly with the parents to let them know what skills they should be supporting. You might even videotape your lessons or invite them for a classroom visit to show them how to teach specific skills or use behavior modification methods. Bear in mind that the autistic child may not be a reliable conveyor of messages or carrier of notes. If so, set up a time to talk with the parents on the phone or meet them in person.

2. Obtain Help from a Specialist in Autism or Communication Disorders

Given the specialized nature of autism, you will most likely benefit from consulting with a specialist. This person may guide you in establishing appropriate expectations, developing lessons to enhance his language development, and using strategies to manage his behavior. Talk with your principal or the director of special services about attending a workshop or having a consultant meet with you in school. It is especially important that you obtain help from an expert in the field if the student is exhibiting self-injurious behaviors.

3. Provide Structure and Consistency

Autistic children learn best in a highly structured setting. In the classroom, this means following predictable routines, using consistent language and gestures, communicating clear instructions, and providing a familiar physical setting. Keep the classroom materials organized and in the same place so that the child quickly learns to locate them. In this way, he learns to master his environment and become more independent. Make sure to coordinate with others working with the child in school so that your approaches to the child are consistent.

4. Speak Simply and Directly

Keep the structure of your sentences simple and avoid including extraneous information. Saying "I do not want you to scream like that" conveys your message more effectively than "Why are you screaming so loud?" In trying to change his behavior, state clearly the behavior that you want him to stop, but also offer an alternative ("I do not want you to yell out when you want my attention. If you need me, I want you to raise your hand high without making any noise.") Because the autistic child has difficulty processing visual and auditory information simultaneously, use one approach at a time. Avoid asking him to look at something while you are also talking to him. Keep in mind that speaking simply and directly should not keep you from being warm and friendly, even though the child may seem unaffected by your nurturing approach.

5. Avoid Using Abstract Ideas

The autistic child may understand language in a very concrete and literal manner; phrases such as "hands of a clock" or "please wrap it up" will confuse him. Concepts will be better understood if you reinforce them with visual cues, actions, and gestures.

6. Use Visual Aids to Communicate

Autistic children are typically visual learners; they tend to think in pictures rather than words. Auditory processing is often deficient, so you must reinforce your lessons with visual images or aids (but try to avoid presenting auditory and visual information to the student at the same time). This is especially true with abstract concepts. For example, in teaching the concepts of "in" and "out," you might use a small figure entering and leaving a doll house while repeating the word. In showing the student what an object looks like, be aware that he may not understand line drawings, so use real objects or photographs instead. When you give instructions, if the child is able to read, write the directions down in addition to giving them orally. Try to design tasks so that the child can tell what he has to do by looking at the task. In this way, he will need little explanation from you and can learn to work more independently.

7. Promote the Use of Spoken Language

The child with autism may need to learn the most basic purpose of language—to communicate one's needs. If the child has not learned this lesson, show him in a very concrete way that his speech leads to action or fulfills a need. Encourage the student to use language rather than pointing or tantrumming to get something he wants. Provide opportunities for the student to interact with younger children. The language development of younger children may be comparable to that of older autistic children, so the autistic child is more likely to communicate in the presence of younger children.

8. With Nonverbal Children, Find Alternative Methods of Communication

The child who cannot speak may learn to communicate using sign language, a communication board, or a computer with voice-output capability. You might also teach him to express basic ideas through the use of pictures or gestures. In some cases, the child who does not speak may communicate through singing. You may find that the child's behavior will improve as he learns other ways to communicate, since the nonverbal child often expresses his needs through his behavior. Autistic children who have little language are especially prone to behavioral outbursts and even aggressive behavior.

9. Prepare the Student for Changes in School Routine

The autistic child may become anxious if the classroom routine is changed or the setting is altered. Let him know ahead of time of changes that are likely to set him off (for example, a shortened day, an assembly, a substitute teacher, and indoor recess because of the weather). The emergence of behavior problems may signal to you that he is experiencing stress. If so, consider removing him from the source of the stress and allowing him to go to a place where he feels at ease, to have an object that comforts him, to be with a familiar person who calms him down, or to engage in a familiar activity.

10. Provide Environmental Protection

Identify problems in the environment that are likely to cause the child distress and take steps to protect him. You may find that specific sounds, particularly if they are sudden and unexpected, elicit screams or behavior problems. Examples of school sounds that may be distressing to the autistic child are the school bell, the buzzer in the gymnasium, the fire alarm, chairs scraping on the floor, and messages on the public address system. Some of these sounds can be controlled. Try putting slit tennis balls on the bottom of chair legs to lessen the scraping noise. Also, you may be able to muffle the sound of a bell by stuffing it with tissue or paper towels. Carpeting will, of course, be a big help in the classroom. While you will want to try to keep classroom noise to a minimum, there will no doubt be times when the class is loud. Consider giving the child some headphones to listen to music during especially noisy periods. Some autistic children are particularly sensitive to fluorescent lights, especially if they flicker or hum. If there is no alternative to using these lights, try placing the child near the window or use new fluorescent lights, which tend to flicker less.

11. Build on the Student's Interests

Use the student's interests to grab his attention. For example, if he is fascinated with baseball statistics, exploit this interest to teach him about fractions and decimals and find books that feature baseball players with impressive statistics. You may find that his attention to task will increase and any behavior problems he is having may decrease as he works in an area that he enjoys. Children with autism often find art activities and computers appealing.

12. Promote Generalization of Skills to Outside Settings

An important challenge for educators working with autistic students is to encourage them to use the skills learned in the classroom outside of school. This process is called generalization. Autistic children have difficulty transferring the skills they learn in the classroom to the outside world. Research shows that the child's ability to maintain the skills he learns in school is directly related to the number of times he uses these skills outside the classroom. It is thus vitally important that you find ways to encourage the child to practice these skills in other settings. The parents are a key part of this process. Help them understand the skills you are teaching so they can reinforce these same skills at home. In this way, students will learn to become more independent and more capable members of their community.

13. Teach the Student Some Waiting Activities

The autistic child may experience behavioral difficulties during those times when he is waiting for an activity to begin (for example, waiting for the school bus, for an assembly program to begin, or for the school day to start while sitting in class). To help him avoid problems during these times, teach him strategies for using his time in an enjoyable and appropriate manner. Find activities that are within his ability level and compatible with his interests. This might include playing cards, reading a book, listening to music on a Walkman, or playing on a computer.

14. Help Organize the Student

The autistic child tends to be disorganized and forgetful. Find ways to remind him without making him stand out. At the end of the day, check to make sure he is bringing the proper materials home and has written the assignments down correctly. Consider taping a 3″ by 5″ card on his desk or bookbag, listing the things to do or bring home at the end of the day. If he does not read, draw pictures as reminders. The autistic child may also have problems keeping his materials neat (although other autistic children may be obsessed with neatness and become upset if their order is disturbed), so you may have to help him learn to locate and organize his materials. Keep in mind that he may have little control over his disorganization, and should not then be punished for his messiness. You can help the student keep track of the day's activities by giving him a schedule that either is written or has pictures of the activities.

15. Encourage Use of a Computer

Autistic children often have fine-motor problems, which may give rise to sloppy handwriting or very slow production. Using a computer to write may lessen their frustration and speed up their pace.

16. Talk with Your Other Students

If the parents and the student give you permission, find a time when the autistic student is out of the class to talk with your other students about the nature of autism and the behaviors they may see from their classmate. Help them understand that the student lacks control over much of his behavior and that his lack of friendliness and withdrawn behavior are a part of his disorder, and not a sign that he is mean or upset. Encourage them to include him in classroom and playground activities, and request that they be patient and tolerant of his behaviors.

17. Coach the Student to Handle Social Situations

The autistic child will need specific instructions in relating to other children. This is especially important in promoting the child's success in getting along with nondisabled children. Make sure that what you are teaching is within the child's ability to learn and is a practical skill. You may have to start with very basic skills such as making eye contact, and eventually move on to dealing with situations in the classroom or during recess. For example, you might rehearse with the child how to ask if he can join in a soccer game during recess.

18. Find Opportunities for Interaction with Nondisabled Peers

Autistic children are able to observe appropriate language and social skills when they interact with students who are not disabled. At the same time, students with autism are prime targets for ridicule because of their unusual behaviors, and may be shunned by their classmates. This can happen, for example, when students are asked to pair off. In these situations, arrange the pairing yourself or find another child who is willing to choose the autistic child. If the autistic student has special skills or interests, use these to win favor with other students. For example, if he enjoys collecting things (as many autistic children do), have him bring in his collection and talk about it.

19. Develop a Thick Skin

The autistic child is likely to be unresponsive to you and seemingly unappreciative of your efforts. You may put forth much effort in teaching and reaching out to him, and he may continue to be self-absorbed and react to you as he does to a stranger. Don't take this personally. He may respond the same way to his parents. He is not intentionally trying to make your life miserable. Rather, his aloof behavior is the result of a condition that he has little control over and is his way of protecting himself from stressful situations and a feeling of being out of control. Don't let his unappreciative attitude stop you from being supportive. Your support is vitally important to his development.

FOR FURTHER INFORMATION

Fullerton, A. (1996). *Higher Functioning Adolescents and Young Adults With Autism: A Teacher's Guide.* Austin, TX: Pro-Ed.

Hart, C. A. (1993). *A Parent's Guide to Autism.* New York: Pocket Books.

Koegel, R. L., and Koegel, L. K. (1995). *Teaching Children With Autism.* Baltimore: Paul H. Brookes.

Powers, M. D. (ed.) (1996). *Children With Autism: A Parents' Guide.* Bethesda, MD: Woodbine House.

Quill, K. A. (1995). *Teaching Children With Autism.* Albany, NY: Delmar.

ORGANIZATIONS

Autism Network International
P.O. Box 448
Syracuse, NY 13210-0448

Autism Services Center
The Prichard Building
605 Ninth Street
P.O. Box 507
Huntington, WV 25710-0507
1-304-525-8014

Autism Society of America
7910 Woodmont Avenue, Suite 650
Bethesda, MD 20814-3015
1-800-3-AUTISM
1-301-657-0881

Institute for the Study of Developmental Disabilities
Indiana Resource Center for Autism
2853 East 10th Street
Bloomington, IN 47408-2601
1-812-855-6508

See also:
  Attention Deficit Disorder
  Auditory Processing Problem
  Speech and Language Problems

THE DISORGANIZED STUDENT

The biggest challenge many students face is not learning to read or mastering the multiplication tables but rather getting organized. They may have good reasoning ability and well-developed academic skills, but they get failing grades when it comes to the nuts and bolts of learning—bringing the proper materials to class, keeping track of papers, using time wisely, writing down assignments correctly, turning them in on time. Such a seemingly simple task as bringing a pencil to class may elude the disorganized student. The lack of these school survival skills may affect almost every phase of his school performance as well as frustrate his teacher, who may need to spend considerable class time keeping him on track.

A student can lack organizational skills for a variety of reasons, including poor motivation, stress, and depression. In addition, a child with a learning or attentional disability will often exhibit this problem. Disorganized behavior may also reflect disorganized thinking, which may manifest itself in the form of difficulty seeing patterns, organizing and classifying information, and understanding sequence. As a result, the student may have problems retrieving information, keeping track of materials, and planning things out.

It is not hard to recognize a disorganized student. His desk is usually a sure giveaway. A kind of black hole, it swallows up papers almost as quickly as teachers can distribute them. His backpack may be just as much of a jumbled hodgepodge of school materials. Displaying an almost magical ability, the disorganized student can make papers disappear in the blink of an eye. As a result, he may spend much time in school searching for materials and redoing lost papers. "Everything in its place and a place for everything" are clearly not the words the disorganized student lives by.

While the disorganized student may excel at making objects disappear, he does not juggle very well. He may be overwhelmed by having to keep various times, dates, and assignments in his head, and even have difficulty remembering his schedule. Forgetfulness is the hallmark of the disorganized student. Upon entering middle school, he may struggle in finding his way around a larger school, recalling the names of all his teachers, and keeping his assignments straight.

171

The problems of the disorganized student are often most apparent in his homework habits. He may forget to write down the assignment and not remember what to do. Or he may write it down, but record it incorrectly. Or he may write it down accurately, but forget to bring the correct materials home. Or he may complete it, but forget to bring it in to school. Getting the disorganized student to develop good homework habits can exasperate the most experienced of teachers.

CHARACTERISTICS OF THE DISORGANIZED STUDENT

The disorganized student may exhibit the following characteristics in your class:

- forgets to bring the proper materials
- is not ready to work when the bell rings
- is inattentive and distractible
- is often confused about what to do
- has trouble remembering information such as his school schedule
- has a messy desk and backpack
- loses papers and school materials
- turns work in late and sometimes not at all
- uses time inefficiently
- produces written work that is hard to follow
- has a problem getting started with a project or report
- has a poor sense of time
- writes down assignments inaccurately or does not write them down at all
- has difficulty expressing himself in an organized, sequential manner
- is at risk for a learning disability

HOW TEACHERS CAN HELP

The ability to be organized is one of the key building blocks of school success. It is also a skill—one that can, and should, be taught in school. You can use the following practical strategies to help your students manage their school responsibilities:

1. Provide Structure and Routine

Disorganized students often have trouble keeping things in order and retaining information. You can lessen their confusion by providing structure and establishing routine. Spell out the rules of your classroom clearly and simply, and tell your students what materials they must bring to class daily. Class schedules can be confusing to students, especially if they have a number of teachers or leave class for school programs such as music lessons or speech therapy. Try to schedule activities at the same time every week (for example, give science assignments every Tuesday or spelling tests every Friday). Have students with complex schedules write them out and tape them on their desks or inside their binders. Make sure they know how to read the schedule.

2. State Directions Clearly and Simply

Use a minimum of words to explain what the student must do. Do not give him every detail, or he will miss the key points. Also, avoid giving him multistep directions. Have him repeat your directions to ensure that he understands them. If you are explaining a complex task, demonstrate it to him, and then have him do it while you observe.

3. Require Students to Use a Three-Ring Binder

Consider requiring your students as early as third grade to organize their materials and schoolwork in a three-ring binder with subject dividers, blank notebook paper, and a plastic pouch for pens, pencils, and erasers. Suggest that they get a binder with pockets, one of which can be designated "To bring home" (for assignments to be completed, notes to parents, and papers to bring home and leave there) and the other "To bring to school" (for completed assignments, notes from parents, and signed parent permission slips). Three-hole-punched folders with pockets can also be used for this purpose.

4. Have Students Use a Container for Small Items

These items are easily lost in a desk or backpack. In trying to find a pencil, a student may create a disruption in the classroom—and a greater mess in his desk—as he rummages through his desk. Make sure your students have a case for such items as pencils, pens, erasers, and scissors. This might be a plastic zippered pouch kept in the binder or a box or resealable plastic bag kept in the desk.

5. Have Students Keep Their Work in Folders

Many students use the "crumple and cram" method of storing papers. To help them organize their papers so they can get them when they need them, suggest that they keep them in folders in their binders or their desks. They might have a folder for completed work, one for work to be done, and one for parent information—or they might have different color-coded folders for each subject. Three-hole-punched folders that have pockets and fit into binders are useful ways to store papers. Help students figure out what to do with papers they no longer need. You might have them bring folders with completed work home on a specific day of the week. Let parents know when to expect the folders. After the parents review the work, their children can decide whether to store them at home or to discard them.

6. Present Assignments Clearly

Pay attention to how you communicate assignments to your students to ensure that they get the correct information. Be clear about the due date, the page numbers, the format, the expected length, and the required materials. Write the assignment on the board in the same place every day, and keep it posted there. If you hand out papers to be completed, include the due date on them. Ask students if they have any questions about the assignment, and give them time to write it down. Have them start difficult assignments before they leave your class, in case they have any questions. Emphasize that you expect assignments to be handed in on time. If they are not, let students know they must still complete them anyway.

7. Require Your Students to Write Assignments Down

Give them a choice of how—but not whether—they will do this. They might use a small assignment pad or datebook, which can be kept in the backpack or binder. A monthly assignment calendar also works well (make sure they know how to read a calendar). The calendar should be placed near the front of the binder and is most effective if it is made up of two pages that face each other, to allow more room for the recording of assignments. You might develop and hand out to your students monthly an assignment and events calendar, perhaps using a computer software program such as Calendar Maker by Prairie Group to create it. Note birthdays, vacations, and special events on the calendar. Be sure the calendar squares are big enough to allow students to write in assignment information. Another option for recording homework is a three-hole-punched student planning book, which can be placed into a binder. Whatever system your students use, instruct them to record assignments on the due dates, and to note tests and projects. Make time to check the assignment-recording methods of your students.

8. Record Your Daily Assignments on a Telephone Message System for Students to Call

Talk with your principal about looking into a program that allows you and other teachers to do this. Once it is implemented, students will not have the excuse that they did not copy down the assignment. In addition, it will allow students who are absent to keep up with schoolwork.

9. Minimize the Clutter on Your Handouts

Students can be distracted not only by the clutter in their desks but also by the clutter on their papers. Simplify the visual presentation of the papers you hand out by limiting the amount of information you put on a page, or by having the student fold the paper to allow him to concentrate on one part or problem at a time. When giving a test of more than one page, consider giving the student one page at a time. Also, direct his attention to key information through highlighting or underlining.

10. Model the Way to Approach a Project or Assignment

Students who are disorganized can find large projects overwhelming. Just figuring out where to start can be a challenge. Walk the student through the process by having him brainstorm on paper the various steps needed to complete the project and helping him decide on the order in which they must be done. Then, have him work out a realistic schedule of when he will work on each step of the project. Suggest that he make a list of the needed materials and gather all of them before beginning. Similarly, if he is confused by an assignment, help him break it into smaller, more doable parts, and then take it one step at a time. For long-term projects, set up interim due dates for parts of the project (for example, completion of notecards) to help keep students on track.

11. Provide a Place in Your Classroom for Students to Turn in Their Work

To lessen the chance that students will lose papers, tell them to turn in classwork as soon as it is completed to a designated spot in the classroom. This might be a box, crate, file divider, or file drawer. Have a folder for each student, and arrange the folders alphabetically. As an alternative, have students place assignments into a folder specific to that assignment and color-coded to lessen the chance of misfiling. Instruct students to indicate on a sheet on the bulletin board or next to the folders that they have turned in the assignment by placing a check next to their name and under the column for that assignment.

12. Teach the Student How to Keep a Neat Desk

Keeping a desk neat does not come naturally to a disorganized student. He will probably need instructions on how to reduce the chaos. Bear in mind that the goal is not to have him keep his desk meticulous but rather to have him keep it neat enough so he can find what he needs with little effort. Explain in a concrete, specific way strategies for keeping a neat desk—perhaps even listing them on a poster for display. You might have him make a list, with your guidance, of the items allowed in his desk and then have him tape the list on his desk or in his notebook. Consider implementing a "no toys" policy to lessen the clutter. Also, suggest that he write the subjects on the spines of his textbooks so he can locate them quickly. If his desk has gotten out of control and the student is overwhelmed by the prospect of cleaning it, have him dump the contents into a bag and take them to a table to sort through. Help him figure out what to do with the contents. Rarely used items might be brought home or placed on the classroom shelf. Allow him to keep in his desk a maximum of two or three silent-reading books. Train him to clear extraneous materials from his desk before he begins to work.

13. Build Desk-Cleaning Time into the Class Schedule

Some students will not be able to keep their desks clean unless time is set aside for this task. For students whose desks are already clean or who end early, provide enjoyable activities they can do while their classmates finish up. Build in spot checks of the students' desks—praising those who have kept them neat. Those who have not can stay in during recess to complete the cleaning job. Do not take class time to have students organize their backpacks, although you might have them clean them out as a homework assignment.

14. Encourage Students to Be Responsible for Their Materials

If a student forgets to bring the proper materials to class, lend him what he needs, but consider asking him for some "collateral," to be returned when he gives back the borrowed materials. Maintain a list of items students borrow and return. If a student often forgets materials, take him aside and let him know in a gentle manner that you expect him to bring the required materials to class in the future. If the problem continues, contact his parents or give him a school consequence (for example, detention or loss of part of his recess). If he is constantly losing his pencil, have him put a piece of velcro on his desk, as well as on his pencil, to help him avoid misplacing it. Conduct spot checks to see if students have the proper materials and to put them on notice that you expect them to come to class prepared.

15. Have a Class Discussion in Which Students Share Their Ideas about Keeping Organized

Students can be creative in coming up with ways of staying on top of school responsibilities. Have them share organizational tips with their classmates. You may find that your students are more likely to use strategies that they know other students are using. Record their suggestions and post them, or distribute them to the class.

16. Encourage the Student to Solve Problems with Minimal Teacher Involvement

A disorganized student can consume much of your time. Encourage him to solve the problem on his own to minimize the disruption to your teaching as well as to foster self-reliance. If he has forgotten an item needed for class, suggest that he borrow it from a classmate. If he has forgotten a pencil, tell him to get one from a "pencil stubs" box kept on your desk or near the pencil sharpener. Keep an extra textbook on your desk that a student can borrow by noting his name and the date on a sheet of paper. Let your students know that borrowed items are to be returned at the end of the period or the day.

17. Assign the Student a Classroom Buddy

Arrange for an especially responsible classmate to assist a student with organizational or learning problems when you are unavailable. Tell the student to first see his "buddy" if he needs help before coming to you. A variation of this is to group students at tables, with group members expected to assist others in their group who need help.

18. Encourage the Use of Checklists

Have the student make a checklist to keep track of school tasks he must complete. Suggest that he keep it in an accessible place, perhaps on his desk or in his binder. Show him how to put the checklist in priority order so that he tackles the most important tasks first. Also, tell him to cross out items on the list once they are completed. You can have a younger student draw pictures rather than use words as reminders.

19. Teach the Student Memory Aides

Suggest that he use tangible items such as a rubber band around his wrist or a note attached to his backpack to remind him of tasks he needs to do. If he has a watch with an alarm, have him set it to go off at the time of a schedule change (for example, when he needs to go to a remedial reading class). You might also develop, or have the student develop, an acronym to help him keep track of school responsibilities. For example, suggest he use the acronym PANTS to remind him of what he must bring to school every day (P = Parent notes, A = Assignments, N = Notebook, T = Textbooks, and S = Student—himself!).

20. Monitor the Assignment Sheets of Students with Homework Problems, and Have Parents Do the Same

If a student has a history of not completing homework, require that he come to you at the end of the period or day so you can check the accuracy of his assignment sheet and initial it. Let the parents know that you would like them to review his assignment sheet and initial it daily when they have checked that the recorded assignments have been completed and placed in his backpack. This process can be discontinued after a few weeks if the student is completing homework regularly.

21. Intervene When There Is a Pattern of Incomplete Assignments

Talk with the student privately to identify the source of the problem. Is he not copying down the assignments? Is he not bringing home the proper materials? Is he confused by the directions? Does he not understand the work? Does he not have enough time to complete the work because of excessive involvement in outside activities? Is he completing it, but forgetting to bring it in? If necessary, meet with the parents along with the student to work out a specific plan to correct the problem. Follow up to make sure the student is doing what he agreed to do.

22. Allow the Student to Experience the Consequences of His Forgetfulness

If you excuse his forgetfulness or continually bail him out, he will have little incentive to remember. Allow the student to experience the natural consequences of his behavior—within limits. For example, if he forgets to bring in a signed permission slip allowing him to be on the safety patrol despite repeated requests, consider dropping him from this activity. At the same time, avoid keeping him from going on a class trip because he brought back the permission slip after the due date.

23. Praise and Reward Students for Improved Organization

If disorganization is a significant problem for one or more of your students, consider implementing a behavior modification program to spur improvement. Describe to them in a clear, concrete way the behaviors they must focus on (for example, "copies down assignments accurately for five straight days") and then assign positive consequences for their attainment (for example, an item from the school store, a classroom privilege, or a "no homework" pass). Of course, you may find that verbal praise for improved performance is sufficient to motivate some students. See the chapters Attention Deficit Disorder and The Disruptive Student for a more thorough discussion of behavior modification strategies.

24. Suggest Organizational Strategies for Parents to Use with Their Children

Parents play a key role in helping to organize their children. Send a letter home early in the school year to describe your classroom and homework policies, as well as the materials required by students. Include in the letter some of the following suggestions of steps they can take to help their children stay on track:

- Encourage your child to put his school materials in the same place every day.

- Ask your child daily for notes from school, or look in the part of his binder or backpack reserved for parent information.

- Establish a "homework-comes-first" policy.

- Set limits on your child's television watching.

- Tell your child that you expect him to write down all assignments.

- Have your child do the harder assignments earlier in the evening when he is most alert.

- Put up a checklist in a prominent place to remind your child of materials to be brought to school daily.

- Mark on the family calendar tests, projects, and important school activities.

- Have your child put all school materials inside his backpack before going to bed.

25. Some Miscellaneous Organizational Tips

The following are some additional strategies for helping your students stay organized:

- Make sure your students can tell time using a nondigital clock.

- Use paper of different colors for different tasks so students can locate the papers easily.

- Have students use self-stick notes to mark the pages they are on.

- Punch holes in the handouts you give to students so they can easily put them in their binders.

- Require disorganized students to check with you before they go home, to make sure they have the proper materials and have correctly recorded assignments.

For Further Information

Archer, A., and Gleason, M. *Skills for School Success*. North Billerica, MA: Curriculum Associates. (Separate books available for grades 3, 4, 5, and 6. Contact Curriculum Associates at 1-800-225-0248.) (*Note:* Publication dates range from 1989 to 1994.)

Archer, A., and Gleason, M. *Advanced Skills for School Success*. North Billerica, MA: Curriculum Associates. (Separate books available for secondary school teachers on following topics: behavior; completing daily assignments; classroom instruction; and classroom presentations. Contact Curriculum Associates at 1-800-225-0248.) (*Note:* Publication dates range from 1989 to 1994.)

Clark, F., and Clark, C. (1989). *Hassle-Free Homework*. New York: Doubleday.

Clemes, H., and Bean, R. (1990). *How to Teach Children Responsibility*. Los Angeles: Price Stern Sloan.

Dodge, J. (1994). *Study Skills Handbook: More Than 75 Strategies for Better Learning*. New York: Scholastic.

Schumm, J. S., and Radencich, M. (1992). *School Power—Strategies for Succeeding in School*. Minneapolis: Free Spirit Publishing.

See also:
   Attention Deficit Disorder
   Handwriting Problem
   The Unmotivated Student

THE DISRUPTIVE STUDENT

The disruptive student goes by many names. He may be called acting out, oppositional defiant, passive aggressive, behavior disordered, even emotionally disturbed. What most teachers call him, however, is frustrating. The disruptive student makes the job of the teacher far more difficult, and often takes considerable time away from instruction. Studies show, and teachers know, that students make greater academic progress in a classroom with few disciplinary problems. Children simply cannot learn in a class filled with unruly students.

Disruptive behavior can take many forms in the classroom. The following is a partial list of behaviors that an acting-out student may exhibit:

- makes distracting noises
- talks at inappropriate times
- blurts out answers
- talks back to staff
- uses inappropriate language
- defies the teacher
- wanders around the room
- throws objects
- bangs his books

What these behaviors have in common is that they disrupt classroom instruction. The teacher may have difficulty teaching effectively, and her students may have trouble concentrating. As a result, it is critical that teachers find ways to minimize these disruptions. Despite the importance of maintaining an orderly classroom, however, teachers typically receive minimal instruction in discipline in their formal teacher training. This is not because of a lack of useful information on student discipline. Indeed, there is an abundance of research on how to discipline students effectively, as well as a range of formal classroom discipline programs.

WHY STUDENTS MISBEHAVE

Pinpointing why students misbehave allows us to figure out how to help them behave more appropriately. Rudolf Dreikurs, a psychiatrist, developed a useful, although somewhat simplistic, framework for understanding the goals of students who misbehave. He contended that students who are unable to obtain recognition and approval through appropriate school behavior may misbehave in an effort to obtain four possible goals.

The most common goal of a student who misbehaves is to gain attention from either peers or adults. Unable to obtain recognition in positive ways, he may seek attention through undesirable behavior. While, of course, most children seek attention, the misbehaving student may come to believe that his need to be center stage can only be met by creating a disruption. From his perspective, negative attention is better than no attention at all. His behavior may take the form of yelling out, making noises, tapping his pencil, or using inappropriate language. As a result, the teacher may spend considerable time reprimanding or coaxing the student to behave better.

Some students who misbehave have as their goal the attainment of power. Often feeling powerless and insecure, the student with this objective aims to show that he is in control and can do what he wants—in effect, that he is the boss. To this end, he may refuse to comply with the teacher's rules and defy her authority. To cooperate is, in the eyes of this student, to be defeated. This may result in a battle of wills, marked by angry confrontations between student and teacher. If the teacher is successful in overpowering the student, this only confirms to him the value of attaining power.

Other students who misbehave may be trying to gain revenge. Motivated by feelings of being mistreated, the student is determined to get even by hurting others. He may taunt his classmates, call the teacher names, threaten physical harm, and even damage the property of others.

The fourth possible goal of a misbehaving student is to project an image of inadequacy. This is often seen with the student who despairs of ever achieving success in school or acceptance by his classmates. By convincing the teacher that he is incapable and can't learn, he hopes to lower the teacher's expectations and thus avoid being exposed to situations in which he will experience further humiliation. In short, he wants the teacher to back off. This student's misbehavior takes the form of withdrawal rather than disruption.

While these goals do not account for every case of student misbehavior, this framework is a useful way of understanding what underlies the behavior of acting-out students and how to respond to their disruptions. The guiding principle, as discussed further below, is to find ways for the student to satisfy his emotional needs through cooperative, responsible behavior.

HOW TEACHERS CAN HELP

Because behavior problems can be difficult for teachers to deal with and consume a great deal of instructional time, it is critical that they put time and effort into preventing them. Teachers must also know what to do when students act out. The strategies listed below include ways of preventing problems as well as dealing with them when they do occur. In deciding which measures to use, give preference to positive over negative strategies. Keep in mind that your goal is not just to stop the student from misbehaving, but also to foster self-control. Also, note that the purpose of discipline is to teach appropriate behavior rather than to punish. Indeed, the word *discipline* is derived from the Latin word *disciplina,* meaning instruction.

1. Become Familiar with Your District's and School's Disciplinary Policies

Find out whether the school district has any restrictions on how teachers can discipline students. Also, check with your principal about disciplinary policies and procedures specific to your school.

2. State Clearly and Simply Your Rules for Classroom Behavior

Students are more likely to behave appropriately when they know what you expect of them. An absence of explicit rules is an invitation to students to test the limits to find out what they can get away with. Establish a maximum of six rules of behavior for your students. Communicate them clearly, concretely, and specifically in the beginning of the year, and review them periodically. Consider posting them on the wall. Explain to your students briefly the reasons for these rules. You might give them some input into these rules, although you, of course, retain the final decision. Consider sending home to parents a form that lists your classroom rules. Ask them to review the rules with their child and sign the form to indicate they agree with the rules and have discussed them with the child. When a student violates a rule, refer to the wall chart and have him read the rule to you. Make sure to praise students who comply with the rules, especially those who are prone to violate them. Before special situations (for example, an assembly or a field trip), spell out your rules of behavior for that activity.

3. Make Sure Your Students Understand Classroom Procedures

Students are especially prone to misbehaving when they are not sure what they should be doing in class. This may happen when class procedures are unclear or unspecified. Transitions between activities are particularly problem-prone. The more orderly and predictable the classroom setting, the less likely that students will experience behavior problems. Uncertainty, however, may give rise to noncompliance, which may give rise to misbehavior. Explain classroom assignments clearly and concretely. Err on the side of over-explaining. What may seem clear to you may be confusing to your students. Telling your students to "choose a partner and interview him about his interests and hobbies" may seem unambiguous to you, but raise questions from students (for example, How do they choose partners? How long should each interview take? Should they write the information down?). Make sure your students know what to do when they first arrive in school, where to turn in homework, how to get help from you, what to do when they have finished their seatwork, and what to do if they finish a test early. Spend time in the beginning of the year teaching students these and other classroom procedures. Consider posting them on the bulletin board.

4. Increase Your Influence Quotient with the Student by Showing Respect and Caring for Him

Students are less likely to disrupt class and more likely to cooperate if they feel you care for them. In addition, they will be more receptive to your disciplinary efforts if they perceive they have been treated with respect and dignity. Build a strong bond with a student who is prone to misbehavior by praising him and showcasing his accomplishments, joking around with him, and finding a few minutes every day to talk with him about his interests. Give him an opportunity to share with you his feelings and concerns, and listen attentively to what he says. If your schedule allows, attend an extracurricular event (for example, an athletic, musical, or theatrical activity) in which he is participating, and find something positive to say about his performance. When appropriate, involve him (and other students) in making decisions in the classroom. If he disagrees with a classroom rule, explain to him its rationale without allowing a lengthy debate. Pay attention to your tone of voice and body language when talking with him. If he misbehaves and you reprimand him, do not embarrass or humiliate him—especially in the presence of his peers. This is likely only to incite his anger and perpetuate his disruptive behavior.

5. Recognize Good Behavior

Highlight the behavior of students who are acting appropriately, and try to ignore students who are acting inappropriately, unless they are disrupting your ability to teach or upsetting other students. In this way, you are teaching students that they are more likely to get your attention through cooperative than disruptive behavior. In praising them, describe their behavior to the class (for example, "I am impressed with how Megan raised her hand to answer rather than yelling out."). Praise them as soon as possible after the behavior and avoid adding a discouraging comment such as "Why can't you act that way all the time?" Make a special effort to recognize positive behaviors of students with a history of acting out, even if it means highlighting behaviors that are routine for other students. Vary the form of the positive reinforcement. In addition to praising the student, you might send a note home to his parents or phone them in his presence, allow him to overhear you saying something positive about him to another individual, give him a good-behavior certificate or award, or select him as your student of the month due to improved behavior. If you sense that a student is uncomfortable being praised in front of his classmates, tell him privately. Keep a record of your positive reinforcements to make sure you are acknowledging every student in some way every week.

6. Find Positive Ways to Satisfy the Student's Need for Attention

It is a fact of school life that a student will often misbehave to gain the attention of his teacher or classmates, even if it means risking reprimand or rejection. While you cannot expect to lessen the student's need for attention, you can help him find more appropriate and cooperative ways of gaining recognition. The chapter entitled Low Self-Esteem lists a number of activities, from handing out papers to serving on the safety patrol, that a student can do in the classroom and school to gain a sense of importance. Try to match the activity with the student's particular needs. For example, if he likes being the class clown, offer him a few minutes at the end of the day to tell some jokes to the class, or give him a funny role in the school play. If he seeks status with peers, find an opportunity to highlight his talents or achievements to the class. If he enjoys being in control, give him opportunities to serve in leadership roles, while stressing to him the need to act responsibly.

7. Support the Student Academically, if Needed

Some students misbehave because they are frustrated by their academic deficiencies, are confused about what to do in class, or feel overwhelmed by a task. If a student has a pattern of misbehavior, consider whether he is having academic difficulties. If so, find ways of helping him feel that he is a capable learner and giving him support, perhaps through after-school help, peer tutoring, or parent support. If the classwork is too hard for him, give him work at a lower level—but do this without the knowledge of his peers, to lessen his feelings of self-consciousness. When giving an in-class assignment, make sure he understands the directions, perhaps doing the first problem or task with him, and ask him if he has any questions. If necessary, break down the task into smaller, more doable steps. Consider assigning him a class "buddy" to help him out when he is confused. Find ways that he can contribute meaningfully to the class to give him a sense of belonging. If you suspect that he has a learning disability, talk with the principal about referring him for an evaluation by the school's evaluation team. Also, consider the possibility that his misbehavior is related to boredom in class because the work is far too easy for him. If so, consider giving him more challenging or stimulating work.

8. Decide Whether to Ignore or Respond to the Behavior

You cannot respond every time a student misbehaves, nor should you try. Focus on those misbehaviors that interfere with your ability to teach or your students' ability to concentrate. In some cases, you may have to work on modifying your tolerance level rather than the student's behavior. For example, a student who gives you an angry look, laughs at inappropriate times, or mutters under his breath is better left alone. In addition, try to avoid responding to mild misbehaviors that you conclude are the student's way of gaining your attention. Avoid giving him eye contact, talking with him, or even being in his presence. As soon as he begins to behave appropriately, however, give him some attention and comment positively on his behavior. There is a third option, other than responding directly to the behavior or ignoring it. This is to encourage the student to solve the problem himself. Do this in situations where you are confident he can deal with the problem without your intervention. In this way, you are showing trust in his ability to think through the problem and make the right choice. Students often rise to this challenge.

9. Redirect the Student's Attention

With some misbehaving students, particularly those in the early elementary grades, it is better to quietly guide them to another activity rather than confront them or give them a consequence. You might divert their attention by asking them a question, letting them assist you, having them do a class chore, or sending them out to the water fountain. In this way, the students' energy is redirected toward a useful activity and away from the misbehavior and a likely confrontation.

10. Tell the Student Clearly and Directly What He Must Do, and Not Do

Teachers usually respond verbally to a student's misbehavior, but their reactions are often vague and indirect. Comments like "How many times do I have to ask you to stop that?" or "Just go ahead and try it" are unlikely to elicit compliance. Similarly, phrases like "Give some thought to" or "Try to" do not convey your insistence that the student stop his behavior. Rather, say to the student clearly, firmly, and unemotionally that he must stop his disruptive behavior, but avoid lecturing or belittling him. When you say it in this way, the student will learn to respect your authority and understand that you mean business. In giving a directive, try to be near the student without getting in his face, make sure you have eye contact, and use his name to gain his attention. After giving a directive, turn away and continue on with the lesson to avoid a confrontation and allow him to save face. If he continues to misbehave, use the broken-record technique of repeating the directive without being drawn into secondary issues. You might explain the directive, but avoid long-winded justifications. Vary your degree of firmness depending on the student, his history of misbehavior, and his sensitivity level. Some students may call for gentle reminders; others require firm, no-nonsense statements. One way of reminding students with little risk of triggering anger or distress is to tell them what they must do next time ("Allison, please remember next time to raise your hand rather than yelling out.").

11. Talk with the Student Privately to Seek His Cooperation

In a calm, supportive way, explain to the student specifically what he is doing that is disruptive and how it is bothering his classmates. Use "I" statements to help him understand its impact on you (for example, "I find it very hard to help students when there is so much noise in the classroom."). Request his cooperation in understanding and stopping the behavior. Allow him to voice his concerns. If he complains about your classroom practices, offer a brief explanation. If he complains about your actions toward him, let him know that you treat him the same as other students. Ask for his suggestions about classroom changes that might lessen the problem. End the discussion by expressing your confidence that he can learn to cooperate and having him summarize what he is going to do differently. Let him know you will follow up with him after a short period to discuss how he is doing. Praise him when he has made strides.

12. Use a Gradual System of Disciplinary Consequences

If your efforts to win the student's cooperation are unsuccessful and he continues to misbehave, consider giving him a negative consequence that is proportional to the frequency and severity of the behavior. Let him know in advance what these consequences will be and, if he misbehaves, follow through with them in a timely, consistent, and matter-of-fact manner. Some examples of consequences: loss of recess, detention, loss of class privileges, denial of extracurricular activities, or the student's phoning his parents or writing them a letter to explain his behavior. Be gradual in your disciplinary measures. For example, the first consequence might be a loss of ten minutes of recess. Every subsequent consequence might be ten additional minutes of lost recess until he has missed the entire recess. After that, his misbehavior might result in a call home or a visit to the principal's office in addition to the loss of recess. When choosing a consequence, avoid taking away from the student something that is very important to him, or the student may become even less cooperative. Also, do not punish the entire class for the actions of one student, although you may want to reward the whole class for the appropriate actions of one student. The former strategy will cause classmates to be angry with the student, while the latter will cause them to encourage him.

13. Modify the Classroom Environment

The best way to change the student's behavior may be to change aspects of the classroom setting, schedule, or procedure that are likely to trigger the behavior. Keep mental or written notes about his misbehaviors and try to discern patterns. Once you have identified factors that contribute to the problem, take steps to modify them. For example, if you observe that the student has behavioral difficulties first thing in the morning, make sure to have appealing activities for him at the beginning of the school day. Consider the following questions about your classroom environment to identify contributing factors:

- Does the student misbehave more when he is sitting near certain students?

- Is he more cooperative when you are near him?

- Should his desk be moved closer to yours or to the front of the room?

- Should students' desks be spaced farther apart?

- Is he in possession of objects that are contributing to his disruptive behavior—objects that need to be removed?

- Is his disruptive behavior being reinforced by the reaction of his classmates? If so, do classmates have to be instructed to ignore his behavior?

- Is he more likely to act out in certain situations and at certain times of the day (for example, between classes or activities, right before lunch, in the afternoon, during free time, on field trips, or when there is a substitute)?

- Does he tend to misbehave when he experiences academic difficulties (for example, when he struggles with a test or is confused about directions)?

- Is he more difficult on some days than others?

14. Enlist the Help of Your Other Students

A disruptive student often alienates his classmates. They may be put off by his obnoxious behavior or have a hard time concentrating because of his antics. As a result, they may avoid and even shun him, which may only intensify the student's misbehaviors. If you see this pattern in your classroom, arrange for the student to be called out of the room, and have a candid conversation with the rest of the class. Let them know that you are aware that the student can be very annoying, while helping them understand that he is only trying to get their attention—even if negative—and is probably hurt and angry from their rejection. Ask their cooperation in trying to help him change by ignoring his annoying behaviors, avoiding making nasty comments, and reaching out to him in a friendly way. Tell them some positive things about the student that they may not know (for example, his special talents, accomplishments, or interests). Ask for suggestions, and offer some of your own, about what they could say or do to reach out to him. Soon after talking with the class, meet privately with the student. Point out to him his specific behaviors that are most annoying to his classmates, and tell him he must stop them if he wants to have more friends in class. Accentuate his positive qualities, and suggest some things he can say or do with his classmates. Agree on a special signal you will give him when he is exhibiting a negative behavior. Have a follow-up meeting with the class (without the student), as well as with the student to assess progress.

15. Make Your Presence Felt by the Student

The student will be less likely to act out when you are near him, so consider placing his desk near yours, or try to stand near him when he is likely to misbehave. If you are unable to be near him, call out his name and catch his eye when he is getting out of line to let him know that you expect him to behave. Another option is to have him bring his chair near you when he is acting out and disrupting those around him. Tell him he is to sit there quietly until you allow him to return to his seat. Alternatively, you might tell him he can return to his seat when he feels ready to behave appropriately.

16. Signal the Student That He Is Being Disruptive

Establish with the student a subtle way to alert him when he is disrupting the class and you want him to stop. This private signal will allow you to inform him of his behavior without interrupting the lesson or embarrassing him in front of his peers. Ask him for suggestions about possible signals. Some examples: making eye contact, scratching your nose, raising your eyebrows, touching your lips, winking your eye, pointing to a posted rule, or touching him on the shoulder. Tell him that you may say his name softly to get his attention prior to signaling him. Of course, if he continues to disrupt class despite your repeated signals, take some stronger action. (You can also develop a signal to use with the entire class as a way of quickly getting their attention or telling them to stop talking—for example, turning off the lights or raising one hand to be copied by students who see the teacher.)

17. Monitor the Frequency of the Student's Behavior

You may be surprised how simply keeping track of the frequency of a behavior and giving this feedback to the student can make him more aware of the behavior and be a powerful incentive for him to change. This process is even more effective if the student monitors the behavior himself—a process called self-monitoring. Even children as young as 7 or 8 can do this. Choose a behavior that is easy to observe (for example, yelling out without raising his hand). If the student is willing to self-monitor, have him put a check on a 3″ by 5″ card taped to his desk every time he exhibits the behavior. As an alternative, he might tally the number of times you have given him a silent signal to alert him about his behavior. Review with him at the end of the day how he did and compare it with the previous day's tally, perhaps having him graph or chart each day's count. Talk with him about what he did well and what he needs to do differently. You can use the results as the basis for a behavior modification program in which you reward him for attaining a certain prearranged goal.

18. Require the Student to Complete a Behavior Improvement Form

When a student misbehaves, have him fill out a form that asks him to describe specifically what happened, how it disrupted the class, and how he could have handled the situation more appropriately. Take a few minutes to review and discuss with him his responses. Design this form to suit your needs and your students' age level.

19. Avoid Power Struggles

Students who misbehave are expert at drawing teachers into battle. Resist the invitation. While it is easy to lose patience with a student who is disrupting your class and react with anger and sarcasm, this may only stiffen his resistance and result in continuing noncompliance. Avoid arguing or negotiating with him. Try pausing momentarily before reacting to a defiant student to avoid losing your temper. When you feel the impulse to raise your voice, try lowering it while insisting firmly, but quietly what the class rule is and what he must do. If he brings in secondary issues, briefly acknowledge his concerns, but refocus him on what he must do (for example, "I know that you feel that I'm being unfair, but I want you to stop making noise in class right now."). If a consequence is warranted, carry it out in a calm, unemotional manner without expressions of anger. After the incident is over, wipe the slate clean and do not hold a grudge.

20. Implement a Behavior Modification Plan

The chapter on attention deficit disorder describes the basic principles of behavior modification and strategies for implementing such a program in your classroom. While praise is certainly important in promoting appropriate behavior, it is not always sufficient, and you may have to provide a program of incentives and consequences tied to the student's behavior. There are many variations of behavior modification programs that you can use in the classroom. Consider designing your own, bearing in mind the principles discussed in the chapter on attention deficit disorder. Some examples of incentives that you might build into your behavior modification program: special school or class privileges, time in a favorite school activity such as the computer, or choice of an item from a class treasure box or the school store. A list of negative consequences is provided earlier in the chapter.

You can use the following examples of behavior modification strategies to spur students to improve their behavior. Of course, you can adapt these strategies to your own needs and the age of your students. Some can be used with your entire class, while others are intended for use with individual students.

- *Assertive Discipline:* This is a formal discipline program developed by Lee and Marlene Canter. To use this approach, begin by establishing and posting four or five rules for class behavior. Explain these rules to your students, and then describe the rewards for complying and the consequences for not complying. When a student violates one of these rules, place his name on the board; for subsequent violations, place a check next to his name. When he has two checks by his name, give him the prearranged consequence. If he meets the established standard for compliance (for example, three days without his name on the board), provide a reward. See the book by Lee and Marlene Canter listed in the references at the end of the chapter for a more complete description of this approach.

- *Point System:* Have students start each week with the same number of points. Deduct points for misbehaviors from point cards they carry with them or have taped to their desks. (Let them know in advance the point deductions for particular behaviors). With the points remaining at the end of the week, they can purchase rewards, each of which carries a specific point value. Unused points can be carried over to the next week.

- *Color-Coded Cards:* Each week, all students receive a green card. If a student misbehaves, he is given a warning. If he misbehaves again, his green card is replaced by a card of another color, and he is given a consequence. Additional misbehaviors result in cards of other colors with more severe consequences. The cards are kept in a visible place, so you can see everybody's status at a glance. You can reinforce students in various ways, for example, by rewarding the students who maintain the highest color all day or week.

- *Behavior Contract:* This is a written contract in which a student agrees to behave in a certain manner in exchange for a reward or privilege provided by the teacher. The contract should describe one or more specific behavioral goals for the student, the way the behavior will be measured, the precise reward, and a date on which the agreement will be reviewed. The parties to the agreement should sign the contract. Work out the details of the contract with the student so he has a sense of ownership of the agreement.

- *Class Rewards for Individual Behavior:* Giving the class a reward such as extended recess for a student's positive behavior may help him win support and encouragement from classmates.

21. If Necessary, Remove the Student from Class

Removing a student from class or moving him away from other students—giving him "time out"—is a last-resort measure to be used when, despite your disciplinary efforts, he continues to disrupt the class, and you and the other students need some relief. A student in timeout sits apart from other students, either in the class or in another room, for a short period and is not allowed to engage in any activity. It is most commonly used with young children and to help angry or acting-out students settle down. Before using this strategy, check with the principal to get her or his approval and also to find if there is a supervised, unappealing area outside the classroom where a student can be sent. Prior to sending him to the timeout, give him a warning, so he has a chance to remedy the problem. You might present this to him as a choice: "John, you can either sit in your seat quietly without making noise, or you can go to timeout." If you send him to timeout, tell him in a brief, matter-of-fact way without lecturing that he is being sent to timeout to help him calm down and gain control. If there is no timeout room in your school, you might get permission from another teacher to send a misbehaving student to that class, where he is to sit quietly in the back of the room for a short period, perhaps 15 minutes. (Offer to do the same for the other teacher.) You might also have a timeout area in your classroom—perhaps a chair in the back of the room or behind a wall divider, but make sure that the student is visible. If you use this approach, do not have him stay there very long—perhaps five minutes. Of course, if he continues to be disruptive while sitting in the chair, he should be made to stay longer. Rather than setting a time limit, you might tell the student he can return to his seat or the group when he feels he is ready to cooperate. When he returns from timeout, talk with him briefly about what he did that prompted his removal and what he must do differently. If a student refuses to go to timeout and continues to disrupt the class, call the principal.

22. Get Ideas from the Previous Year's Teacher

Ask the teacher which strategies worked with the student and which did not. Also, find out what seemed to trigger his disruptive behavior. You might review his school cumulative file for information to help you identify previous behavioral patterns and give you ideas for managing him.

23. Seek Assistance from Other School Personnel

The following are some ways that other staff members can help you manage a disruptive student:

- Ask the school psychologist to observe in your class to give you some ideas for modifying your approach to the student or the class environment.

- Arrange for the student to talk with the school's guidance counselor, psychologist, or social worker about his behavior or underlying personal concerns.

- Arrange for the principal or vice principal to meet with the student to convey that his class behavior is inappropriate, and to insist that he cooperate in class.

- If you are aware that the student has a strong connection with another staff member (for example, a coach), have him talk with the student to encourage his appropriate behavior in your class.

- Have the student work with another staff member to gain a sense of importance (for example, helping the custodian set up chairs for an assembly, helping the school secretary by serving as a school messenger, or helping the librarian by shelving books). This staff member may take a special interest in the student and be able to wield some influence in curbing his disruptive behavior.

- Ask a colleague to videotape your class so you can analyze the student's behavior pattern and the contributing factors. You may want to show this tape to his parents to give them an understanding of his behavior. Make sure to get their permission before you videotape the child.

- If you have a particularly difficult student who can get out of control, arrange in advance for another staff member to assist you if the student becomes unmanageable or violent.

24. Involve Parents in Resolving the Problem

If your efforts to lessen the student's disruptive behavior have been unsuccessful, contact the parents. While they may sometimes be hard to get in touch with, be persistent; parent support can spell the difference between a cooperative and a disruptive student. In talking with the parents, take the approach that you and they must work together as a team to help their child improve. They will be more receptive to working cooperatively with you if they perceive you as an ally who cares about their child. Strenuously avoid an adversarial relationship with them. Your efforts to discipline the child will be more effective if you have a good working relationship with them, and the student sees that his parents are supportive of your classroom decisions. To this end, set up a meeting with the parents. Describe your concerns with the child's behavior and ask them if they can help you understand why he is behaving this way. Tell them it would be helpful to you if they would express to the child their support for your rules and disciplinary approach and, additionally, would state clearly, directly, and specifically how their child is to behave—and not behave—in your classroom. If they are willing, bring the child into the meeting so he can see and hear that his teacher and parents are of one mind about the importance of his following your rules. Arrange to to talk with the parents after one week, and periodically after that, to review his progress. Make sure the student knows that you and his parents will be in communication. A note of caution here: If you suspect that the parents are abusive of their child, you may want to avoid informing them of their child's misbehavior. Check with other school staff members, such as a previous teacher, the nurse, the guidance counselor, or the principal to find out if there is a history of abuse.

25. Have Parents Reinforce the Child for Appropriate School Behavior

Develop with parents a plan in which you send home with the student a daily note or rating form, the results of which are used by parents to reward the child for positive school performance. Meet with the parents and the child to work out the details, including the following:

- what kind of rating form will be used

- where the form will be kept during the day

- when it will be completed by the teacher

- what behaviors will be targeted

- how the point system will work (consider using a five-point scale for each behavior, where 1 is "poor" and 5 is "excellent")

- what rewards will be provided at home

- how many points are needed to obtain these rewards

- what happens if the form is not brought home by the student

Involve the student in the discussion of these issues, including the determination of the rewards. If this system is to be effective, it is important that parents adhere strictly to the plan. In particular, the reward should not be given by parents unless the student has achieved the agreed-upon goal.

26. Arrange for a Classroom Aide

The presence of another adult in the classroom can be an effective way of curbing student misbehavior. Talk with your principal about obtaining an aide—perhaps the parent of one of your students or a volunteer from a community organization. Give explicit instructions to the aide about his or her role in dealing with your students. You might use the aide to grade papers so you have more time to work with your students, to provide extra academic help to the disruptive student, or to stay near him to discourage misbehavior.

For Further Information

Canter, L., and Canter, M. (1993). *Succeeding With Difficult Students*. Santa Monica, CA: Lee Canter & Associates.

Evertson, C.; Emmer, E.; Clements, B.; and Worsham, M. (1996). *Classroom Management for Elementary Teachers* (4th ed.). Boston: Allyn & Bacon.

Goldstein, S. (1995). *Understanding and Managing Children's Classroom Behavior.* New York: John Wiley.

Jones, V., and Jones, L. (1997). *Comprehensive Classroom Management* (5th ed.). Boston: Allyn & Bacon.

Kazdin, A. (1994). *Behavior Modification in Applied Settings* (5th ed.). Pacific Grove, CA: Brooks/Cole.

Sprick, R. S. (1985). *Discipline in the Secondary Classroom: A Problem-by-Problem Survival Guide*. West Nyack, NY: The Center for Applied Research in Education.

Walker, H. M. (1995). *The Acting-Out Child: Coping With Classroom Disruption* (2d ed.). Longmont, CO: Sopris West.

Organizations

Council for Children With Behavioral Disorders
The Council for Exceptional Children
1920 Association Drive
Reston, VA 20191
1-703-620-3660

See also:
   The Aggressive Student
   Attention Deficit Disorder
   Low Self-Esteem

LOW SELF-ESTEEM

Self-esteem is one of the key building blocks of school success. Also referred to as self-worth, self-esteem is not a measure of a person's capabilities, but rather her evaluation of those capabilities. It reflects her feelings of being accepted and valued by others, her perception of how she measures up to others, and her confidence in her ability to cope with challenges. In short, it represents her satisfaction with herself as a person.

How a person views and values herself can have a significant impact on almost everything she does—the way she relates to others, the way she approaches activities, the way she copes with adversity. It can also have a marked effect on her academic performance, notably her motivation to learn, her ability to focus, and her willingness to take risks. Healthy self-esteem thus provides a firm foundation for learning.

SCHOOL AND SELF-ESTEEM

High self-esteem empowers individuals to take on life's challenges and weather life's storms. A student with healthy self-esteem is comfortable with who she is and confident in her abilities. Optimistic about the future, she believes she can overcome most obstacles. She may have shortcomings, but she is not consumed by them and does not let them define her. She may experience disappointments, but she is forgiving of herself when she doesn't meet her goals. She may get frustrated, but she has an inner strength that keeps her from giving up. In this sense, self-esteem helps to innoculate the student against the despair—and even depression—that can accompany low self-esteem.

Low self-esteem is the result of a gap between the way a person would like to be—her ideal self—and the way she perceives she is—her perceived self. The student with low self-esteem feels that she cannot do anything right. Her perceptions, however, are often distortions of the truth. Frequently putting a negative spin on her accomplishments, she may discount as unimportant what she does well and give undue weight to what she does poorly. She may misinterpret comments of others as negative or critical. Errors or mistakes serve to confirm her negative view of her abilities, rather than to be perceived as a normal part of learning. Her beliefs and perceptions may give rise to a self-fulfilling prophesy: Expecting to fail, she puts forth little effort, resulting in poor performance, which reinforces her expectation of failure. The student with low self-esteem may experience social and emotional problems. Fearful of rejection, she may be tentative in relating to peers and prefer solitary activities. She is also at increased risk for disciplinary problems in school, drug and alcohol abuse, depression, and teen pregnancy.

The student with low self-esteem may exhibit some of the following characteristics in school, which may contribute to academic difficulties:

- approaches new situations with anxiety and trepidation
- believes that she is unlikely to succeed, even with hard work
- gives up easily when frustrated (for example, with homework)
- is very discouraged by experiences with failure
- is especially sensitive to the judgments of others
- is timid in relating to peers
- puts herself down
- shies away from academic challenges
- has difficulty concentrating in class
- hesitates to seek teacher assistance when confused
- is reluctant to speak up in class
- is at increased risk for dropping out of school

Self-esteem wanes as children go through school. During preschool and the early elementary years, children are typically confident, as evidenced by their curiosity and eagerness to learn. As they move into higher grades, they become increasingly aware of how their performance compares with that of their peers, and more realistic about their capabilities. Confidence and self-esteem take a downward turn for many students during their middle and high school years. According to one study, about one of two elementary students felt consistently proud of her or his work, compared with one of six high school students.

A child's self-esteem is affected by her perceptions of success or competence in four basic areas:

- *Family:* Does she feel valued and respected by parents and siblings?

- *Peer Interaction:* Does she feel accepted and sought out by classmates?

- *Academic Ability:* Is she confident of success with most academic tasks? Does she feel capable relative to other students?

- *Physical Attributes:* Is she content with her physical appearance? Does she feel confident and skilled in athletic activities?

Some students feel unsuccessful in any area, and experience a pervasive sense of worthlessness. Others may feel confident in some areas and unconfident in others. A student may see herself as a good athlete but lack confidence in her academic skills. Another student may be secure in her ability to read but feel inept in math. Still another may feel valued and accepted at home but sense a lack of belonging in school. If a student feels competent in the areas that are important to her, she is likely to have high self-esteem; conversely, if she is deficient in those areas—or perceives herself as deficient— she is likely to have low self-esteem. The areas that are important to her will most likely reflect the values of her family and community. Thus, a child who is physically awkward in a sports-oriented family may have low self-esteem. Similarly, a slow learner in a high-achieving family may feel especially self-conscious about her academic deficiencies.

Students with learning disabilities often experience low self-esteem. Many are confused by the mixed messages they receive as a result of their ability to do some tasks and inability to do others. They may wonder how it is they can be whizzes in math yet stumble along in reading. They may be baffled about why they have such difficulty getting their thoughts down on paper when they excel in class discussions. As their failure experiences mount and they become increasingly discouraged, they may write off their strengths and conclude they are dumb or there is something wrong with them. They may feel helpless when presented with difficult schoolwork and hopeless about achieving success. The challenge for their teachers is to restore their belief in themselves so they persevere in the face of academic challenges. Teachers must not only express confidence in their ability to succeed, but also arrange instruction so they experience success.

SOURCES OF SELF-ESTEEM

Self-esteem is not inborn, but rather is learned. Indeed, the building blocks for self-esteem are laid early in life as children learn to feel loved and valued. They begin discovering about themselves as a result of the feedback they receive from important people in their lives, as well as the success of those people in meeting their needs. Children use their experiences in dealing with challenges, the feedback they receive from others, and their interpretation of this information to begin developing notions of their own competence.

The key adults in a child's life, notably parents and teachers, play a vital role in promoting feelings of confidence and competence. While they can foster the child's self-esteem through supportive words and actions, they can also cause her self-esteem to plummet by, for example, suggesting she has limited ability or conveying low expectations. It is not unusual for children to receive mostly negative feedback from adults. By one estimate, children receive an average of ten times more negative messages than positive messages. They may be bombarded with a constant stream of "don'ts," "can'ts," and "shouldn'ts." This may be true in school as well as at home.

As the child grows and becomes less egocentric, she shows increasing awareness of how she measures up against her peers. Research shows that, as early as kindergarten or first grade, students are already making judgments about their competence relative to classmates. They are also becoming more aware of how they are viewed by others. Their perceptions of being accepted by peers and their ability to get along effectively with them help to shape their feelings of self-worth. This is especially true during the teen years. The child who is popular with her peers is likely to feel that she has qualities that are appealing, while the child who has few friends or is rejected by peers is likely to feel socially inadequate.

Their experiences also help to shape their belief in themselves as competent and capable. In particular, their success in school plays a crucial role in how they perceive themselves. The child who has consistent difficulty in school is likely to experience low self-esteem, especially if she comes from a family where education is highly valued and she has friends who are high-achieving. She may begin to perceive herself as slow or stupid and come to feel helpless in school, giving rise to a loss of motivation and a drop in concentration.

It is not just the student's experiences with failure that lessen self-esteem, but also her interpretation of these experiences. She is likely to dwell on her failures and dismiss her successes. When she does well, she may attribute it to luck; when she does poorly, she may attribute it to incompetence. Young children, in particular, tend to view things in absolutes, and thus may develop a skewed view of their abilities; they may see themselves as either smart or stupid, good or bad, fast or slow. If a student fails at one task, she may conclude she will be a failure in all tasks. If she has difficulty with one subject, she may conclude she will have difficulty with all subjects. Part of the task for teachers, then, is to help the student see herself more realistically.

GIRLS AND SELF-ESTEEM

Girls are especially prone to low self-esteem. In elementary school, they typically feel capable of tackling any task, but as they enter middle school, they may experience a decline in confidence. While a fourth-grade girl often has her hand raised, eager to answer a question, the same girl in seventh grade may feel unsure of her answers and thus volunteer infrequently. Even when she does offer a response, she may preface it by saying "This is probably wrong." She may also be reluctant to ask a question and, if she does, may begin it with "This may be a stupid question." Girls' tentativeness in school can in large measure be traced to the societal messages they receive. They are often told in subtle and not-so-subtle ways that they are not expected to excel in school.

Girls' lack of confidence is especially evident in the areas of math and science. Teachers may contribute to this slump in confidence among girls by the way they interact with them in these classes. Research shows that math and science teachers' responses to students are often gender-based. They may face boys more often than girls, call on boys more often, wait longer for their responses, take their questions more seriously, and give them more feedback on their performance. Interestingly, female teachers are as likely as male teachers to react in this way.

HOW TEACHERS CAN HELP

While schools generally recognize the importance of promoting self-esteem, they have not always agreed on the best way to do this. Formal self-esteem programs are available, complete with curricular goals and materials, but some of these programs have been criticized for fostering self-preoccupation. You do not need a formal program to promote self-esteem; you shape self-esteem every day as you interact with your students. Though you cannot teach your students to feel good about themselves, you can nurture their self-esteem through a continual process of encouragement and support. This process requires much more than simply the awarding of gold stars. At its most basic, it demands that you show appreciation for the things students do well and express confidence that they will improve in the areas they don't do well. You will find the following strategies useful in helping students become more confident academically and socially:

1. Set a Warm, Supportive Tone in Your Classroom

While you cannot give students self-esteem, you can create a climate that nurtures it. Provide an accepting atmosphere in which students feel valued, supported, and free to take risks. Show respect for all students, especially those who are different. Let your class know that mistakes are expected and a normal part of learning. Encourage your students to compliment their classmates, and do not allow them to make fun of or put down others.

2. Consider the Impact of Your Actions and Comments on Your Students

It is hard to overemphasize the teacher's potential impact on a student's self-esteem. Even small actions or offhand comments have the ability to lift a student's spirits or send them on a downward spiral. The power of teachers to shape the self-confidence of their students is evident from the many people who can recall either encouraging or discouraging teacher statements years after they were made. Get in the habit of trying to anticipate the impact on your students' self-esteem of what you say and do in the classroom. Keep in mind that they may interpret ambiguous comments in unintended and often negative ways, so be clear in your communication. Avoid using language that students may perceive as belittling or criticizing them in front of their peers.

3. Offer Praise That Is Specific and Genuine

Praise that conveys real appreciation for the student's work will be more meaningful to her than vague, nonspecific compliments. Let her know in particular what you like about her work or behavior. This not only tells her specifically what she has done well but also demonstrates your genuine and thoughtful appreciation of her effort. If she is progressing slowly, praise her for small steps forward. Keep in mind that a student may be uncomfortable being praised in front of her classmates; if so, praise her in private or send her a note. Consider developing a formal recognition program in your class, for example, certificates of achievement signed by you and the principal for specific academic or behavioral accomplishments that are awarded to the student in class and then sent home to parents. You might even call the student's parents in her presence with the good news. Some teachers send postcards home or place self-stick notes on students' desks or notebooks with positive messages (for example, "Congratulations on a terrific oral report!" "That was very thoughtful of you to help Jason," or "I missed you and your sense of humor when you were sick.").

4. Avoid False Praise

Students are skilled at distinguishing valid feedback from empty compliments. Vague, general words of praise may mean little to them and even sound phony. Constantly telling a student that she is special or making a big deal out of a small accomplishment may make her uncomfortable and lessen your credibility. She may learn to dismiss your compliments and tune out your words of support. Moreover, if you praise her all the time, she may interpret your failure to praise as indicative of a poor performance.

5. Bolster the Student's Academic Skills

A student who consistently struggles with schoolwork will understandably begin to lose confidence in her academic abilities. The most effective way to lift her confidence is to help her improve her skills. Success is the best antidote to low self-esteem, and academic mastery is the best remedy for low academic self-confidence. Carefully analyze where her weaknesses are, and find ways to support her in these areas. This support may take the form of a change in your classroom approach, peer tutoring, extra help after school, outside tutoring, remedial instruction, or special education. When helping her in class, try to give her work that is not seen by her as overwhelming, is within her ability, and is likely to lead to success. If you are unavailable, ask a classmate who is responsible to assist her. Pay special attention to her understanding of directions—an obstacle to academic success for many students.

6. Help the Student Gain a Realistic Understanding of Her Strengths and Weaknesses

Students with low self-esteem tend to focus on their failures and dismiss their successes. Try to modify her perceptions by having her make a list of her strengths. Review her list, and have her add strengths that she omitted. At the same time, talk about a few areas where she needs to improve, noting that every student has weaknesses. You might give a name to these weaknesses so they seem more manageable and less overwhelming (for example, "You have a difficulty in phonics."). This approach will help her learn to separate her weaknesses from her overall competence. Suggest the analogy of a student who has a vision problem and wears glasses but is healthy. Express your optimism that with hard work she will improve in these areas.

7. Replace Negative Self-Talk with Positive Self-Talk

The internal messages of a student with low self-esteem are often negative. The public comments she makes about herself most likely reflect her private speech. If you hear her saying things like "Other kids can do this. Why can't I?" "I got lucky with that one," or "Nobody likes me," you can be sure she is also saying these things to herself. Try to counter her negative self-talk by exposing her misperceptions and offering a more positive and realistic view of her abilities. Give her feedback that she can turn into positive self-talk such as "I'm in the high reading group, so I must be pretty smart," "I was elected to the student council so other kids must like me," or "If I work hard, I'll eventually get it."

8. Show the Student Evidence of Her Progress

It is important that you show confidence in the student's ability to be successful, but pep talks may not be enough. Children with low self-esteem often misperceive their skills, giving excessive attention to what they do poorly and discounting as unimportant what they do well. Try to redress this balance by focusing on the student's strengths and helping her appreciate the progress she has made. Show her visible evidence of her growth by keeping a chart of her progress, comparing papers from earlier in the year with later papers, or demonstrating how the math problems she struggled with during the first marking period now come so easily to her. You might show her progress in reading by taping her oral reading at the beginning of the year and comparing it with her performance later on. Also, have her place cards with spelling or reading words she has learned in a "mastery" box to document her growth.

9. Challenge the Student

Children see through the efforts of adults to make them feel better by giving them easy or frivolous tasks to do. Self-esteem is not something that teachers can give to students . Rather, it results from real effort and genuine accomplishment. It comes from meeting what they perceive to be real challenges—in short, from earning it. Give the student work that engages her mind and stretches her abilities, but make sure it is within her ability. Presenting tasks that are too difficult will quickly discourage an unconfident learner; presenting tasks that are too easy will leave her feeling unfulfilled. Use your knowledge of the student and her frustration tolerance to determine the appropriate difficulty level. Be sure she has the prerequisite skills or knowledge needed to do the task successfully. Make sure she completes it, even if prompting and additional time are needed. As she gains confidence, give her somewhat more difficult work and lessen your involvement.

10. Showcase the Student's Strengths

Find opportunities to highlight her accomplishments to the class. This might take the form of reading one of her compositions, putting her artwork on the wall, asking her to demonstrate a difficult math problem, or having an ESL student talk to the class in her first language. Make sure to get her permission before you do this. You might have to do some planning to ensure success (for example, having the student rehearse the math problem at home before presenting it to the class). Also, encourage her to talk to the class about a particular hobby or interest. "Show and Tell" should not be limited to kindergarten.

11. Take the Student's Questions and Comments Seriously

A sure sign of a student's lacking in confidence is her reluctance to ask a question or volunteer an answer. Encourage class participation by giving thoughtful answers to her questions and respecting her comments. Reinforce her asking of questions by saying, "That's an interesting point" or "That's something I haven't thought about." You might even come in the next day with a more complete response, saying that her question was such a good one that you decided to get more information. In terms of her answering questions in class, do not call on her if she does not volunteer unless you are certain she can answer correctly. If she takes time in responding, wait more than you usually do for her answer. For example, if you normally wait a second or two before providing the answer or moving on to another student, consider waiting four or five seconds. You might also provide a clue to prompt a correct answer from her.

12. Create Opportunities for the Student to Feel Important

Assign the student classroom or school tasks that give her a sense of importance. Tell her that you have given her this job because you are confident she can do it well. Seek out opportunities in which she can help others; it is hard not to derive self-esteem and personal satisfaction from the act of giving to another person. Some possible activities follow:

- serving as line leader
- being class messenger
- handing out papers
- serving on the safety patrol
- having responsibility for audiovisual equipment
- becoming the class computer expert
- taking care of the class pet
- answering the school phone while the secretary is at lunch
- reading the school's morning announcements
- explaining directions to a student who is confused
- tutoring a classmate or a student in a lower grade
- being a "buddy" to a classmate who speaks little English
- taking a new student on a tour of the school
- participating in a school or community project (for example, a canned food drive, a winter coat drive, or an adopt-a-grandparent program at a local nursing home)

13. Give Special Attention to the Student's Interests

Students gain self-esteem and a sense of purpose from being involved in activities that are meaningful to them. Find a few minutes every day to talk with the student about her interests and concerns. If necessary, contact her parents to find out about her favorite hobbies, collections, television programs, or musical groups to give you a basis for initiating a conversation with her. Bear in mind that what seems trivial to you may be important to her. Offer ways that she can pursue her interests in greater depth, and suggest that she become involved in related extracurricular activities. You might even bring in a book or item from home relevant to her interest. Consider making this a classroom practice by setting aside time to have one-on-one or small-group discussions with all your students to learn about their concerns and interests.

14. Spotlight a Student Every Week or Month

Put up a poster in the classroom with the student's picture and a description of her interests, talents, and accomplishments. You might also ask her parents to write a paragraph or two about her. A variation of this is to trace an outline of her body on paper, attach it to the bulletin board, and encourage classmates to write positive information about her on the paper. Give it to the student to take home after you take it down. This "Student of the Week (Month)" display is an effective way to celebrate the academic or nonacademic accomplishments of your students as well as boost the morale of those who are lacking in confidence. You can spotlight only select students in your class, or do it for all your students.

15. Be Especially Encouraging of Girls in Secondary School

As girls enter middle school, they often experience a slump in confidence. Make a special effort to promote their self-esteem and be aware of any subtle tendencies on your part to expect more from boys than from girls. Make sure that you call on girls as often as boys, that you are as patient in awaiting their responses, and that you are as serious in responding to their questions. Avoid particularly gender-based teaching practices in math and science—subjects in which girls are generally less confident than boys. Find ways to make math and science classes more female-friendly. Students who like these subjects in high school tend to be much more self-confident in school.

16. Lessen the Negative Stigma When Marking Papers

Grade the student's papers accurately, and point out areas needing improvement, but do so in a way that does not discourage her or deflate her self-esteem. Consider using some of the following strategies:

- Use blue or green ink rather than red ink, which may elicit negative reactions from students.

- Mark only the answers that are correct.

- When putting a numerical grade on a paper, put the number or percentage of answers right rather than the number wrong.

- Put only comments on some papers without giving them a grade or a number.

- Indicate what she has done well, while suggesting how she can improve weak areas without making negative comments.

17. Minimize the Negative Effects of Competition

Students with low self-esteem can be disheartened by performing poorly in class competitions, whether by being first to be disqualified from a spelling bee or last to finish a race in gym. If you have competitions in your class, try to recognize or reward as many students as possible—or plan the competition so that students are competing against an attainable standard rather than against each other. If a student is having difficulty keeping pace with her classmates academically, suggest that she evaluate herself by comparing her progress with her earlier performance rather than with the performance of her classmates.

18. Encourage Peer Involvement

Students with low self-esteem are often withdrawn or isolated from their peers. Find ways to integrate the student into peer activities, either in or out of school. Orchestrate the activities so she is likely to meet with success and is involved with students who are accepting. You might break the class into year-long groups of three or more students to give them a sense of belonging as well as a support system. Let them know that you expect them to provide constructive feedback to members of their group, help one another with difficulties, applaud the efforts of members of their group, and give one another information when someone in the group is absent. Choose group members randomly or based on your knowledge of the students.

19. Help the Student Cope with Failure

Your role is not just to show the student how to minimize difficulty, but also how to cope with it constructively. Help her appreciate that failure is a normal part of learning and that accomplishment rarely comes without set-backs—perhaps citing as an example that Debbie Fields had to give her cook-ies away before Mrs. Fields Cookies became a success or Lincoln lost seven elections before being elected President. Convey to her your belief that her failure is temporary, and that with perseverance and new strategies you are confident she will succeed. Ask her to recall a time when she had difficulty with a task but with hard work finally mastered it. Allow her to express her frustration and acknowledge her feelings, but then move on to helping her understand the source of the problem and giving her strategies for improving.

20. In Disciplining the Student, Be Sure to Focus on the Behavior Rather than the Individual

A student with low self-esteem may sometimes misbehave in class. You should not treat her differently from other students if she does, but be sure to convey that your concern is with her behavior, and not with her as a person. For example, if a student is disrupting your class by talking with another student, you might say something like "Megan, your constant talking is making it hard for me to teach. I'd appreciate it if you would be quiet" rather than "Megan, you are being a rude and inconsiderate student."

21. Encourage Other Teachers to Bolster the Student's Confidence

Keep in mind that there are opportunities to promote the student's self-esteem in her nonacademic classes. Talk with the art, music, and physical education teachers about your concern, and ask them to find ways to make the student feel important or successful in their classes.

22. Inform Parents of Their Child's Successes

Teachers are usually very conscientious about letting parents know when a child has a problem, but not nearly as diligent about notifying them when she has a success. Send a note home or call them when the child does something especially well. Let the student know you are doing this. A gesture that may take you only a couple of minutes can brighten a student's day and generate positive responses from the parents to the child.

FOR FURTHER INFORMATION

Canfield, J., and Siccone, F. (1995). *101 Ways to Develop Student Self-Esteem and Responsibility.* Boston: Allyn & Bacon.

Glenn, H. S., and Nelsen, J. (1988). *Raising Self-Reliant Children in a Self-Indulgent World: Seven Building Blocks for Developing Capable Young People.* Rocklin, CA: Prima Publishing.

Marston, S. (1992). *The Magic of Encouragement: Nurturing Your Child's Self-Esteem.* New York: Pocket Books.

Pope, A. W.; McHale, S. M.; and Craighead, W. E. (1988). *Self-Esteem Enhancement With Children and Adolescents.* Boston: Allyn & Bacon.

Silvernail, D. (1985). *Developing Positive Student Self-Concept.* (2d ed.). Washington, DC: NEA Professional Library.

Van Ness, R. (1995). *Raising Self-Esteem of Learners.* Bloomington, IN: Phi Delta Kappa International.

See also:
> The Disruptive Student
> Math Anxiety
> Mild Mental Retardation
> The Perfectionist Student
> Reading Disability
> The Shy Student
> The Unmotivated Student

THE PERFECTIONIST STUDENT

Sarah is never quite satisfied with her work. In school, she will labor endlessly over a composition as she tries to produce the perfect paper. Her mother says it's the same at home; she will redo assignments countless times, and even then rarely feels that her final effort is good enough. To say that she is tough on herself is putting it mildly. Sarah considers anything less than perfection a failure. When she gets back a test, the first thing she does is look for mistakes. Even when she gets an A, she is upset if it is not the top grade in the class.

You probably have had students like Sarah. She is a perfectionist, a student who is not satisfied with merely doing well. Relentlessly self-critical, perfectionists set impossibly high standards for themselves and become frustrated when they fail to meet them. Usually bright and often gifted, perfectionist students are more motivated to avoid failure than to pursue success. Their wants and desires take second place to achieving the top spot in every activity. Extrinsic measures of success—grades, scores, records, awards, trophies—are of paramount concern to them. Even when they succeed, however, they find reason to be dissatisfied. The perfectionist athlete who wins the race may fret about not breaking a record. The perfectionist violinist who makes the regional orchestra may complain about not making first chair. The perfectionist student who wins the spelling bee may be upset because she got one word wrong.

The following are common characteristics of the perfectionist student:

- bases her self-worth on what she does rather than who she is
- exaggerates her failures and downplays her successes
- is easily discouraged and upset by minor failures
- avoids taking risks and shies away from new experiences due to fear of failing
- is very influenced by the perceptions and expectations of others
- becomes anxious in evaluative situations such as tests and oral presentations

- works at a slow pace and starts over frequently

- procrastinates in starting tasks that will be evaluated

- hesitates in responding to questions unless certain of answer

- reacts defensively to criticism or suggestions for improvement

- has difficulty making decisions because of a need to find the perfect solution

- is critical of others who do not meet her high standards

EFFECTS OF PERFECTIONISM

Students respond differently to their perfectionist impulses. Some become compulsive workaholics, pouring every ounce of their energy into their work. Others have a markedly different reaction. Frightened of failing and being exposed as an impostor, the perfectionist student may put forth minimal effort and take few risks, opting for activities she can do easily and well. What on the surface appears to be apathy may actually be the student's way of protecting her self-esteem. She may conclude that it is safer not to try than to try and risk making a mistake. According to the perfectionist's code, failure is simply not an option. As a result, she may not complete a project for fear of getting less than an A, or she may not sign up for an advanced-placement class in high school because she worries that she will not be the top student in the class. The perfectionist student who shies away from challenges may perform at a level well below her potential and be tagged as an underachiever.

Perfectionism is not the same as task commitment. There is nothing unhealthy about setting high standards or striving for lofty goals. Indeed, the determined pursuit of excellence can provide the energy and focus that ultimately give rise to outstanding achievement. But the healthy striving for excellence is far different from the unhealthy pursuit of perfection. The striver for excellence reaches for challenges, while the perfectionist avoids them. The striver for excellence derives pleasure from the process of working on a task, while the perfectionist focuses almost exclusively on the end product. The striver for excellence attributes success to hard work and ability, while the perfectionist credits it to luck and good timing. The striver for excellence perceives a failure as a reflection of a weakness in a particular area, while the perfectionist attributes it to her weakness as a person. The striver for excellence celebrates an accomplishment, while the perfectionist experiences relief that she did not meet with failure.

The drive to excel can be a double-edged sword if the student becomes consumed with being the best at everything she does. When taken to an extreme, the pursuit of excellence can lead to emotional difficulties. Unable to live up to her unrealistic expectations, the perfectionist student may experience intense disappointment and feelings of worthlessness. Some may experience debilitating anxiety, and even depression, which may stifle their imagination and hamper their performance. In some cases, the anxiety may manifest itself through physical problems such as tics or ulcers.

CAUSES OF PERFECTIONISM

What causes perfectionism in a child? While it is not easy to pinpoint the source of a particular child's perfectionism, we can identify some potential contributing factors. The perfectionism in some children seems to be part of their natural temperament. They may have a compulsive need for order and be bothered when their performance is flawed or has blemishes. Gifted students are especially prone to perfectionism. Even with their superior intellect, they may establish goals for themselves that are unreachable. They may find it especially frustrating when they do not meet their high expectations, because they typically have little experience with failure. These high standards may result from their friendships with older children, their association with other gifted students, and their intellectual confidence stemming from the ease with which they handle most school challenges.

The expectations conveyed at home can also affect the goals the child sets out for herself. Parents who are preoccupied with their child's achievement and constantly and effusively praise her accomplishments may be sending her a message that she is valued more for what she achieves than who she is. Parents at the other end of the spectrum, namely those who are almost impossible to please or whose approval requires perfect performance, may give rise to a child who is driven to obtain the elusive recognition of her parents. Some children learn their perfectionism by emulating their parents; perfectionist children tend to come from high-achieving families and have perfectionist parents. Factors outside the home can also play a role in the development of perfectionism—most notably the constant exposure to media images of perfection. This bombardment makes it hard for children not to want to have and be the best.

HOW TEACHERS CAN HELP

The challenge in teaching a perfectionist student is to maintain a delicate balance between encouraging her pursuit of excellence and avoiding the negative consequences of perfectionism. The following strategies will help you channel her drive to excel in a way that enhances achievement without creating pressures for perfect performance:

1. Provide a Supportive, Encouraging Climate

Adopt a sympathetic, patient approach with your students so they feel safe about taking risks and are not afraid of the teacher's or students' reactions if they make a mistake. Convey through both your words and your reactions that errors are accepted in your class and the contributions of all are valued. Encourage your students to take risks and explore new topics. At the beginning of the year, let them know that your goal for them is to improve rather than to perform perfectly.

2. Avoid Putting down the Student

While disparaging criticism should be avoided with all students, it can be especially disheartening for the perfectionist student. Focusing on her flaws may only intensify her determination to perform perfectly, and stifle initiative and imagination. If you must correct the student, do so in a way that helps her understand the source of the problem without speaking negatively of her performance.

3. Accentuate the Student's Successes and Downplay Her Failures

Help the student achieve success in school by giving her work that is somewhat challenging but not so difficult that she will lose confidence or become anxious. Find opportunities to demonstrate her talents and successes to classmates, for example, by displaying her artwork on the wall or reading one of her essays to the class. (Be sure to get her permission before you do this.) Praise the student for her efforts or accomplishments, but be selective in your praise; do not fall into the trap of praising her only for perfect performance. When she performs poorly on a task, do not sympathize with her or draw attention to her performance. If it was a tough assignment, let her know that you expected students to struggle with the task because of its difficulty.

4. Let the Student Know That Mistakes Are Expected

Give the student permission to make mistakes by explaining that mistakes are a normal part of learning and imperfection a normal part of living. Help her view mistakes as minor setbacks rather than major catastrophes. Show her how a mistake usually reflects a specific weakness that can be corrected rather than a general lack of ability. Point out errors in books and newspapers, and help her see how even accomplished people are not without blemishes. For example, you might point out that Babe Ruth struck out 1,330 times or that Grandma Moses was an octogenarian when she became nationally known for her primitive folk art. You might even have your students share mistakes they have made (make sure to chime in with your own). Remind students that mistakes are a normal part of living by posting such sayings as the following in your class: "Making mistakes is part of being human, so if you don't make mistakes you are not human." "We all make mistakes; that's why they put erasers on pencils." "There are no mistakes, only learning experiences."

5. Explain to the Student the Downside of Perfectionism

Explain to the student how her perfectionism can hamper her performance and productivity. Give her examples, perhaps citing her tendency to start over frequently or begin projects too late. Discuss how much time and energy it takes to try to produce perfect work and how she will miss out on important and enjoyable activities as a result. Also, let her know that students do not produce their best work when they are worried and anxious, and that her work may actually improve if she learns to relax.

6. Help the Student Set Realistic Goals

Talk with the student about how she is being unnecessarily hard on herself by aiming for unreachable goals. Help set her sights on goals that are achievable and viewed positively by the student. Suggest that she develop concrete goals that represent realistic progress from her current level. You can show her the progress she has made by saving her earlier work and comparing it with her later work, or by using tapes or charts to demonstrate improvement.

7. Encourage the Student to Set Priorities

Students who are perfectionist feel they have to excel in all areas. Let the student know that it is virtually impossible to be a star in everything and that life is a matter of making choices about where to put your energies. Help the student identify areas she wants to focus on, and encourage her to abandon pursuit of excellence in other areas.

8. Challenge the Student's Faulty Beliefs

The need some students have to be perfect is driven by the way they think. They may believe that others will perceive them as weak or flawed if their performance is anything less than perfect. They may think that a suggestion or criticism means that they are incompetent or bad. Talk with the student to find out if she has beliefs that must be challenged. For example, if she is terrified of making an error, ask her what is the worst thing that could happen as the result of a mistake.

9. Stress Effort and Learning in Addition to Evaluation

Help the student appreciate that there is more to an educational task than the grade she earns or the recognition she receives. Comments such as "It seems that you really learned a lot from working on that report" or "I'm impressed with how much work you put into this project" convey to the student that schoolwork is not just about earning high marks. Make sure to praise students who have put forth strong effort, even if their final product is weak. Bring to the attention of the class not only those who have outstanding results but also those who have made significant improvement or had particularly creative efforts.

10. Monitor the Student's Performance Closely

Help the student get off to a good start—often a problem for the perfectionist student. Keep an eye on her to see if she is becoming frustrated or distressed with her performance. If so, consider intervening by adjusting the difficulty level of the task or suggesting a change in strategy. Perfectionist students often become bogged down with minor aspects of an assignment, so you may have to help her refocus on the more important parts of the task. Find a way to turn failures into successes; for example, if the student wants to throw away a composition or picture, try to salvage her effort by showing her what is good about it and encouraging her to build on it.

11. Spell out Your Expectations to the Students

When giving an assignment or project, describe in detail what you expect from the students in terms of content, format, and length. In this way, you will lessen the chance that the perfectionist student will set unrealistic standards for herself. Let the students know your primary purpose with the assignment so they do not get hung up with other concerns. For example, in asking students to submit notecards with research information for a term paper, you might tell them that your chief concern with the notecards is content rather than grammar and spelling. If you are giving a test to assess your students' level of mastery in a subject, let them know that they may not be familiar with some of the material on the test, and thus mistakes are expected.

12. Talk to the Student about Coping Strategies You Have Used

Students are curious to hear how adults have dealt with difficulties that they are facing. If you recall being burdened by a perfectionist approach to schoolwork, talk with the student about how you handled it. Let her know what you told yourself to try to counter your perfectionist impulses. Also, give her a sense of how you handle it in the present day by allowing her to see your mistakes in class as well as your constructive responses.

13. De-emphasize the Grading of the Student's Work

Help the student see that her score or grade is not your sole focus. You might make comments on some assignments without giving them a grade or a number. Highlight what she has done well, and indicate how she might improve without making negative or discouraging comments. In marking papers that have answers that are either right or wrong, you might mark only the answers that are correct, or you might mark the incorrect answers so that the marks can be erased when the answers are corrected.

14. Encourage the Student to Trust Her Own Judgments

Perfectionist students are often very dependent on the approval of others, sometimes seeking feedback at every step. Try to lessen the student's reliance on others by building confidence in her own judgments about her work.

15. Encourage Class Participation

The student may shy away from volunteering in class for fear of getting the wrong answer. Spare her any embarrassment, while trying to encourage her participation. Ask her questions that you are confident she can answer or that she has been prepared for in advance, or have her read correct responses from her paper. If you ask her a question and she blanks out or says nothing, you might restate the question or lead her toward the right answer. You might also let her off the hook by giving her the answer while saying something like "That was a tough one" or "That's all right; I'm sure you'll get the next one" and then moving on. Try to come back to her soon with a question you know she can answer.

16. Use a Divide-and-Conquer Strategy with Long Assignments

The perfectionist student can feel overwhelmed by long or complicated assignments. Help lessen her anxiety and get her started by breaking the task into doable steps. For example, if your students are writing a term paper, divide the assignment into the following parts: taking notes on notecards, making an outline, developing a rough draft, and writing the final draft. Set a deadline for completion of each step.

17. Encourage Task Completion

If the student is having difficulty finishing assignments because she is rarely satisfied, use light pressure to get her to finish without punishing her. You might set a firm time limit for the task, or ask her to submit the assignment even if she is not completely satisfied. If she is constantly erasing, suggest she cross out instead, or consider removing the eraser from the pencil. If she is using paper after paper, consider limiting the number of pieces she can use. Many students are also learning how to used copy-editing marks on their writing; you might encourage all your students to do this if they can.

18. Use Humor to Help the Student Lighten Up

If you find the student is taking an assignment so seriously that it is affecting her performance, find ways to relieve the tension. Help her learn to laugh at mistakes, but do it in a friendly and nonthreatening manner.

19. Help the Student Adjust Her Expectations of Others

A perfectionist student may value achievement more than personal relationships, and thus may be as tough on others as she is on herself. She will alienate her classmates if she makes unreasonable demands of them or criticizes their performance. This can be a particular problem in cooperative learning situations, in which students are dependent on the performance of others in their group. Monitor the student's interactions with her classmates and help her see the impact of her comments on them.

For Further Information

Adderholdt-Elliott, M. (1987). *Perfectionism: What's Bad About Being Too Good.* Minneapolis, MN: Free Spirit Publishing.

Elliott, M., and Meltsner, S. (1991). *The Perfectionist Predicament.* New York: William Morrow and Company.

See also:
The Gifted Student
Low Self-Esteem

THE SCHOOL-PHOBIC STUDENT

Many students are resistant to attending school at some point during their school career. Even Shakespeare recognized this problem centuries ago, describing the child "creeping like a snail / Unwilling to school." While parents often worry that this portends long-lasting problems, usually the issue can be resolved quickly. In some cases, however, school resistance can develop into a prolonged absence from school. At its most extreme, this may become school phobia. Also called school refusal, school phobia is an intense anxiety reaction to going to school, resulting in a persistent and determined refusal to attend. It is important that school phobia be confronted quickly by the school as well as by the parents. Prolonged absence from school can give rise to significant academic and social difficulties. In addition, the longer the student is absent from school, the greater her anxiety about returning and the harder it is to get her back in school.

School phobia differs from truancy. The school-phobic student resists school because of anxiety associated with attending. The truant student does not avoid attending because of school-related anxiety, but rather because of an aversion to school and a desire to engage in other activities, which are often of an antisocial nature. The school-phobic student is thus more likely to exhibit an anxiety disorder, while the truant student is more likely to exhibit a conduct disorder.

CHARACTERISTICS OF THE SCHOOL-PHOBIC STUDENT

A student's anxiety about school may be apparent from the first day, when she pleads with the teacher to go home and appears nervous and distracted in class. She may spend much time in the nurse's office with vague complaints of not feeling well, and may be the first one to line up to go home. Eventually, she may refuse to attend school altogether. Persuasion, cajoling, parental threats of punishment, even pressure from the principal may be futile in getting her back in school. The child who is persuaded to finally leave the house may get halfway to school, only to turn around and come back. Or when dropped off at school, she may cry unceasingly until the principal calls the parent to pick her up.

The child with school phobia may exhibit a range of behaviors. She may frequently complain of stomachaches, headaches, or nausea either before she goes to school or during regular visits to the school nurse. If she stays home because of these complaints, they may miraculously disappear by morning's end, and her mood may improve dramatically. She may become argumentative or throw tantrums before school or act withdrawn or sullen after school. In school, she may seem sad and withdrawn—often appearing on the verge of tears. She may be reluctant to interact with classmates and tentative about engaging in academic activities, even though most children with school phobia are of average intelligence and have at least grade-level academic skills.

Kindergarteners and first graders are especially prone to anxiety about school attendance. This should not be surprising; after all, they are going from a familiar, secure setting with a trusted adult to a strange, uncertain setting with unfamiliar adults and children. They may appear timid and tentative in class, and may even display behavior problems. Some do not manifest a reaction until after a few weeks, when they finally realize that going to school is not a temporary arrangement. Most students with beginning-of-school jitters eventually adjust as they begin to feel secure in the setting, trusting of the teacher, and comfortable with their classmates.

Most common during elementary school, school phobia can also affect students in middle or high school, although it may show itself differently. Young school-phobic children often display fears of separating from their parents—separation anxiety—while older children are more likely to show signs of a phobic or depressive disorder. This may be evident in anxiety about the school environment, problems interacting with peers, withdrawal from social or community activities, and difficulties functioning independently. The prognosis for getting older school-phobic students back in school is not as good as it is for younger students.

Children are at particular risk for school nonattendance at certain times of the year and after certain events. Research suggests that school phobia tends to surface at three critical points in a child's school career: the beginning of formal education, namely entry into kindergarten; the move to middle or junior high school; and the end of compulsory education. Children may also experience difficulty returning to school at the beginning of the school year, at the beginning of the week, after a school vacation, and after an absence due to an illness or an operation.

CAUSES OF SCHOOL PHOBIA

School phobia is not a single problem, with one cause. Rather, it is a group of problems with varied causes that share the characteristic of nonattendance at school. School refusal for some children has more to do with fear of school, while for others it has more to do with anxiety about leaving home.

Varying theories have been advanced to explain school phobia. Psychodynamic theory suggests that children who are school phobic have an inflated and unrealistic self-image as a result of an overprotective parent-child relationship. They refuse to attend school, according to this theory, to avoid confronting the reality of their limitations and facing threats to their self-image. Behavioral theory takes a somewhat different slant, explaining school avoidance as the child's way of avoiding the aversive experiences of school (for example, academic and social pressures) and obtaining the rewards of being home (for example, parent attention and the opportunity to watch television and play).

The resistance of some students to school seems to come on without warning. They may seem to be adjusting fine to school, then all of a sudden start finding excuses not to attend. This may suggest that something has happened in school to give rise to anxiety. Think about what may have changed for the student. Watch carefully for any signs of distress. Any of the following examples of potential anxiety-provoking situations in school may engender school resistance:

- academic problems
- apprehension about evaluative situations
- anxiety about appearing stupid in class
- lack of acceptance by peers
- being left out of games during recess
- ridicule or bullying from classmates
- difficulties with peers on the schoolbus or at the bus stop
- loss of a close friend
- anxiety about getting dressed for gym or showering after gym
- fear of a toileting accident

■ departure of a favorite teacher

■ fear of a stern teacher

■ move to a new school district

■ transition to middle or junior high school

The move to middle school can be especially unsettling for many students. They may be leaving a small, familiar school where they had one primary teacher, and entering a large, unfamiliar school where they have six or seven teachers. They may be leaving a school where they attended the same class with the same students most of the day, and going to a school where they change from class to class with a different mix of students in almost every class. They are also entering a school where they face new social pressures and expectations of greater independence. It is not surprising, then, that children are especially prone to school resistance as they enter middle school.

For some students, the anxiety about attending school has less to do with events at school than events at home. For these students, the term "school phobia" is a misnomer. Many school-phobic students refuse to attend school because separating from parents—usually the mother—causes them overwhelming anxiety. This usually stems from an extremely intense relationship between parent and child. Lacking the inner resources to function separately from their parents, these students may have difficulty being apart from them in other settings as well. They may resist being left with a babysitter, hesitate to go over to a friend's house, and refuse to participate in a summer program.

Family events such as the birth of a baby may trigger the child's fear of abandonment and give rise to a strong desire to stay home. In addition, children may refuse to attend school because they are terrified that their parents will experience some harm or catastrophe. This fear may be prompted by a parent's physical illness or emotional problem, the death of a parent, or the separation or divorce of her parents. Afraid that harm may come to the parent in her absence, the child may cling to the home to try to protect the parent, as well as to relieve her anxiety about her parent's welfare. Some parents may even keep a child home under the pretext of her being ill, so she can help care for a family member or assist with family responsibilities. Children placed in this role are taking on adult responsibilities that not only are inappropriate but restrict their social and psychological growth. They are, in effect, being robbed of their chance to be children.

Therapy has proven effective in helping parents return a child to school, even with entrenched cases of school phobia. If the school resistance cannot be quickly resolved, schools should help families obtain outside assistance. (See item 13 under "How Teachers Can Help.") Medication has also been used with some school-phobic students, although typically it is used only when other efforts to get the child back in school have failed. Imipramine, normally used for depression, is often the medication of choice for these students. It has been effective in lessening the anxiety and panic attacks associated with school attendance and easing students' return to school. Medication is not a substitute, however, for therapeutic help for the family, or for efforts by the school to get the student to attend. If used, it should complement rather than supplant other efforts to help the student.

HOW TEACHERS CAN HELP

The most pressing concern with a school-phobic child is to get her back in school as soon as possible. The longer she remains out, the harder it is to get her back in, so the school must work closely with the parents to try to resolve this problem quickly. The strategies described below are intended to help school staff get the child back in school and, once back, maintain her attendance. Some of the strategies are designed for milder cases of school resistance, while others are for more serious cases of school phobia.

1. Have an Orientation for Kindergarten Students and Their Parents Prior to the First Day of School

The first day of school can be anxiety provoking for kindergarteners, especially those without preschool experience. Some of this anxiety can be lessened by having students and their parents visit the school prior to the first day to tour the building and meet their teachers. This may be done in conjunction with kindergarten registration programs. The school might also provide this service to newcomers to the school.

2. Respond Promptly to School Absenteeism

It is important that the school respond quickly to attendance problems. While some students with high absenteeism are out because of genuine physical problems, others may be showing the initial signs of school resistance. You or the school nurse should contact the parents if the student has been out for even a short period to find out if the student is experiencing any anxiety about coming to school.

3. Urge the Parents of a School-Resistant Child to Send Her to School, Even if She Is Upset

The parents are the key to getting the child back in school, so set up a meeting with both parents, if possible, immediately. Be empathetic and understanding in talking with them; they will have their own anxieties about the child's attendance problem. Make sure to work in the following points in your discussion with parents:

- It is vital to get the child back in school as soon as possible to ensure that the problem does not get worse.

- The school has dealt with this problem many times, and most children adjust after a short period of discomfort.

- The school will try to make the child as comfortable as possible, and will cope with her distress—and even tantrums.

- Children generally calm down soon after parents leave, so it is best if they leave immediately after they drop the child off and avoid becoming upset in her presence.

- The child is likely to feel a little more comfortable each day, as she adjusts to the school routine and becomes more trusting of the teacher.

- Advise them not to argue with or yell at the child in the morning before school, but rather to tell her in a calm, matter-of-fact way that all children must go to school and that it is not possible for her to stay home.

4. Problem-Solve with the Parents and Student

Meet with the parents to brainstorm about possible reasons for the child's school resistance. You might involve the child in part or all of this discussion. She may have difficulty putting into words what is bothering her, or she may be embarrassed to tell you. If so, mention some potential sources of anxiety in school, using the above list of aversive school situations as a guide, and ask her whether any are upsetting her. While she may deny that she is upset by them, you may get some clues to the contrary by observing her reactions; she may look down, hesitate, or become teary-eyed at the mention of a sensitive issue. If you are able to pinpoint her concern, find out from the child if she has any ways of making the situation better. Suggest some ideas of your own, and get the child's reaction. It is important that the child see that you are taking her concerns seriously and that you are intent on resolving them. When she returns to school, monitor the problem area closely, and watch for other possible trouble spots. As an example of this process, a teacher of a school-resistant student found from talking to her parents that she was anxious about school because she did not think that she could wait until her class went to the bathroom, and she feared having an accident. This was quickly resolved by changing the bathroom time.

5. Encourage the Parents to Rule out Any Medical Concerns

You or the school nurse might advise the parents to have the child examined by a physician to determine if there is a physical basis to the child's complaints. Suggest that the exam include a check of her vision and hearing. If the doctor gives her a clean bill of health, then the parents will be more confident in taking the strong steps that may be needed to get the child back in school.

6. Reward the Student for School Attendance

Work out a plan with the parents to provide incentives to the child for attending school. These rewards might be provided at home or in school, or both. Work out the specifics of the plan with the parents, allowing the child to have some say in the reward. What the child has to do to earn the reward should depend on the degree of the attendance problem. For example, if the student is not attending at all, the parent might provide the reward after one day's attendance. You might also provide rewards in school in the form of special privileges or activities. Have the student choose from a menu of rewards that you suggest. As her attendance stabilizes, gradually phase out the rewards. Be creative in designing behavior-modification plans.

7. If Necessary to Ensure School Attendance (and if Possible), Allow the Student to Go Home for Lunch

The risk with this strategy is that the student will go home for lunch and not return. If you and the parents agree to use this strategy, try to cut back on or eliminate the midday trips home as she feels more comfortable in school. An alternative is to have the parent come into school and eat lunch with the child or take her out for lunch one or two times a week. You might also use lunch with her parent as a reward for the student's attending a set number of times. For example, if the student has attended school Monday through Thursday, she might earn lunch with her parent on Friday.

8. If Necessary (and if Possible), Arrange for the Parent to Volunteer in School

It may be that the student is willing to attend only if she knows that her parent is nearby. If so, ask the parents if either mother or father is able to volunteer in school for a short time each day. This may be sufficient to get the student to come to school and stay there. As the student adjusts to being in school, the parent can lessen her or his volunteer efforts.

9. Consider Allowing the Student to Call a Parent from School

You may be able to relieve some of the student's anxiety by having her call her mother or father at a set time every day. You might begin by having the student call every day, then gradually cut it down to two or three times per week. To aid the child in cutting down the number of calls, you might arrange for parents to send money with the child to make the call. If she decides not to call, she can be allowed to keep the money. Use the telephone call with caution, since calls home can upset children and make them more determined to go home.

10. Encourage the Child to Carry a Security Item to School

Many children are made more comfortable by having a picture of the family—or perhaps of a pet—or a favorite doll, book, stuffed animal, or toy while they are in school.

11. Consider a Partial-Day Program

While the goal should be to get the student back for a full day as soon as possible, you may conclude that a full-day program is too ambitious initially. In this case, try to get her to come in for the morning or afternoon only. As she settles in, expand to a full-day schedule.

12. Arrange for Classmates to Contact the Student

If the student is absent for a prolonged period, have your other students send her notes telling her they hope she returns soon, and describing some of the exciting activities they are doing in school. When the student returns to school, instruct your other students to say simply that they are glad that she is back in school, and not to bombard her with questions about why she was absent.

13. If the Student Remains Absent from School, Suggest That the Parents Obtain Outside Help

Ask the school's social worker, psychologist, or guidance counselor to recommend an outside counselor to the parents—one who is experienced in working with children and families. While there will probably be significant family issues to work on in counseling, the immediate goal should be to energize the parents to take firm and strong steps to get the child back in school as soon as possible. It is inappropriate for a counselor to spend weeks getting to know the family and the child before tackling the issue of returning the child to school. The counselor should help the family lessen any rewards associated with staying at home (for example, unlimited television) and, if appropriate, deal with the issue of parental overprotectiveness. Once the child returns to school, the counselor might work with the school to put into place a support system for maintaining her school attendance.

14. Do Not Place the Student on Home Instruction

Strongly resist a parental request that the school provide a teacher to instruct the student at home. Home instruction makes staying home more comfortable for the student and lessens the incentive for parents to get the child back in school. The end result is that it will be much harder to get her back in school.

15. If the Student Exhibits Distress in School, Weather the Storm

Brace yourself for a crying episode or tantrum once the parent leaves—although you may be surprised at how quickly the student calms down. These behaviors may be the student's way of testing your resolve. While you may need some support from a classroom aide or the principal if the student's behavior is disrupting the class, strenuously avoid the impulse to call the parents to have them pick up their child; that will only make the next day that much harder. Make sure to have some pleasurable activity for the student to engage in after her parent leaves. As the child appears more comfortable in school, give the parents a call to reassure them that their child is adjusting better.

16. Help the Student Feel More at Home in School

Make the climate in the classroom as inviting as possible for the student. Avoid yelling at your students and adopt a positive, supportive attitude. Find out from the parents of the school-phobic student what kinds of things are comforting to the child, and try to incorporate them into the class routine; ask them what things are upsetting to her, and try to avoid them.

17. Build Trust in the Student and Acknowledge Her Fears

Talk with the student in a calm and reassuring manner, and let her know that you understand that she is nervous about being in school and away from home. If she is experiencing beginning-of-school jitters, tell her that many children find the first days of school hard because it is an unfamiliar place with people they may not know. Let her know that school will feel a little bit better each day and that with time she will feel comfortable in school. Listen intently to her concerns and fears, reassuring her and giving her suggestions for resolving them. Bear in mind that her fears may be fueled by exaggerated tales or school horror stories she has heard from other students. If so, reassure the student that her fears are unfounded. Also, try to find a few minutes each day to talk with her about activities that she does well or enjoys, so she does not come to associate you primarily with her fears and anxieties.

18. Foster Friendships with Classmates

It is important that the child feel comfortable with her classmates and develop a sense of belonging and acceptance. Look for opportunities to involve the student with classmates in enjoyable school activities, and to highlight her accomplishments in their presence. You might consider assigning each of your students a buddy to whom they can read stories or share experiences for a short period each day. If you do this, make sure to pair up the school-resistant child with a classmate who is friendly and gentle. This relationship may help to lessen the intensity of the parent-child relationship.

19. Help the Student Understand the Daily Routine

The school-phobic student needs to feel that school is a safe and predictable place. To this end, explain the class schedule and routines to the student; you might even write this information down and tape it to her desk.

20. Arrange Counseling for the Student in School

The child may receive comfort and confidence from talking privately with the school's guidance counselor or school psychologist. Let the parents know of this arrangement. If the student seems uncomfortable with seeing a counselor in school, don't push it.

For Further Information

Chiland, C., and Young, J. G. (eds.). (1990). *Why Children Reject School*. New Haven, CT: Yale University Press.

Kahn, J. H.; Nursten, J. P.; and Carroll, H. C. (1981). *Unwillingly to School* (3d. ed.). New York: Pergamon Press.

King, N. J.; Ollendick, T. H.; and Tonge, B. J. (1995). *School Refusal: Assessment and Treatment*. Old Tappan, NJ: Prentice Hall/Allyn & Bacon.

See also:
   Low Self-Esteem
   The Shy Student
   The Unmotivated Student

THE SHY STUDENT

The shy child is not hard to recognize. Typically very quiet, she may speak only with her teacher, and even then in a soft voice or tremulous tones. When asked a question, she may gaze downward and give monosyllabic responses. Sometimes she will nod or gesture in place of speaking. When she arrives in the morning, she may take time entering the classroom and be the last to remove her jacket. While your other students gather noisily on the rug in the morning for calendar activities, she may sit quietly toward the back, preferring to watch rather than join in. During recess, she may keep to herself, perhaps sitting against the wall or silently wandering the playground. More spectator than participant, she tends to hang back rather than dive in. The shy child is anything but a risk taker.

Shy children often have little self-confidence and low self-esteem. They embarrass easily, and are often reluctant to speak up in class. Fearful of appearing foolish, they prefer to blend into the background. While many of their classmates work hard to get attention, shy children work just as hard to avoid it. Reading aloud, giving oral reports, and doing Show and Tell can cause shy children much anguish. If they have a bad experience in front of the class (for example, freezing up when talking), they become even more reluctant the next time.

Shyness may be misinterpreted by classmates. They may perceive the shy child as unfriendly and even stuck-up, and conclude that she doesn't want to play with them. While these perceptions miss the mark, classmates may begin to avoid her, which may reinforce her shyness and deny her the opportunities to learn how to relate to her peers. In reality, the shy child generally wants to be involved with her classmates, but the social skills may simply elude her. She may not know how to begin playing with a classmate or how to enter into or sustain a conversation. As a result, making friends can be a major issue for the shy child. In some cases, social isolation can be a long-term problem.

Even teachers may misread the shy child. They may mistake her reluctance to volunteer for lack of understanding. They may assume she is a step behind her classmates academically and hesitate to call on her in class. Low teacher expectations may become a self-fulfilling prophesy as her effort declines and grades suffer, causing her to withdraw further. Studies indicate, however, that the shy child is on average as intelligent as children who are not shy. In other cases, the teacher may conclude that the shy child is simply a serious, well-behaved student who needs little attention. While it is true that shy children are often conscientious students, they often need special attention from the teacher.

SOURCES OF SHYNESS

Some children are shy by temperament. Simply put, they are born shy. Studies suggest that heredity contributes to shyness more than any other personality characteristic. Children who are temperamentally shy are timid and reticent as early as age 2, and may manifest this behavior in a variety of situations and settings. Jerome Kagan, a psychologist who has studied the temperament of children, estimates that 10 to 15 percent of children are born with a predisposition to become shy. He concludes, however, that for these children biology is not destiny. His research indicates that for every ten children who inherit a tendency to shyness, eight will be shy as preschoolers, four will be shy as second graders, and two will be shy as teenagers.

It is apparent that, with time, many shy children learn to feel more comfortable with their classmates and more confident speaking up. As the shyness fades, however, these youngsters may retain subtle signs of cautiousness and timidity. This may be evident in their choice of friends, their post-high school plans, and their career decisions. Structure and security may be sought, and stress and uncertainty may be avoided.

That shyness is an inborn trait for some children does not mean that what teachers or parents do is irrelevant. A student who is temperamentally shy inherits a predisposition to be shy. Whether that student becomes shy, and if so to what degree, depends on her environment, notably the key adults and peers in that child's life. A child who is temperamentally shy but has a warm, supportive family, as well as understanding teachers who gently encourage her and try to draw her out, is less likely to be quiet and withdrawn and more likely to overcome her fears. In short, the right environment can empower the shy child.

CAUSES OF SHYNESS

Some children, however, are not shy by nature, but rather become shy because of life experiences. Some possible situational causes of shyness follow:

- *Parenting Style:* The reticence of some children may reflect their parents' conversational style. If their parents subscribe to a "children should be seen and not heard" approach, and thus reinforce quiet behavior, their children are not likely to be comfortable with or skilled in verbal interaction. In addition, overprotective parents may give rise to timid and cautious children.

- *Stress at Home:* Shyness in school may be related to stress at home. Family conflict, divorce, unemployment, and illness are just some of the situations that may cause a student distress and result in quiet, timid behavior in school.

- *Cultural Differences:* A child from a different cultural background may feel awkward interacting with peers and need time to adjust to their different social styles. If English is not her first language, she may be self-conscious about speaking. While she may be reticent in school, you may observe her to be much more talkative when interacting with other children from the same cultural background.

- *Adjustment to a New School:* Children who are new to a school are often tentative in class until they adjust to the styles of their classmates, make friends, and learn the school and classroom routines.

- *Learning Problems:* Students with learning problems may try to hide their academic deficiencies by not volunteering in class and letting others take the lead in academic activities. Lacking confidence in their abilities, they may feel they have little worthwhile to contribute in class.

- *Peer Ridicule:* A child who fears being teased or bullied by peers may withdraw socially in an effort to avoid becoming a target. Her classroom participation may also be greatly inhibited by classmates' laughing at her comments.

- *Speech Problems:* A child may try to conceal a speech articulation problem by speaking only when necessary.

Understanding the source of the child's shyness can provide clues about how to respond to her supportively. While a child who is temperamentally shy may look the same in the classroom as a child who is shy because of other factors, talking with parents may help you make the distinction. If they tell you that the child has always been timid around people and new situations, this is a strong clue that the shyness is a basic part of her personality. If the parents express surprise at your description of this child—or tell you that she began to show these qualities only upon going to school or that she is shy only in specific situations—this suggests that her shyness is not part of her basic temperament but rather caused by other factors.

If you conclude that the child is shy by nature, your approach should be geared toward adapting to what is basic to her personality. Acceptance and encouragement are called for, because temperamental shyness is hard to change—especially in older children. If you conclude that the child's shyness is due more to environmental causes, then you will want to observe the child carefully to identify the specific sources of the child's timidity and withdrawal.

In determining what steps to take with a shy child, assess whether her shyness is causing her problems, and if so, in what areas. Keep in mind that being cautious and reserved can be a normal, adaptive response to difficult social situations. Ask yourself the following questions:

- Does she seem happy in class?

- Does she know what to say to classmates to get them to interact with her?

- Does she play with her classmates during recess, even if she is slow to get involved?

- Does she seem comfortable and confident around other children?

- Does she volunteer to speak in class?

- When she speaks, does she seem confident in what she is saying, even if she volunteers infrequently?

- Can she give an oral report in class without being very flustered?

- Does she speak to you without anxiety or apprehension?

- Does she adjust adequately to new situations or changes in routine?

If you are able to answer most or all of these questions positively, then you should consider leaving the situation alone. Negative responses to these questions may suggest areas where you must intervene. Consider whether her shyness is interfering with her ability to make friends, her academic performance, her confidence in speaking up in class, and her willingness to take advantage of school opportunities.

HOW TEACHERS CAN HELP

You can take the following steps in the classroom to help the shy child become more comfortable when interacting with others, and less threatened by novel experiences:

1. Seat the Student Near the Front of the Room

If she is in front of the room and near you, the reticent child may be more willing to speak up in class because she will be less aware of the rest of the class. It also gives you a chance to talk with the student easily. Choose students to sit next to her who are friendly and accepting.

2. Accept the Child's Shyness

It is difficult to alter the basic personality of children who are naturally shy. Trying to eliminate a child's shyness by constantly pushing her to be more involved may place unnecessary pressure on her and cause her to feel that she has disappointed you if she does not meet your expectations. You don't want to convey that being outgoing is the most desirable social style, nor do you want to label the child as shy in her presence or have her feel that there is something wrong with her being shy. Find a private moment to let her know that everybody has a different style, and that being quiet and reserved is a normal, acceptable way of interacting. If she is struggling socially, reassure her that making friends is not always easy and that the situation is likely to improve with time.

3. Have Private Conversations with the Student Often

Private speaking can be as intimidating to the shy child as public speaking. Even a few minutes of daily discussion can help her develop her conversational skills. Find out her interests and use these topics to generate conversation with her. Listen attentively and ask questions about things she talks about.

4. Reduce the Stress of Public Speaking

Speaking in front of the class can be frightening for many students, not just those who are shy. The following strategies may lessen their fears and increase their comfort level:

- Ask her questions in class that you are confident she can answer successfully.

- Let the student know ahead of time that you will be calling on her so that she can prepare her response. You might also speak with the parents the day before to ask them to rehearse with their child.

- If she is willing, have her speak to the class about a topic she knows well and enjoys.

- Rather than having her stand in front of the class, have her speak from her seat.

- Do not criticize the student for her oral reports in the presence of other students.

- Do not grade the student for oral reports or penalize her for lack of class participation.

- Allow her to make a presentation as part of a group. Once she feels comfortable making a group presentation, encourage her to make an individual presentation.

- Allow students who are very anxious about oral reports to satisfy the requirement in another way (for example, a written report, an oral report to the teacher only, or an audiotape of the presentation made at home).

5. Gently Encourage Involvement

While you don't want to push the shy student into very stressful or potentially embarrassing situations, you shouldn't shield her from awkward social situations either. You may have to nudge her to engage in activities that are mildly uncomfortable for her but that you are confident she will enjoy or do successfully. For example, you might encourage her to be a class messenger, a job that is valued by students and that requires talking with school staff.

Make sure to praise her performance even if she struggles with the task. Find something about her performance to highlight or compliment her on. Give assistance if necessary, but withdraw your support as she begins to feel more confident. With a reinforced sense of independence, she will be more willing to tackle new challenges.

6. Encourage the Student to Ask for Help

Shy students are often reluctant to seek assistance from the teacher, even if it means not understanding a homework assignment or classroom activity. Assume that this is a problem for the shy child; take her aside and tell her that it is important that she let you know whenever she does not understand something. Give her permission to come up to you at your desk or when you are working with a group.

7. Build Trust with the Student

The child who develops a trusting relationship with her teacher and comes to view school as a safe place will gradually gain the courage to reach out to peers. When possible, find time to engage in some activities alone with the child that she enjoys and does successfully. Perhaps she can teach you a skill that she does well. Be warm and nurturing, and praise her accomplishments. Shy children are in special need of stroking, particularly if they view themselves in a negative light. At all costs, avoid a loud, critical approach. Strong reprimands will shut a shy child down.

8. Foster Confidence by Finding Areas Where the Student Can Succeed

Talk to her parents or give her an interest inventory (which the school psychologist can provide) to find particular talents or interests that you can highlight in class. Showcase her accomplishments by, for example, displaying an art project she did on the bulletin board or reading to the class a particularly good paper she wrote. You might also give her valued class jobs to give her a sense of importance. Take your cues from the student, and provide activities that interest her and in which she can be successful. At the middle or high school level, encourage her to get involved in after-school activities that tap her interests and abilities. Because she may be reluctant to pursue them on her own, you may have to do some of the initial legwork for her in terms of identifying possible activities and finding out when the groups meet. You might also give this information to her parents. Make sure that the activity you are recommending is led by an adult who is supportive and encouraging. Speak to the staff member beforehand about the student.

9. Provide Classroom Activities That are Nonthreatening and Noncompetitive

Large groups may cause shy children to clam up. They are likely to join in more easily in small-group situations that are noncompetitive, where the children work cooperatively with one another. Arrange for her to be in a group with students with whom she is likely to feel comfortable. Even in these situations, however, you may have to sit with her at first and encourage her involvement. As she settles in and grows more confident, you can gradually pull away.

10. Prepare the Student for New Situations

New situations or activities often throw the shy child for a loop. If she has adjusted to a setting and the routines, a change may set her back, and she may start to withdraw once again. Do not push her into threatening situations without preparing her and giving her some time to warm up to the new challenges. Let her know what she is likely to encounter. If she has concerns, listen attentively and try to resolve them in advance. You might also have the child rehearse an unfamiliar activity (for example, if she is going to do an oral report, have her do a dry run with you or a parent). This will give her increased confidence when she has to do the real thing.

11. Arrange Social Interactions with Classmates

The child who keeps to herself most likely wants to be involved with other children but the prospect of interacting with them scares her off. Keeping to herself is often the less painful option. This may call for you to put on your social director's hat and orchestrate the child's involvement with her classmates. For example, you might ask a couple of kind and mature students to ask her to play during recess or join them at their lunch table, or you might organize an activity for a group of students, including the shy child. If you have students pair up in class, assign her a friendly and easygoing partner. Of course, the parents play an important role here and you will want to encourage them to help their child develop friendships by arranging social contacts with classmates. Also, suggest that they get their child involved in community activities that interest her and in which she is likely to do well.

12. Teach the Child Social Skills

The shy child may lack awareness of the basic skills of peer interaction. Entering social situations may be particularly hard for her, especially if she does not know the right words to use to ask another child to play. Talk with her privately and suggest to her some "door openers" (for example, "Would you like to play a game with me?" or "Do you want to be my partner?"). Emphasize the importance of smiling and maintaining eye contact. Also, give her ideas for things she can talk about with classmates during recess or after school. If she is comfortable, role-play with her some common social situations.

13. Encourage the Student to Take a Leadership Role with Younger Students

The child who is anxious about interacting with children her own age is often surprisingly at ease with younger children. If so, arrange some activities in which she can work with younger children. For example, you might send a third grader into a kindergarten class to read a story, help a small group of students learn the alphabet, or lead a game on the playground. These kinds of activities may bolster the student's confidence to interact with students in her own grade.

14. Consider a Referral to Your School's Speech-Language Pathologist

If your efforts to elicit speech from the student are unsuccessful or there are signs of a language-related problem, consider referring the student to the speech-language pathologist, who may be able to identify whether the reluctance to communicate is related to a speech or language problem.

15. Place Students with the Same Teacher for Two Consecutive Years

Some districts follow this practice in the early elementary grades to enhance continuity in the students' program. For example, a first-grade teacher will move to second grade the following year with the first-grade students, while the current second-grade teacher moves back to first grade. This practice allows teachers to develop an in-depth knowledge of students, and to form a solid bond with the parents. Shy children, who generally find transitions anxiety provoking, especially benefit from this practice by not having to adjust to a new teacher and new students during the second year. As a result, they may be may be more secure socially, more confident academically, and more likely to join in class activities.

FOR FURTHER INFORMATION

Cheek, J. M. (1990). *Conquering Shyness.* New York: Basic Books.

Daly, J. A., and McCroskey, J. C. (1984). *Avoiding Communication: Shyness, Reticence, and Communication Apprehension.* Beverly Hills, CA: Sage Publications.

Schneier, F., and Welkowitz, L. (1996). *The Hidden Face of Shyness: Understanding and Overcoming Social Anxiety.* New York: Avon Books.

Zimbardo, P. G., and Radl, S. L. (1981).*The Shy Child: A Parent's Guide to Preventing and Overcoming Shyness From Infancy to Adulthood.* New York: McGraw-Hill.

See also:
    The ESL Student
    Low Self-Esteem
    The School-Phobic Student
    Speech and Language Problems
    Stuttering

STUTTERING

Stuttering is a common problem among schoolchildren. It is estimated that 4 percent of children exhibit this problem, with boys about four times more likely than girls to stutter. Many children outgrow these speech disfluencies, but others continue to struggle with the problem. Teachers play an important role in identifying students who may be stuttering and obtaining help for them through the school's speech-language pathologist. Just as important, teachers can help students who stutter feel accepted in the classroom and become more at ease speaking with others.

While we do not know the precise causes of stuttering, we do know that stuttering is not a disease, is not caused by emotional trauma, and is not the result of a personality or thinking disorder. In fact, children who stutter have the same psychological makeup and mental capacity as those who do not. What distinguishes them from other children is that they struggle to get words out even though they know precisely what they want to say. More specifically, stuttering occurs when a child involuntarily repeats a sound (for example, "pa...pa...pa...paper"), prolongs a sound (for example, "ppppppppencil)," or experiences a speech block so that he may not speak for several seconds.

Many children experience disruptions in the flow of their speech. For example, a preschooler might ask, "Daddy, daddy, daddy, can I, can I, can I play catch with you?" These disfluencies are to be expected as children go through the process of learning how to communicate, and usually are not a cause for concern. Speech disfluencies typically begin between the ages of 2 and 6, although they may occasionally emerge after a child begins kindergarten. It is during this preschool period that children are experiencing an explosion of language development. Disfluencies during this period often go away on their own by the time a child enters school. These normal disfluencies are different, however, from the abnormal disfluencies of stuttering.

DISTINCTIVE FEATURES OF STUTTERING

What distinguishes stuttering from normal speech disfluencies? While normal speech disfluencies typically involve the repetition of whole words or phrases, stuttering is characterized by the repetition of initial sounds or syllables. A child who stutters may use a starter or filler word or phrase (for example, "um" or "you know") either prior to speaking or prior to saying a feared word. Or he may substitute an easy-to-pronounce word for an anxiety-producing word. In an effort to conceal his stuttering, he may talk quickly or use an awkward phrase.

Children with normal speech disfluencies may also have hesitations, repetitions, or insertion of words, but their speech is relatively tension-free. In contrast, children who stutter experience a frantic struggle to get words out. The tension that accompanies stuttering may take the form of quivering lips, raised pitch, and higher volume. Facial expressions may signal anxiety or fear. Children who stutter may also exhibit nonverbal cues such as blinking or closing of the eyes, tapping of the finger or foot, jerking of the head, or unusual breathing.

Stuttering can have a marked effect on a child's emotional adjustment and self-esteem. To understand the discomfort that children who stutter may feel, you might try an experiment that is often given to speech-language pathologists in training: Pretend to stutter while in a public setting and monitor your own level of discomfort as well as the reaction of the person to whom you are speaking. You may find yourself riding the same emotional roller coaster experienced by people who stutter—from shame to embarrassment to frustration to anger. Children who stutter may also experience confusion. Unable to point to any physical cause for their stuttering, they have trouble understanding why they can't speak like their peers. As they talk with others, they are often unsettled and on edge because they are never quite sure when their stuttering will emerge.

Not surprisingly, children who stutter are often very self-conscious about their speech. Fearful of humiliating themselves, they may shy away from talking with their peers. It is easier for them to withdraw socially than risk embarrassment. They may go to great lengths to conceal their stuttering, but beneath their silence is a strong desire to talk like their peers. As they enter adolescence, when the desire to fit in is of paramount concern, dating and social pressures can be overwhelming for them.

PROFESSIONAL HELP

If you suspect that one of your students is stuttering, it is important that you refer him to your school's speech-language pathologist. Your job is not to determine whether the student is exhibiting stuttering or just normal speech disfluencies, nor is it your job to help correct his speech problem. Helping the student learn to control his stuttering is a task better suited to a specialist in speech.

Referrals to a specialist are important because children who stutter can be helped. While many children outgrow stuttering, others do not—and those who do not will benefit from special attention. Stuttering is a learned behavior and, while stuttering is not likely to be cured, experienced professionals can help children learn to adjust to their stuttering and talk more comfortably with others. More specifically, speech-language pathologists can help lessen children's speech tension, develop methods to control their stuttering, and alter their attitude toward stuttering. The overriding goal, then, of speech therapy is not as much to promote stutter-free speech as it is to promote effective speech.

Professional help is especially important with young children when speaking habits are not as firmly entrenched. While a child who is still stuttering after puberty is likely to continue to stutter in some form in later years, adolescents should still be referred to the school's speech specialist—even though they may be reluctant to talk about their stuttering or may reject efforts to help them. If you are not certain whether to seek help for a child, err on the side of referring.

HOW TEACHERS CAN HELP

While the speech-language pathologist can help a child develop methods to control his stuttering, you play a key role in helping him adjust in the classroom; a teacher, after all, spends much more time with the child than a speech specialist does. Don't try to correct the stuttering; leave that to the specialist. Your primary task is to lessen the child's fear or avoidance of stuttering. Stuttering is an avoidance reaction; a child stutters in an effort to avoid stuttering, and you can do more harm than good by trying to "fix" a child's stuttering. One adult recalls a teacher who worsened her stuttering by insisting that she repeat each word that she stumbled over until she pronounced it fluently.

Help the child feel more comfortable while speaking and, in effect, give him permission to stutter. His stuttering will decrease as his fear of stuttering lessens and he puts less effort into trying to prevent its occurrence. Your role is to promote free speech rather than fluent speech—to serve as a role model to your students on how to become an accepting, noncritical listener. You may find the following specific strategies helpful in working with a child who stutters:

1. Listen Attentively and Patiently to the Student

Children who stutter are very sensitive to the reactions of the listener and have their antennae out for possible signs of discomfort. If a child senses that you are uncomfortable, he will try even harder not to stutter, which may actually increase his disfluency. As he talks, try to give him your undivided attention and respond encouragingly with nods and smiles. In addition, maintain natural eye contact, respond patiently and calmly, and do not interrupt him. Avoid rushing him or conveying time pressure. If you have trouble understanding what he said, repeat it back to him to see if you understood correctly, or ask him to repeat it to you. *Don't* guess at the meaning, or pretend you understood when you did not.

2. Avoid Drawing Attention to the Student's Stuttering

You do not want to finish his sentences, supply him with words during speech blocks, give him suggestions or tricks for avoiding stuttering, or even comment on his speech. Many teachers try to help a child who stutters by suggesting that he "relax," "slow down," or "start over." These suggestions are unlikely to lessen his stuttering. More important, the underlying message to the child from these suggestions is that you are uncomfortable with his stuttering, which may make him more self-conscious about his speech and more likely to stutter.

Do not even praise him when he speaks fluently. By saying, for example, "good speaking," you are telling him that you are monitoring his speech. In addition, he may come to see lack of praise as a sign of poor performance. It is much better to focus on *what* he is saying rather than *how* he is saying it. Comment on the substance of what he says rather than the manner in which he says it. Do not refer to him as a "stutterer" in his presence; indeed avoid using the word "stutterer" altogether. Stuttering is something he *does*, not something he *is*.

3. Consider Talking with the Student Privately

If he is receptive, talk with him briefly about his stuttering, but don't belabor the issue. Bringing his speech difficulty out in the open may help to diffuse some of his anxiety and lessen the shame he may be feeling. Your goal is to convey acceptance of his stuttering and thus give him permission to stutter. Let him know that it is not a problem if he gets stuck on some words or takes time to get the words out (at the same time, avoid use of the word "stuttering" in his presence unless he uses it). Reassure him that other students often get tangled up in their words and that he will have as much time as he needs when speaking. You might let your other students know that they will have plenty of time as well when speaking, so that the student who stutters does not feel he is receiving special treatment. Ask him if there are particular situations in school that concern him and if so problem-solve with him to find solutions that ease his fears.

4. Adjust Your Rate and Style of Speech

Children are more likely to stutter if the person they are speaking with speaks rapidly, and uses complicated syntax and unfamiliar vocabulary. Interestingly, studies indicate that parents of children who stutter speak much faster than normal. Model a relaxed, unhurried, easy-to-understand communication style when speaking to a student, but not so slow as to sound abnormal. Pause a second or two before answering questions. Also, avoid classroom discussions or games that place a premium on rapid responses or shouting out of answers.

5. Have the Same Expectations for the Child Who Stutters as for Other Students

Do not excuse a child from academic requirements because he stutters. He should be expected to do the same assignments as other students, although specific tasks that cause him anxiety may require some adjustments. If he is overwhelmed at the prospect of giving oral presentations, for example, have him tape the presentation or do a written report instead. In terms of reading aloud, consider having him read with another student or a small group. He is less likely to stutter if accompanied by others. You may want to do this with other students as well, so he does not feel singled out.

6. Identify Situations That Trigger a Student's Stuttering and Make Changes Accordingly

The situations that may prompt stuttering vary with each student; reading aloud and giving an oral report are two of the more common ones. Some children are more likely to stutter when talking with an unfamiliar adult or meeting other children for the first time. You may also notice that stuttering increases when a child is engaged in another activity (for example, coloring) at the same time he is talking. If so, have him stop the activity while he is speaking. Fatigue, illness, or stress can also bring on stuttering. So, too, can excitement, so it may be helpful to inform the child in advance of changes in the class schedule or upcoming events. Also, bear in mind that there are situations in which children are less likely to stutter, including singing, reciting rhymes, and using puppets.

7. Provide the Child with Comfortable Speaking Experiences in Class

A child who stutters is often terrified of speaking in front of the class and usually finds ways to avoid it. As a result, he may have little experience speaking before a group. Getting him to the point where he feels comfortable speaking in class will require some planning on your part. The key is to arrange experiences that ensure success as a way of bolstering his confidence. When appropriate, allow him to talk about areas of interest to him, and avoid bombarding him with questions. You might rehearse with the child before he reads aloud or makes a presentation, or arrange to call on him for an answer you are confident he knows. If you do this, call on him early in the class so that his anxiety does not build up. The anticipation of being called on can be agonizing for a child who stutters. For the same reason, avoid calling on students in alphabetical order.

You must strike a balance here. If the idea of speaking in class throws a child into a panic, do not push the issue. On the other hand, if a student who stutters wishes to speak in front of the class, don't stand in his way. A student who stutters needs practice talking in front of a group. In particular, he may need help explaining things because of his limited speaking experience.

8. Gradually Introduce the Student to Tasks That Are Anxiety Producing

Begin with tasks he is comfortable with, and then gradually increase the level of difficulty. For example, you might have him read to his parents at home, then read alone to you, then read aloud with a group, and—when he feels ready—read in front of the class. When asking him questions in class, initially you might ask him questions requiring one- or two-word answers, and then as his confidence grows, ask him questions demanding longer responses.

9. Find Positive Things to Highlight about the Student

The child who stutters often feels that he has come to be defined by his stuttering—that his other qualities go unnoticed or unappreciated. Find ways to highlight his special interests, skills, or talents so that his classmates come to see him in a new light.

10. Help Your Students Become Sensitive to a Child Who Stutters

You may want to talk to your students to help them understand how to respond, and not respond, when a student stutters. You can do this with the student present or absent, depending on his preference, but do not speak to the class unless you have first obtained the permission of the student and his parents. He may even surprise you by offering to talk to the class about his stuttering, but make sure he does this in the spirit of educating the class about stuttering rather than apologizing for it. If he is open to talking with the class, you may want to discuss with him what he is going to say, and even rehearse. When you talk with your students, let them know that stuttering is common, perhaps giving examples of famous people who stuttered, including Bo Jackson, Carly Simon, Lewis Carroll, Winston Churchill, Marilyn Monroe, and Bruce Willis. You may also want to remind them that we all have things we do well and things we don't do so well, and that those things may be different for each of us. Encourage them to be patient, not to try to help him when he has difficulty getting words out, and—above all—to treat him as they would want to be treated.

11. Be Alert for Any Signs of Teasing or Lack of Sensitivity by Classmates, and Intervene Immediately

If you observe any students engaging in ridicule, talk with them privately, and try to elicit their understanding of how teasing can be hurtful and how it can worsen the stuttering. If the ridicule persists, consider having the principal talk with them, or contact their parents. If a student who stutters is being left out of social activities (for example, he is sitting alone at lunch or is not being chosen for a team during recess) or is voluntarily choosing not to participate, arrange for some children to invite him to participate.

FOR FURTHER INFORMATION

Johnson, K. L., and Heinze, B. A. (1994). *The Fluency Companion: Strategies for Stuttering Intervention*. East Moline, IL: LinguiSystems.

Treiber, P. M. (1993). *Keys to Dealing With Stuttering.* Hauppauge, NY: Barron's Educational Series.

The Stuttering Foundation of America (address and phone number listed under "Organizations") offers the following publications:

- *Do You Stutter? A Guide for Teens*

- *If Your Child Stutters: A Guide for Parents*

- *Stuttering and Your Child: Questions and Answers*

- *Treating the School Age Stutterer*

- *Treatment of the Young Stutterer in School*

Organizations

American Speech-Language-Hearing Association
10801 Rockville Pike
Rockville, MD 20852
1-800-638-8255

National Stuttering Project
5100 E. La Palma, Suite 208
Anaheim Hills, CA 92807
1-800-364-1677

Stuttering Foundation of America
P.O. Box 11749
Memphis, TN 38111-0749
1-800-992-9392

Stuttering Hotline
1-800-992-9392

Stuttering Resource Foundation
123 Oxford Road
New Rochelle, NY 10804
1-800-232-4773

See also:
  Low Self-Esteem
  The Shy Student
  Speech and Language Problems

PHYSICAL PROBLEMS

This section describes common physical problems that you may encounter with your students. While it is, of course, not your job to provide them with medical assistance, it is nonetheless important that you understand the nature of the problem, how it may affect their school performance and behavior, what precautions to take, and what to do if they exhibit difficulties in class. Keep in mind that you are not alone in this responsibility: the school nurse and the parents are key resource people, and you should take full advantage of their expertise and support.

Students with physical concerns may face emotional difficulties beyond the normal challenges of growing up. In particular, their self-esteem may suffer from perceptions of being different from their peers. It is thus essential that you help them feel comfortable in the classroom and accepted by their classmates. While this may call for more than the usual amount of emotional support, at the same time you don't want to shower them with excessive concern or attention, or excuse them from the normal classroom responsibilities. This may only reinforce their perceptions of themselves as different.

Children with physical problems are often defined by their condition. Remind yourself that the student is not diabetic but rather a student with diabetes, that the student is not epileptic but rather a student with epilepsy. In general, you should have the same academic and behavioral expectations for them as for other students, and you should avoid drawing attention to their condition or sin-

gling them out for special treatment, unless their medical problem dictates otherwise. If you shield them from the normal challenges of childhood or do for them what they can do for themselves, they will become excessively dependent and develop feelings of inadequacy. Your guiding principle should be to help them become resourceful and independent.

AIDS AND HIV

The acronym AIDS stands *for acquired immunodeficiency syndrome,* a disorder that destroys the body's ability to fight disease. It is caused by infection with a virus called HIV, or human immunodeficiency virus. A person with HIV is diagnosed as having AIDS when the immune system breaks down and can no longer ward off infections, placing him at risk for developing a number of life-threatening illnesses.

Many more people have HIV than have AIDS. It takes an average of ten years before a person with HIV develops AIDS, although the length of time between infection with HIV and the onset of AIDS can vary dramatically. A person who has AIDS is highly vulnerable to infection, especially from pneumonia, and may experience fever, fatigue, loss of appetite, weight loss, diarrhea, and enlarged lymph glands.

It is estimated that approximately 5,000 children in this country have AIDS and an additional 10,000 to 20,000 more have HIV. The majority of children with HIV attend school. The number of students with HIV has increased in recent years due to improved treatment methods that have prolonged the lives of children with this illness.

As a teacher, you may not know that one of your students has HIV, either because the parents and school district have chosen not to inform you out of concern for confidentiality, or the parents are not aware that he has HIV. If you are informed that you have a student with HIV or AIDS in your class, it is important that you learn about the illness, understand confidentiality requirements, and know what precautions to take. While this chapter will discuss these issues, you must also find out what your local school district policies are for dealing with a student with HIV or AIDS.

HOW DO CHILDREN GET HIV?

HIV is transmitted by direct contact with body fluids. This may result from having unprotected sexual intercourse with a person infected with HIV, sharing a drug needle or syringe with someone who is infected, or receiving the virus during pregnancy or birth or through breast milk from a mother who is infected. Most children with HIV have become infected as a result of being born to mothers with the virus. While some people have developed HIV by receiving transfusions of contaminated blood, this risk was virtually eliminated in 1985 when the screening of blood to detect HIV became standard practice. (You also cannot receive HIV by donating blood.)

A person may be infected with HIV and appear and feel completely healthy. As a result, most people with HIV will not be aware that they have the infection unless they are tested. Even if a person with HIV has no symptoms, he can still infect others.

Research to develop new ways of treating HIV and AIDS is ongoing. While there is no cure or vaccine, some very promising developments slow the damage caused by HIV to the immune system. As a result of new medications, individuals with HIV and AIDS are living longer, and some now view HIV as a manageable although long-term illness.

SCHOOL ATTENDANCE

There is very little risk that a student with HIV will transmit the virus to other students. As a result, the U.S. Public Health Service recommends that children with HIV or AIDS be allowed to attend school. This right to attend school is supported by Section 504, a federal law that prevents discrimination against those with disabilities. Courts have taken the position that children with HIV or AIDS can be segregated from their peers only when their attendance poses a significant health risk to other children.

It is thus inappropriate to exclude a student from school or otherwise segregate him from other students solely because he has HIV or AIDS. He should thus attend the same school and class that he would have been assigned to if he did not have the illness. In addition, he should be provided with the same rights, privileges, and activities as other students.

At the same time, special circumstances may call for the student's removal from a regular school program. This step should be taken only when a student with HIV or AIDS is believed to pose a serious health risk to other students (for example, he has a secondary illness that can be transmitted to others, such as tuberculosis) or he is unable to attend class because of physical problems. Courts have allowed students to be removed from regular classes when they demonstrate extremely aggressive or self-abusive behavior or present unusual problems involving body fluids. Schools should make these decisions on a case-by-case basis, consulting the student's physician, public health officials, and of course the parents. If the decision is to remove the student from school, the school district should provide an appropriate alternative program until a physician concludes that the risk has abated, at which time the student should be permitted to return to school.

The education of students with HIV and AIDS involves complicated and sensitive issues. School districts are well advised to develop committees to establish policies for managing these students. These committees should be composed of school staff, board of education members, medical professionals, and community members. The community should be apprised of the school district's policies.

ISSUES OF CONFIDENTIALITY

Because of the risks of prejudice toward students who have HIV or AIDS and ostracism by their classmates, information about their medical status must remain confidential. If parents or students do not have confidence that this information will remain confidential, then they will be reluctant to report it to school officials, thus denying students the support and understanding of concerned school staff members.

Whether school districts are informed about a student with HIV or AIDS may depend on state law. Some states have laws governing the dissemination of information about students with HIV. In some states, medical personnel are required to inform school districts that a student has HIV, even if the parents and the student do not consent. In states without such a requirement, medical personnel typically will inform a school district that a student has HIV only with the consent of the parents or the student. There is no law requiring that parents of classmates be informed if a student in the class has HIV or AIDS.

If a parent informs the school district that a child has HIV, this information should be given only to those staff members who have a vital interest in knowing it and who are approved by the parent or the student to receive it. In addition, parents or the student should have the right to control specifically what information is released. In sum, where a student has HIV or AIDS, the school staff members who are aware of this information will vary. In some cases, no one in the school district will know of the student's medical condition; in others, only the superintendent will know; in still others, such staff members involved with the student as the school principal, nurse, and teacher will be informed.

Those who receive this information must treat it with the utmost confidentiality. School staff members must be very careful not to include information about the student's medical condition in his standard educational records. Any documents containing information about this condition— including medical reports, letters, or notes from meetings or conversations— must be kept in a locked file, with access allowed only to those approved in writing by the parents or student.

As a result of these safeguards, it is very possible that you could have a student in your class who has HIV or AIDS and not be aware of his condition. You may disagree with this practice, or even be angry that this information is withheld from you. But where there is little risk of harm to you or your students, the need to preserve confidentiality takes precedence over the need for school personnel to know of the student's condition. Even if you are informed that one of your students has HIV or AIDS, you are not allowed to divulge this information to anyone else without the consent of the parents or student. Indeed, in some cases, you can be held liable for violating the student's confidentiality.

If a parent informs you that a child has HIV or AIDS, you are placed in an awkward situation. Find out what your district policy is, as well as any relevant state laws, by checking with an informed school official without disclosing the name of the student. If district policy is that all communicable diseases must be reported to the school district, inform the parents of this policy and encourage them to disclose their child's status to school officials. If you have any questions about a conflict between district policy and your obligation to maintain confidentiality, obtain the opinion of the school district attorney.

WHAT ARE THE RISKS TO STUDENTS AND TEACHERS?

Much confusion and misinformation about AIDS and HIV have been sown by fear and mistrust. In some communities, teachers and parents have reacted with apprehension and even panic to the news that a student in their school has HIV or AIDS. In some cases, parents have even removed their children from the school.

It is important that the facts about HIV and AIDS be clearly understood. This is what we can say with assurance. You cannot get HIV from:

- being coughed or sneezed on by an infected person.

- touching, shaking hands with, hugging, or kissing (with a closed mouth) an infected person.

- using a toilet, water fountain, or doorknob touched by an infected person.

- touching the materials (for example, clothes or books) of an infected person.

- sharing eating utensils or a drinking glass used by an infected person.

- eating food touched by an infected person.

- being bitten by an insect or animal.

In short, a child infected with HIV cannot give the virus to other students through ordinary school activities or everyday contact. You cannot "catch" HIV as you can the flu. There is no evidence that HIV can be transmitted through saliva, tears, or sweat. Children with HIV thus do not pose a risk to their classmates except under special circumstances.

The issue of teens with HIV playing sports has generated considerable controversy. The American Academy of Pediatrics recommends that youngsters with HIV be permitted to play sports, but advises them to avoid such contact sports as football and wrestling, which may lead to blood exposure. A student with HIV should not be excluded from a school team, however, unless a physician advises school officials that he poses a direct threat to the health of other students. If the student is injured and bleeding results, he should of course be removed from the game until the bleeding is completely under control. Coaches should be taught the precautions recommended by the Centers for Disease Control (CDC) for dealing with injuries involving blood (see below). HIV cannot be transmitted through sweat.

TAKING PRECAUTIONS IN SCHOOL

It is important that schools establish routines for handling body fluids of *all* students. If school officials take precautions only with students they know to be infected, they will be taking unnecessary risks. Students with HIV may attend school without knowledge by school officials of their medical condition.

In addition, body fluids can also transmit other illnesses such as hepatitis A, a cold, a flu, and a virus.

The following precautions should be taken in dealing with body fluids from students, based on recommendations by the Centers for Disease Control and the National Association of School Nurses. These precautions are not cumbersome or difficult for school staff to follow.

- Wear disposable, waterproof rubber gloves during contact with blood or body fluids that may contain blood such as urine, feces, or vomit. Wash your hands vigorously for ten seconds or more with soap and warm water after disposing of the gloves and dry them thoroughly. While not all situations will call for using gloves, it is best to err on the side of caution.

- Any parts of your body that come into contact with the child's blood or other body fluids should be washed vigorously for at least ten seconds with soap and warm water and then dried thoroughly. There is no risk of HIV infection from coming into contact with saliva or wiping a runny nose.

- Make sure to cover any broken skin (for example, cuts or sores) on either your own or the child's body. Encourage students to care for their own minor injuries by washing them and applying bandages. Keep in mind that HIV cannot penetrate unbroken skin, so there is no risk of infection from getting blood on your own unbroken skin.

- Dispose of potentially contaminated items such as tissues or diapers. Handle these items with gloves.

- Any surfaces that are soiled with body fluids, including floors and furniture, should be washed and disinfected. A solution made up of one cup of bleach to one gallon of water is an effective disinfectant.

SPECIAL EDUCATION FOR THE STUDENT WITH HIV OR AIDS

A student with HIV or AIDS often has special needs beyond those that are medical. While he should not be placed in a special education program simply because he has HIV, he may have learning or emotional problems resulting from his medical condition that warrant special education. The nature of the special education program should derive from his learning or emotional problems rather than his physical problems. If a school evaluation team determines that he is eligible for special education, then the decision about the student's educational program will be made by a special education placement team, which by law must include the parents and the teacher. The decisions of this team must conform with state and federal special education laws. This team will also be responsible for deciding whether a special education student who has HIV or AIDS is to be removed from school. In making this decision, the team must consult with medical professionals to assess the degree of risk to other students.

AIDS EDUCATION

While there is no vaccine for HIV or AIDS, it is nonetheless a preventable illness; HIV is transmitted by behavior that individuals can choose to avoid. Unless people learn to modify their behavior, however, many more people will become infected with HIV and develop AIDS. This is especially true with adolescents, who tend to engage in high-risk behavior, notably unprotected sex, and are thus vulnerable to HIV infection. The Centers for Disease Control reports that about three of every four adolescents has had sexual intercourse by twelfth grade, with less than half reporting use of adequate protection. It is apparent that many teenagers believe that they are impervious to disease.

The best way we have to fight the transmission of this infection is through education. And schools, which educate 95 percent of children from ages 5 to 17, are the most efficient way we have of reaching the greatest number of children. It is important that schools teach about HIV and AIDS as part of their regular health program, beginning at least by seventh grade and continuing through high school. School districts should involve community members in designing this program so that the curriculum reflects community values.

While outlining a comprehensive AIDS education program is beyond the scope of this book, it is important to discuss some basic principles of AIDS education. Classes should ideally be small to allow for student questioning and discussion of sensitive issues. The content of the lessons and the materials used should be scientifically accurate and appropriate to the students' age and level of understanding. It is especially important that the teacher debunk some of the myths about how HIV is transmitted as a way of lessening student fears and prejudices. Students need to be reassured that HIV is very hard to get and that there is no reason to have concerns about interacting with students who have this illness.

You must also help students understand that their behaviors can have a significant impact on their health, and that the key to avoiding infection is to make wise choices by resisting pressure to engage in risky behavior. The program should include role playing as well as discussion. Simply giving students pat phrases such as "just say no" or telling students what to do and what not to do is not sufficient to change behavior.

The Centers for Disease Control (see Organizations at end of chapter) offers information to teachers who are providing AIDS education in schools, including curriculum guides and audiovisual materials. Your state may also have curriculum materials for schools providing AIDS education.

HOW TEACHERS CAN HELP

If you are informed that a student in your class has HIV, you may find the following strategies helpful in working with the student:

1. Find out the School District's Policies

Your school district should have policies and procedures to guide school personnel in working with students who have HIV or AIDS. The state department of education may also have regulations as well as recommended practices for managing these situations. Ask your principal how you can obtain this information.

2. Obtain Training in Working with Students with HIV or AIDS

If a student in your class has HIV or AIDS, it is important that you understand the nature of the illness, the way it is transmitted, the requirements of confidentiality, and the precautions that you must take in the classroom. This training should be provided not only to teachers but to others who have direct involvement with the student, including teachers of special subjects, athletic coaches, and staff on the bus and playground. The state departments of education and health may have staff who provide this training or consult with schools about specific concerns relating to HIV or AIDS. Make sure that as a result of this training you are clear about the procedures to be followed in the event of an incident involving the student's body fluids. You will also want specific information about the student—in particular, special learning needs, equipment he requires in school, and restrictions on his school activities.

3. Work Closely with the School Nurse

The school nurse will be a key resource person for you, as well as an advocate for the student. In addition to serving as a likely liaison with the parents and the student's physician, the nurse may provide you with important information, teach you how to take precautions in the classroom, and take the lead in dealing with incidents involving body fluids.

4. Keep the Student's Medical Status Confidential

Out of respect for the privacy of the student, and in an effort to prevent prejudice toward him, this information should not be released to anyone without parent or student consent. Because the risk of transmission of HIV is generally very low, there is little need for many school staff members to have this information.

5. Consider Eligibility for Special Services under Section 504, or for Special Education

If you believe the student warrants special school services or classroom accommodations, recommend to the principal that the student be considered for eligibility for Section 504 of the Rehabilitation Act of 1973, a federal law that requires school districts to provide needed special services to students who are disabled. Examples of special services or accommodations are the use of an FM trainer to enhance classroom hearing, shortened assignments, oral test administration, and peer tutoring. In terms of special education, the student with HIV or AIDS will not qualify for special education simply by virtue of his illness. To qualify for special education, he must be evaluated by a team of school professionals and determined to have a disability that is adversely affecting his ability to learn. If he is deemed eligible for special education, a team of people, including the teacher and parents, will design an educational program appropriate to his educational needs.

6. If Classmates Are Aware of the Student's Medical Condition, Talk with the Class in a Reassuring Manner

Speak with the student with HIV or AIDS and his parents and let them know that you would like to talk with the class about the student's medical condition. Apprise them of what you plan to say and ask them if that meets with their approval. Inquire whether there is anything they want you to add and whether they want to be present when you talk with the class. In talking with the students, be honest but reassuring. Let them know that the student has an illness that may result in periodic absences but reassure them that they can't "catch" the illness from the student in the same way that they can catch a cold. Encourage them to treat the student the same as they do other students. Let them know that if the student gets hurt or starts to bleed an adult should be contacted immediately.

7. Treat the Child the Same as You Do Other Students

There is no reason to treat the student differently than other students, unless he has special learning needs or requires emotional support. By treating him like other students, you are conveying a message to his classmates that, other than his illness, he is just like other students. In addition, you will be helping the student feel as normal as possible.

8. Make Physical Contact with the Student

It is important that you demonstrate to the student and his classmates that you have no hesitation in being near and touching the student. A touch on the shoulder or a gentle squeeze of the hand in a natural way will comfort and reassure the student, help to lessen any stigma about physical contact with him, and encourage classmates to reach out to him.

9. Provide Emotional Support

Find an opportunity to talk with the student privately and let him know that you are aware of his illness and that you would like to make him feel as comfortable as possible in class. Ask him whether there is anything he would like you to do—or not do—in class and whether he has any special concerns. Listen attentively and show understanding for the student but be careful about expressing sympathy in a way that makes him feel abnormal or helpless. Let him know that you are available to talk with him whenever he has a concern and that your discussion will be kept confidential. Ask the student whether he would like to meet with a guidance counselor on a periodic basis. If so, obtain approval for this arrangement from the parents. Keep in mind that a child with HIV or AIDS may have a parent or sibling who also suffers from this illness, and that the child may be dealing with various emotional issues.

10. Do Not Allow the Student to Be Ostracized

If the other students are aware of his medical condition, they may perceive him as an outsider and avoid interacting with him. He may be bypassed by classmates when they are choosing sides for a game, or left without a partner when you ask students to pair up. If this is a problem, avoid classroom situations in which students choose other students, or encourage one of your more mature students to select him. Also, alert staff on the bus and the playground to monitor his peer relationships and encourage these staff members to get him involved with other students. Intervene immediately if you observe the student being ridiculed.

11. Inform the Student's Parents When a Classmate Has a Potentially Serious Contagious Illness

Children with HIV or AIDS are especially vulnerable to infection because HIV impairs the immune system. Thus, other children who are sick pose a risk to children with HIV or AIDS, who may need to be excluded from school for their own protection when communicable diseases such as chickenpox or measles are spreading through the school population. Obtain medical advice or consult with the nurse to determine which illnesses are threatening to the student with HIV or AIDS.

12. Make Accommodations for Frequent Absences

The child with HIV or AIDS may be absent from school often because of health problems or medical testing. As a result, he may fall behind in his schoolwork and miss instruction in key skill areas. If possible, arrange for instruction to be provided at home during the periods of nonattendance. When the student returns, provide the student with instruction in skills that he missed through after-school instruction, peer tutoring, or parent assistance.

13. If the Student Is Hospitalized, Have His Classmates Send Letters

These letters will mean a lot to the student, and will help to teach classmates the importance of reaching out to and showing compassion for others.

FOR FURTHER INFORMATION

Bogden, J. F., and Fraser, K. (1996). *Someone at School Has AIDS: A Complete Guide to Education Policies Concerning HIV Infection.* Alexandria, VA: National Association of State Boards of Education.

Kerr, D.; Allensworth, D.; and Gayle, J. (1991). *School-Based HIV Prevention: A Multidisciplinary Approach.* Kent, OH: American School Health Association.

Noonan, D. G.; Webster, C. L.; and McAlister, R. O. (1996). *AIDS: The Preventable Epidemic Curriculum and Guide.* Portland, OR: Oregon Department of Human Resources. (Address: Division of Health, Department of Human Resources, AIDS Education Program, 800 NE Oregon Street, Suite 745, Portland, OR 97232)

Quackenbush, M., and Villarreal, S. (1992). *Does AIDS Hurt? Educating Your Children About AIDS* (2d ed.). Santa Cruz, CA: ETR Associates. (Address: P.O. Box 1830, Santa Cruz, CA 95061-1830)

Scheer, J. K. (1992). *HIV Prevention for Teachers of Elementary Education and Middle School Grades.* Reston, VA: Association for the Advancement of Health Education.

Stang, L. (1994). *HIV: Health Facts.* Santa Cruz, CA: ETR Associates. (Address: See above)

ORGANIZATIONS

American School Health Association
P.O. Box 708
7263 State Route 43
Kent, OH 44240
1-330-678-1601

CDC National AIDS Hotline
1-800-342-AIDS

Centers for Disease Control (CDC)
National AIDS Clearinghouse
P.O. Box 6003
Rockville, MD 20849-6003
1-800-458-5231

National Association of Persons With AIDS
P.O. Box 18345
Washington, DC 20036
1-202-429-2856

National Association of School Nurses
P.O. Box 1300
Scarborough, ME 04074
1-207-883-2117

ASTHMA

Asthma, a respiratory disease in which the airways that carry air into and out of the lungs become inflamed and blocked, is the most common chronic childhood illness. This illness affects about one child in twenty, so teachers will have, on average, one child per class with this disease. Most children with asthma develop this condition by about age 5. By the age of 15, about half of all children with asthma are free of symptoms, although they can recur at any time. Asthma is not contagious, so it cannot be passed from one student to another.

In children with asthma, the muscles surrounding the airways are unusually sensitive to a variety of factors and agents in the environment. The particular triggers of asthma differ for each person. As you read through the following list of common asthma triggers, consider whether you have any potential triggers in your classroom that may cause a problem for a child with asthma:

- air pollutants (for example, tobacco smoke, perfume, chalk dust, construction dust, and fumes from chemicals used in science experiments)

- substances that cause allergies (for example, molds, pollens, and animal hair)

- specific weather conditions (for example, cold air and temperature changes)

- upper-respiratory infections (for example, a cold and flu), which are the most common triggers for children

- activities that cause heavy breathing (for example, vigorous exercise)

- expression of strong emotions (for example, anger, distress, and excitement)

DEALING WITH AN ASTHMA ATTACK

Derived from the Greek word for panting, asthma manifests itself in the form of an attack or episode in which the person is literally panting for breath. The muscles surrounding the airways tighten, the lining of the airways swells, and excess mucus blocks the airways. As a result of these changes, the airways narrow and breathing becomes very difficult. The symptoms of asthma vary with each child and range from mild to severe. A child in the early stages of an attack may exhibit some of the following:

- wheezing sound while breathing

- chest tightening

- shortness of breath

- frequent coughing

- spitting up mucus

A simple pocket-sized device, called a peak flow meter, can also provide early warning signs of an attack by measuring the flow of air through the airways. To use it, a child simply blows into it and then looks at the scale, which is divided into the colors of a traffic light, to read the result, called a peak flow reading. This number can be compared to the student's best peak flow reading (which should be part of the child's school health file) to determine if an attack is coming on and medication is needed.

Many children with asthma can sense that an attack is coming and will alert you. They will probably experience some anxiety and distress, especially if the episode is severe. Most asthma episodes come on gradually, so the child usually has time to take action. The key is for the child to recognize the attack early and take the medicine immediately to help clear the airways.

If you see a student beginning to experience an attack, it is important that you and your students stay calm. If you become nervous, you may excite the child, which may in turn aggravate the asthma. Provide help if needed in taking the medication, although most children will be able to do this on their own. The child may also perform breathing exercises to slow her breathing, although this is not a substitute for taking the medication. After the episode ends, you may want to have the child rest in the nurse's office or engage in a quiet activity until she feels ready to rejoin the class. You or the school nurse should inform the parents of the asthma attack the day it occurs.

In rare cases, an attack can turn into an emergency situation. If a student displays some or all of the following characteristics, she may be in the throes of an asthma emergency requiring parent contact and medical help:

- no improvement 15 to 20 minutes after medication is given

- trouble breathing (for example, child hunched over trying to breathe)

- difficulty walking or talking

- lips or fingernails turning a blue or gray color

- a peak flow reading significantly below her best peak flow reading

EXERCISE AND ASTHMA

It has been said that children with asthma should not exercise. This is a myth. With proper medical treatment, children with asthma may have few physical restrictions, and many can participate fully in exercise and sports. Indeed, physical activity can be important for the child with asthma in building stamina and lung capacity. In addition, excluding her from physical activity because of the fear of an asthma attack can give rise to peer perceptions that the child is different.

At the same time, it is important for teachers to recognize that exercise—especially extended running—is a common asthma trigger, particularly in cold weather and during pollen season. Physical education teachers must therefore be made aware of the child's asthma, any doctor-recommended physical restrictions, and steps to take in the event of an asthma attack. If the physical education teacher is uncertain of what the student is allowed to do, she should contact the physician directly. The teacher may also have to make some accommodations during gym class. The child with asthma may need to start slowly and increase her physical exertion gradually. She may also need regular rest breaks or have to sit out when her asthma symptoms flare up. During cold weather or high pollen counts, the student may have to be excused from outdoor physical education classes or allowed to do an indoor activity. The physical education teacher may want to find some way of altering the activity for the child with asthma (for example, in place of a running activity, the child could walk or run part of the way or alternate running and walking). The teacher might also find some way that the child can be involved in the class without strenuous physical exertion (for example, as a scorekeeper). Children with asthma who have significant physical restrictions may benefit from taking a modified form of physical education called adaptive physical education.

Children whose asthma is effectively controlled can participate in most school sports and should be encouraged to do so. Indeed, many professional and Olympic athletes suffer from severe asthma. Swimming is especially good for children with asthma because there is minimal loss of body fluids and little problem with allergens. Bear in mind, however, that children with asthma who participate in sports must take special precautions. The coach should be made aware of the child's asthma and how to handle an attack. The coach should also know what signs to look for that suggest the child should take a break. In addition, the student should have medication and the inhaler readily available if she begins to have problems breathing. She may also need to take medication before the activity to avoid an attack. Warmup and cooldown exercises will help avoid an episode.

DIAGNOSING AND TREATING ASTHMA

Asthma can be difficult to diagnose because its symptoms resemble those of other respiratory problems. As a result, cases go undiagnosed and untreated. While there is no one test to establish the presence of asthma, physicians rely on a combination of behavioral symptoms, medical history, physical examination, and various laboratory tests to make the diagnosis.

There is no known cure for asthma, but it can be controlled effectively with good medical care, education, and adequate planning. The keys to managing asthma are to identify asthma triggers, avoid contact with them, have medication available when needed, recognize the warning signs of an attack so that you can take medication, and know what to do when an attack occurs. Children who learn these strategies can lessen the frequency of attacks and live a relatively normal and active life. While asthma can be fatal, the majority of deaths are preventable with proper medical treatment.

Children with asthma are generally prescribed two kinds of medications. *Anti-inflammatory medication,* which lessens swelling in the airways and helps to prevent attacks, is usually prescribed for those with moderate-to-severe asthma and is to be used daily. A *bronchodilator,* which relaxes the muscles around the airways, helps relieve breathing problems related to an asthma attack. The medication is usually inhaled through a machine called a nebulizer or a small device called an inhaler or puffer. Medication, when inhaled, goes straight to the lungs and begins working almost immediately. The child is to take medication when she feels an attack coming on. The doctor may suggest other times when the medication should be taken (for example, before exercising, before coming into contact with an asthma trigger, and when coming down with a cold or flu).

Some children taking asthma medication experience side effects that hamper school performance. These side effects may include poor concentration, handwriting difficulties, lethargy, excitability, headache, and nausea. The school nurse should be able to tell you possible side effects of the particular medication by consulting the *Physician's Desk Reference*. If you observe what you believe to be side effects of the medication, jot down your observations, including the time and specific behaviors observed, and let the parents know. These side effects may suggest the need for a change in medication.

SCHOOL IMPACT

Asthma can cause a student to miss much class time. In fact, asthma is the leading cause of school absenteeism due to illness. Children with asthma are absent from school three times as often as children without asthma. They may make many trips to the doctor's office or the emergency room and may have been hospitalized due to the asthma. In addition, their frequent trips to the school nurse lessen their time in the classroom. Even when they are in class, there may be an absence of attention. The asthma symptoms and the accompanying anxiety may impede their concentration on schoolwork, or asthma-related sleeping problems may cause them to be sleepy in class. As a result, you may find that a child is confused regarding directions or lagging behind in her classwork.

While asthma is not a psychological or emotional illness, it can give rise to emotional difficulties. Children with asthma can become discouraged and, in some cases, depressed by the medical demands of the illness, the frequent attacks, the physical discomfort, and the days spent apart from their peers. In addition, they are most likely aware of the physical risks they face if they are not vigilant about controlling the asthma. They may feel different from their classmates as a result of the asthma episodes, and you may see them start to withdraw and show other signs of low self-esteem. It is important that you provide emotional support for the child as well as reassurance that you offer a "safety net" if she should need one. At the same time, avoid being overly solicitous of her so that you do not accentuate her being different from her classmates.

HOW TEACHERS CAN HELP

If asthma is managed effectively, the child can participate in virtually all activities, and school performance need be only minimally affected. School personnel can take the following steps to help the student adjust in school:

1. Find out about Your School District's Policies Regarding Asthma

Schools vary in their policies about the taking of asthma medication during the school day. The school nurse should be able to tell you the policy in your district. The American Academy of Allergy and Immunology recommends that "students with asthma be permitted to have in their possession inhaled medications for the treatment and prevention of asthma symptoms when they are prescribed by that student's physician." Given the importance of medication to preventing and treating asthma attacks, it must be readily available to the student. It may be appropriate, however, to treat older students differently from younger students. Most middle and high school students are capable of carrying and regulating their own medication, although the school nurse should have a record of the medication. Elementary school students may need supervision to ensure that medication is taken properly, and some districts require it to be taken in the presence of the school nurse.

2. Gather Information from the Parents

It is important that the child's teacher and the school nurse meet with the parents at the beginning of the school year to discuss how to manage the child's asthma in school. While you may be knowledgeable about asthma, you will still have to learn about this student's asthma profile, since asthma differs for each person. You may want to ask the parents the following questions:

- What are the particular asthma triggers for your child? Are there specific foods that may trigger an asthma attack?

- Does she use a peak flow meter? What is her best peak flow reading? What peak flow reading signals that an attack may be coming?

- What are the signs with your child that suggest an attack is coming?

- What should school staff do when the child has an attack?

- When can she return to class after an asthma attack?

- What kinds of medication will she take in school? How is it administered? Can she administer it herself?

- When should the medication be taken?

- What are the potential side effects?

- Does your child have any physical restrictions? Are there times when she should not take gym or go outside for recess?

- Under what circumstances do you want to be called?

- Under what circumstances should medical help be obtained?

- Should your child have a spare inhaler in school?

- What symptoms suggest the child is experiencing an asthma emergency? What should be done? Who should be called?

3. Develop a Written Asthma Management Plan Tailored to the Student

This management plan should be an outgrowth of the meeting with the parents. It should be tailored to the child's particular needs, since asthma manifests itself differently with each child. The teachers, including the physical education teacher, and the school nurse should have copies of this plan. Others in school who work with the child should be aware of the plan and either have a copy or know where to obtain one.

This plan should include the following information:

- phone numbers of parents (home and work), emergency contact, and child's doctor

- school policies regarding asthma medication

- short history of child's asthma

- asthma triggers for this child

- warning signs of an asthma attack

- steps for school staff to follow in the event of an asthma attack

- medications child takes in school and procedures for administration

- potential side effects of medication
- physical restrictions
- signs of an asthma emergency and steps to take
- the child's best peak flow reading

4. Speak with the Student Individually

Find time to talk with the student privately to reassure her that you are aware of her asthma and know what to do if she has an attack. Have her show you how her inhaler and peak flow meter work. Let her know that she can leave class to go to the nurse when she feels an attack coming on or when she feels tired and needs to lie down. Suggest a signal that she can give to you to let you know that she is leaving the class.

5. Educate Your Students about Asthma

Ask the parents and student for permission to talk with the class about asthma. You may want to invite the parents and student to participate in the discussion. Ask the student whether she would feel comfortable demonstrating to the other students how the inhaler and peak flow meter work. Describe for the students what an asthma attack is and what they are likely to see. Let them know that it is important that they stay calm and that the student is likely to get better once she takes her medication.

6. Monitor the Child's Understanding of Lessons and Assignments

The student may have problems with attention due to the asthma symptoms or fatigue. As a result, she may miss directions and have difficulties keeping up with classwork. Check up on her periodically to make sure that she is aware of what she needs to do. You may want to assign a responsible student to sit next to her and help her stay on track.

7. Provide Opportunities for the Child to Make up Missed Work

A child who is absent frequently is likely to miss crucial lessons and begin to fall behind. This can be a particular problem in high school. Develop clear procedures for how the student will make up the work and communicate these procedures to the parents. You might arrange for the parents to pick up the work, have it sent home with another student or a sibling, or give it to the parents over the phone. If the student is going to be absent for a significant period, her parents should contact the principal to arrange for homebound instruction. This is a temporary arrangement in which a teacher works with the student at her home until she is well enough to return to school.

8. Try to Eliminate Asthma Triggers from Your Classroom

Take the parents on a tour of your classroom when school is not in session so they can help you identify possible triggers, which might include animals with fur, chalk dust, rugs, science projects with plants or flowers, or new paint.

9. Consider Whether the Student Qualifies for Special Services under Section 504

Section 504 of the Rehabilitation Act of 1973, a federal law, prevents discrimination against students with disabilities who attend public schools. To qualify as having a disability under Section 504, the student must have a physical or mental impairment that substantially limits a major life activity. If the student meets this criterion for eligibility, the school and parents must develop a plan describing services and accommodations to ensure that the student is provided the same opportunities in school that are afforded to nondisabled students. The accommodations should be based on the student's individual needs. In the case of a student with asthma, this plan might provide an alternate attendance standard and provisions to allow the student to make up work.

FOR FURTHER INFORMATION

Sander, N. (1994). *A Parent's Guide to Asthma.* New York: Plume.

Steinmann, M. (1992). *A Parent's Guide to Allergies and Asthma.* New York: Delta.

ORGANIZATIONS

Allergy and Asthma Network/
Mothers of Asthmatics*
3554 Chain Bridge Road, Suite 200
Fairfax, VA 22030-2709
1-800-878-4403
1-703-385-4403

Asthma and Allergy Foundation of America*
1125 15th Street, NW, Suite 502
Washington, DC 20005
1-800-7-ASTHMA
1-202-466-7643

National Asthma Education Program*
National Heart, Lung and Blood Institute
Information Center
P.O. Box 30105
Bethesda, MD 20824-0105
1-301-251-1222

* The Allergy and Asthma Network offers a *School Information Packet,* the
Asthma and Allergy Foundation of America offers a video called *Managing
Asthma in School: An Action Plan,* and the National Asthma Education Program
offers a free video and three publications about students with asthma for educators.

CEREBRAL PALSY

Cerebral palsy is a condition caused by damage to the brain; it affects muscle control and coordination. "Cerebral" refers to the brain while "palsy" refers to poor muscle control. Cerebral palsy, often described simply as CP, can range from mild to severe and often affects a child's intellect, learning, speech, and vision. It is not a disease and cannot be passed on to other students. It is also not progressive; it does not get worse. While cerebral palsy is not curable, children with this condition can be helped through a combination of family support, medical attention, and appropriate educational programming. Children with mild cases of cerebral palsy often attend regular classes.

DIMENSIONS OF THE DISORDER

The brain damage that causes cerebral palsy can occur before, during, or shortly after birth. Events before or during birth that may cause cerebral palsy include infection of the mother during pregnancy, insufficient oxygen, poor blood flow to the fetal or newborn brain, blood type incompatibility between mother and infant or between mother and father, and premature birth. A small percentage of cases of cerebral palsy—about 10 percent—is caused by events after birth, including head trauma, such infections of the brain as meningitis or encephalitis, and exposure to certain toxins such as lead.

Because cerebral palsy is caused by damage to the brain, it is helpful to understand the brain's role in the movement of the body. The brain controls the movement of our muscles. It enables us to move our legs, bend our arms, raise our heads, and sit up straight. It also directs the use of our fine-motor skills such as grasping a pencil, typing on a keyboard, or using a fork. When part of the brain is damaged, the motor functions controlled by that part of the brain are impaired, even though the muscles themselves and the connecting nerves are normal. As a result, the child has less control of the movements of her body. The precise impact upon motor skills depends on the location and extent of the brain damage.

Types of Cerebral Palsy

Cerebral palsy is not one disorder but rather a group of disorders affecting movement and posture. There are three major types of cerebral palsy. More than half of children with cerebral palsy have a form called *spastic cerebral palsy*. It is characterized by stiff and awkward movements so that the child cannot move the involved limbs effectively. As a result, she may have difficulty shifting positions or letting go of an item she is holding. A child with *athetoid cerebral palsy* displays involuntary, random movement of the arms and legs so that she will have a hard time exercising control over her limbs. Just scratching her head or holding a pencil can present a difficult challenge. She may have an awkward gait and poor balance but will probably be able to walk. She may also experience speech problems, although she will probably have normal intelligence. *Mixed-type cerebral palsy* combines the features of spastic and athetoid forms of cerebral palsy.

Cerebral palsy is also classified based on the location of the motor problem. If you have a student with cerebral palsy in your class, you may come across one of the following terms:

- *Monoplegia:* Involvement of only one limb. Very rare.
- *Diplegia:* Involvement of two limbs, usually both legs.
- *Hemiplegia:* Involvement of one side of the body only. Child will probably walk with a limp. Very common.
- *Quadriplegia:* Involvement of child's entire body. Child will have difficulty with most daily living skills. May also affect facial muscles, so that child has problems eating and speaking.

As an example of the classification system, a child with spastic quadriplegia has spastic cerebral palsy that affects all four limbs.

Associated Problems

The brain damage that causes cerebral palsy may give rise to a range of problems. If you have a student with cerebral palsy, you may see some of the following:

- *Mobility problems:* While some children with cerebral palsy are unimpaired in their gait, others will have difficulty walking. Some may walk unassisted but have a limp or a shuffling gait, while others may need the assistance of crutches or require the use of a wheelchair.
- *Muscle control problems:* Children with cerebral palsy typically have difficulties with muscle tone, namely the ability to stretch their muscles

and resist movement. Their muscles may be so relaxed as to be floppy or they may be unusually tight. The resulting motor problems may affect small as well as large muscles and give rise to difficulty with daily living skills such as dressing, eating, drinking, and toileting. In the classroom, the child may have a hard time grasping objects, writing, and even following the teacher with her eyes. Because of poor muscle control, the child may drool and have problems swallowing, smiling, and even laughing.

- *Involuntary movements:* The child may have involuntary, irregular movements of the head, face, neck, or limbs. These movements may appear random and jerky.

- *Seizures:* About half of the children with cerebral palsy experience seizures. These disturbances in the electrical activity of the brain may give rise to a brief loss of consciousness as well as temporary changes in the child's movements or sensations. She may take medication to control the seizures.

- *Vision impairment:* Children with cerebral palsy have a 75 percent chance of having below-normal visual acuity and a 50 percent chance of having strabismus, an eye muscle imbalance characterized by crossed eyes. Amblyopia, often known as "lazy eye," is also common with children with cerebral palsy. Because visual problems are so prevalent with children with cerebral palsy, alert the child's parents if you see signs of difficulty in using her vision. These signs are discussed in the chapter on visual impairment.

- *Hearing impairment:* A small percentage of children with cerebral palsy experience hearing problems, which can range from mild to severe.

- *Speech problems:* Speech problems are very common with children with cerebral palsy. Difficulties in coordinating speech muscles, called dysarthria, can make it hard for a child to produce speech. As a result, her speech may be slow, slurred, and difficult to understand—or in severe cases may be absent altogether. The child may grimace when trying to talk and her voice may sound unusual. Problems may also occur in her ability to understand speech.

- *Mental retardation:* Studies indicate that approximately 60 percent of children with cerebral palsy are mentally retarded, ranging from mild to profound. It is difficult to assess the intelligence of children with cerebral palsy if they exhibit severe speech and motor problems; special tests may be required.

▪ *Learning disabilities:* Children with cerebral palsy who have normal intelligence are prone to specific learning disabilities as well as attentional deficits. In particular, they may exhibit visual perceptual difficulties or language problems.

▪ *Sensory deficiencies:* Depending on the location of the brain damage, children with cerebral palsy may experience problems processing sensory information. This may take different forms. Some children may be extremely sensitive to touch (tactile hypersensitivity) so that a gentle touch may trigger an emotional reaction. Others may be at the opposite extreme, displaying a relative insensitivity to touch and pain (tactile hyposensitivity). Some with cerebral palsy may have a hard time using their senses to complete motor tasks so that relatively simple tasks (for example, putting on a jacket) can be painstaking.

Diagnosis and Treatment

No two cases of cerebral palsy are exactly the same. At one extreme is the child with barely observable coordination problems who may appear to be simply clumsy. At the other extreme is the child with impairment of her arms, legs, head, and trunk as well as sensory and cognitive deficits. The child with this degree of impairment may not be able to stand or walk and may need assistance with daily living skills such as dressing, feeding, and toileting. Most cases of cerebral palsy are in the mild-to-moderate range.

The course that cerebral palsy follows varies dramatically with the nature and extent of the brain injury, ranging from complete dependence to full independence. While those with severe cases of cerebral palsy may require substantial help as adults, children with mild cases may grow up to live relatively normal and independent lives. They may graduate from high school, go on to college, obtain a job, and eventually get married and raise a family.

Cerebral palsy is usually detected by 18 months of age. While there is no specific test to diagnose cerebral palsy, physicians rely on reports of delays in achieving motor milestones, observations of the child's motor skills, and results of a physical examination to make the diagnosis. The physician must be careful to distinguish cerebral palsy from a general developmental delay. The child with a general developmental delay tends to exhibit delays in all areas, while the child with cerebral palsy is delayed in some areas but not others. She may have significant motor problems, for example, but have well-developed language skills. The diagnosis of cerebral palsy is particularly difficult where the symptoms are very mild, and physicians may sometimes disagree about the diagnosis. Some may conclude that a child has mild cerebral palsy while others may conclude that her motor development is simply delayed.

While there are steps people can take to lessen the impact of cerebral palsy, it cannot be cured. Since the brain damage is permanent, the child with cerebral palsy will have this condition her entire life. At the same time, there are various treatments available to the child that can maximize her abilities and minimize the effects of her condition. Surgery may help to relieve pain, release spastic muscles, and improve the functioning of her arms and legs. In addition, children with cerebral palsy may take medication to lessen spasticity and rigidity, and to control seizures. Physical, occupational, and speech and language therapy, discussed later in this chapter, are also critical components of the treatment program. Because each case is different, the educational and medical management of the child must be tailored to her particular profile.

SCHOOL IMPACT

The student with cerebral palsy will probably need special education or special services while in school, so she should be evaluated by the school's evaluation team to establish her eligibility and determine the needed services. If she has not already been evaluated and she shows signs of learning or other school-related problems, talk with the principal about arranging an evaluation.

In deciding upon an appropriate placement for the student with cerebral palsy, school staff and parents must consider various factors, including the child's intelligence, academic skills, attention span, and the availability of physical, occupational, and speech therapy services if needed. Many students with cerebral palsy who have normal intelligence can perform successfully in regular classes, although you may have to make some classroom adjustments. Students with cerebral palsy who are mentally retarded or learning disabled will probably need special education in a separate setting for at least part of the day. A student who is wheelchair-bound may need the services of a classroom aide who stays with the student throughout the day and accompanies her to the bathroom.

The student with cerebral palsy may have a range of educational needs that must be addressed by the school. As a result, her educational program may require the efforts of specialists. Among the services she may receive in school are physical therapy, occupational therapy, and speech and language therapy. She may also receive a modified form of gym, called adaptive physical education, taught by a physical education teacher who is trained to work with children with disabilities. The extent of these services will of course vary with the nature and degree of the student's difficulties. As with most services for children with disabilities, the earlier these services are begun, the greater the benefit.

Physical therapy is often a critical part of the treatment program for a child with cerebral palsy. PT, as it is often called, attempts to enhance the child's movement skills by increasing muscle control and strength. While the overall goal of physical therapy is to improve large-muscle movements, the specific goals will vary with each child. One child may need to work on improving her balance, another on increasing physical stamina, and still another on learning to coordinate her body parts.

Occupational therapy also targets the child's motor development, but the emphasis is on developing upper-body control in order to improve daily living skills. The overriding goal of OT is to help the child function more effectively in both the home and school environments. For students with severe motor impairments, this may mean working on such practical skills as eating, dressing, grooming, and toileting. The occupational therapist may also work on school-related skills such as cutting with scissors, grasping a pencil, writing, typing on a keyboard, and throwing and catching

Speech and language therapy is also a key part of the educational program, since speech is often impaired in children with cerebral palsy. The speech-language pathologist will evaluate the child's speech and language skills and design a program to remediate her weak areas. The program objectives might range from improving articulation to increasing vocabulary development to learning how to use alternative communication systems, which are discussed later in this chapter.

The focus of these therapies should be on improving the child's practical skills. Thus, the therapist should evaluate the child's abilities within her natural settings, including the classroom, and then target the therapy to improve the child's ability to participate fully and independently in these settings. For example, the physical therapist might help to improve the child's ability to use her wheelchair within school, while the occupational therapist might teach the child how to use a communication board more effectively. The therapist may look to the teacher for guidance in deciding what skills to emphasize.

SPECIAL AIDS FOR THE CHILD WITH CEREBRAL PALSY

The child with cerebral palsy has available to her a wide variety of assistive devices or aids that can enhance her self-sufficiency and provide greater access to her environment. In fact, there has been an explosion in recent years of what is called assistive technology for disabled persons. The following are some of the aids that students with cerebral palsy may use in school:

- *Mobility aids:* Wheelchairs come in many types, from manually operated to battery-powered models. Some children with cerebral palsy may use a walker as a support, while others may use crutches in combination with leg braces. In the classroom, the child may use a stander, which helps a child stand and trains her legs to support some weight.

- *Orthopedic aids:* Most children with cerebral palsy wear orthotics, which are custom-made devices to stabilize the joints or stretch the muscles. A child with cerebral palsy may wear a cast for weeks or even months to enhance a joint's movement and prevent orthopedic problems. Splints may also be worn to ease movement and support a part of the body.

- *Academic aids:* The student with cerebral palsy may be better able to complete academic tasks by using such aids as a pencil holder, book holder, page turner, and adapted computer keyboard.

- *Communication systems:* In addition to sign language, there are various types of what are called augmentative communication devices for children who have limited or no speech as well as those who have difficulty writing. These tools are particularly suited for children who understand language relatively well but are unable to make themselves understood with speech. A simple language board allows a child to communicate by pointing to or focusing on various objects on the board. A much more sophisticated (and far more expensive) version of the language board is the electronic, computerized communication board, which enables children to communicate in ways that were not possible in the recent past. This technology has dramatically improved the quality of life for children with severe speech impairments. The child types out what she wants to say (either on a regular keyboard or an adapted keyboard with symbols), and the computer converts it into print on a screen or into spoken words through a speech synthesizer. (New technology is available that actually enables the computer to simulate the person's voice.) If one of your students uses this kind of system, you will require some brief training to learn how it works. Most likely, the speech-language pathologist will be able to help you with this.

HOW TEACHERS CAN HELP

The following are some classroom strategies to foster independence and self-sufficiency with students who have cerebral palsy:

1. Avoid Overprotecting the Child

Teaching a child with cerebral palsy can trigger strong impulses of wanting to protect the child from failure. It is difficult to watch a child struggle to accomplish what comes easily to others. You may find yourself wanting to shield her from these struggles. You may find yourself tempted to finish her sentence as she struggles to get the words out, or to not allow her to play kickball for fear she may get hurt, or to make a choice for her to save her from the anxiety of deciding. While these actions may feel right, they may convey the wrong message to the child, namely that she can do little on her own and needs the constant assistance of others. Overprotectiveness can cause a child to develop feelings of insecurity and dependence, and to become shy and withdrawn. With many tasks, it is often better to allow the child to struggle and experience her limitations. Give the child confidence that she can eventually master the task, provide some hints, and back off as she learns to find her way.

2. Look for Opportunities to Praise the Student

Frustrated over not being able to control their body or speech, many children with cerebral palsy are in particular need of emotional support and stroking. Their accomplishments may not take the same form as those of other students. Small steps may represent major strides for the child with cerebral palsy. Recognize these gains without being insincere or dishonest.

3. Be Patient in Waiting for a Response

Students with cerebral palsy who have speech, motor, or cognitive deficiencies may be very slow in responding to a question or completing a task. Speech may be slow and labored because of difficulty making the mouth, lips, and tongue work as quickly as normal. Similarly, motor tasks may take longer than usual. In addition to displaying patience yourself, encourage your students to show similar patience when interacting with a classmate with cerebral palsy.

4. If You Do Not Understand What the Student Has Said, Ask Her to Repeat It or Write It Down

Do not pretend that you understand when you do not. The student is likely to be more frustrated by having people pretend they understand than having to repeat or write down what she said.

5. Allow the Student to Participate in Decisions

The child with cerebral palsy may feel a lack of personal control due to her speech and motor impairments, so try to find opportunities to give her a sense of control in other ways. When making decisions that involve her, solicit her opinion and allow her to participate in the decision making. She may make some choices that turn out to be poor ones, but these are learning experiences just as they are for other children. Of course, you have to use some discretion here in deciding on the extent of the child's involvement. Some decisions should be reserved for adults.

6. Promote Peer Involvement

Students with cerebral palsy can become isolated from their classmates because of their speech and motor limitations. Find activities in which the child with cerebral palsy can interact with her classmates successfully. Place her in activities with peers who are likely to be accepting. As a way of promoting acceptance, suggest to the child that she demonstrate to the class some of the aids that she uses. Her classmates will be particularly intrigued by a language or communication board.

7. Use Your Standard, or Adapted, Disciplinary Measures with the Student

The child with cerebral palsy is just as capable of misbehaving as other children. If she does, consider using the same disciplinary measures that you use with other students, or adapt them to the characteristics of the student. Just be sure that the misbehavior is not a result of the child's disability. Also bear in mind that the ultimate purpose of discipline is to teach, not to punish or humiliate. Make sure that the student with cerebral palsy understands what you consider acceptable and unacceptable classroom behavior.

8. Work Closely with Specialists

Physical and occupational therapists and speech-language pathologists can give you ideas on how to reinforce motor and speech development within the classroom. Children retain skills more effectively when they are used and reinforced in the actual settings. In addition, these specialists are good sources of information about how to work the various aids and equipment that the child may use.

9. Encourage the Student to Change Sitting Positions Periodically

Children with cerebral palsy who stay in the same sitting position for a long period may experience increased tightening of their muscles.

10. Allow the Student to Control Her Wheelchair

A child who is pushed in a wheelchair against her wishes may become upset and feel out of control. Check with the student before you push the wheelchair, or wait for her to request help. Similarly, do not push buttons on the wheelchair. Let the student do this. If the student gets out of her wheelchair, make sure it remains within her reach (the same is true of crutches).

11. Check in Advance That Field Trip Sites Are Wheelchair Accessible

While society has made great strides in opening up public places to the disabled, do not assume that all places can accommodate children in wheelchairs. A brief call in advance can avoid an awkward situation.

12. Give the Student a Second Set of Texts

It may be difficult for a student with a physical disability to bring books home. Make it easy on her by lending her a set of books that she can keep at home during the school year.

13. Prepare a Fire Drill Plan for the Student

This is especially important if the student is in a wheelchair and has classes or activities on the second floor.

FOR FURTHER INFORMATION

Aaseng, N. (1991). *Cerebral Palsy* (for grades 9–12). New York: F. Watts.

Geralis, E. (ed.) (1997). *Children With Cerebral Palsy* (2d ed.). Rockville, MD: Woodbine House.

Miller, F., and Bachrach, S. J. (1995). *Cerebral Palsy: A Complete Guide for Caregiving.* Baltimore: Johns Hopkins University Press.

Schleichkorn, J. (1993). *Coping With Cerebral Palsy: Answers to Questions Parents Often Ask* (2d ed.). Austin TX: Pro-Ed.

ORGANIZATIONS

American Academy for Cerebral Palsy and Developmental Medicine
6300 North River Road, Suite 727
Rosemont, IL 60018-4226
1-847-698-1635

American Physical Therapy Association
1111 North Fairfax Street
Alexandria, VA 22314-1488
1-703-684-2782

National Easter Seal Society
230 West Monroe Street, Suite 1800
Chicago, IL 60606-4802
1-800-221-6827
1-312-726-6200

United Cerebral Palsy Association
1660 L Street, NW, Suite 700
Washington, DC 20036-5602
1-800-872-5827
1-202-776-0406

See also:
Epilepsy
Handwriting Problem
Hearing Impairment
Mental Retardation
Speech and Language Problems
Visual Impairment

Cystic Fibrosis

Cystic fibrosis (CF) is a genetic disorder that affects the respiratory and digestive systems. It is the most common life-threatening, inherited illness among children in the United States, affecting approximately 30,000 people in this country. It is not contagious and thus cannot be passed on to other students. If you have a student with CF, he is likely to manifest symptoms of the illness in the classroom. You play an important role in his school adjustment by helping him feel comfortable in class, lessening his illness-related anxiety, and promoting his acceptance by peers.

SYMPTOMS AND TREATMENT

To get CF, a child must inherit a gene for the disease from each parent. If he inherits only one CF gene, he will be a normal, healthy child. CF affects the glands that secrete mucus. Normal mucus is thin and flows easily, helping to remove germs and dust particles, but the person with CF produces an unusually thick, gummy mucus that is hard to remove. This mucus can lodge in the lungs, making it hard to breathe and becoming a breeding ground for infection. The mucus can also block the pancreas, keeping enzymes from reaching the small intestines and, as a result, blocking the absorption of essential nutrients. When this happens, the body does not obtain adequate nutrition. CF can also affect the sweat glands and, under certain conditions, can lead to excessive loss of salt as well as heat prostration.

The child with CF may display both respiratory and digestive problems, or he may display problems in only one area. The extent of the disorder will thus vary from child to child and will range from mild to severe. If you have a student in your class with CF, you may observe the following symptoms: a persistent cough, wheezing sounds, frequent stomachaches, and a tendency to fatigue easily. Children with CF may be small in stature and have problems gaining weight, although they often have large appetites.

While there is no cure for CF, treatment can lessen the discomfort of the disease. The treatment of CF focuses on lung-related problems, since these are the most life threatening. One form of treatment, called postural drainage or chest physical therapy, involves gentle pounding on the back and chest to dislodge the mucus from the lungs and clear the airways. Lung infections are treated with antibiotic medication. In cases where the person with CF is not absorbing enough nutrients because of digestive problems, he may be placed on an enriched diet and given vitamins and digestive enzymes. The child with CF may take as many as eight or ten pills with each meal, and may even have to snack during the day to maintain energy. Salt may also be added to his diet to replace what was lost.

Research into the disorder continues, and there have been some promising developments in recent years. The discovery of the CF gene in 1989 has spurred various research initiatives. In 1993, a new drug therapy was approved by the Food and Drug Administration; it has lessened the number of pulmonary infections and improved lung functioning.

The primary means of diagnosing cystic fibrosis is through a sweat test. Sweat is generated by stimulating a small portion of the skin through heat or medication. If the sweat has more salt than average, it suggests a diagnosis of CF. These test results will be considered in conjunction with chest x-rays and evidence of breathing and digestive problems and infections to reach a definitive diagnosis. Because the symptoms of CF overlap with those of other disorders, children with this illness are sometimes misdiagnosed as suffering from pneumonia, asthma, bronchitis, or allergies.

The person with CF has a shortened life expectancy, although treatment has signficantly extended how long he is likely to live. Thirty years ago only about one in twenty children lived beyond the age of 15. Today the average life expectancy of a child with CF is about 30, and many children with CF have gone on to college, married, and pursued careers.

The quality of life is also much improved for children who suffer from CF. A child who receives proper medical treatment and follows the prescribed regimen can lead a relatively normal life. He may miss relatively few days of school and may be able to participate in most physical activities, although he should be guided by his physician's recommendations. Some physical activities such as running and swimming may even be helpful in removing mucus from the lungs. A student with CF can participate in virtually all sports, although he needs to be guided by what his body tells him in determining when to sit out. His coach must be informed of his illness and the need to monitor his level of fatigue.

SCHOOL IMPACT

Children with cystic fibrosis do not suffer any brain damage, and thus their cognitive skills are unaffected by the disorder. As a result, they are no more likely to have a learning disability than other students. Their school performance may suffer, however, as a result of frequent absences. While children with CF are less likely to be absent now than in the past because of treatment advances, many still experience significant absenteeism. Some CF children have to be hospitalized for weeks at a time for nutritional therapy, chest physical therapy, and antibiotic medication to combat infection of the lungs. In addition, they may have difficulty concentrating in school or be unusually tired because of sleepless nights resulting from persistent coughing.

Cystic fibrosis can also take a toll on the student's emotional well-being and social adjustment. Children with CF may experience depression, low self-esteem, and poor peer relations. They may be socially insecure as a result of their small stature and delays in reaching puberty—both potential consequences of the disorder. They may also experience distress from a feeling of being controlled by their illness. Some may have such a strong response to the physical consequences of cystic fibrosis that they try to deny its existence and resist the treatments. An important goal for parents and teachers is to help the child with CF learn to care for himself so that he develops a sense of control over his illness and becomes less dependent on others. As he assumes more control over the cystic fibrosis, he may start to feel better about himself and relate better to other children.

HOW TEACHERS CAN HELP

You may find the following classroom strategies helpful in working with a student with CF:

1. Learn about the Child from His Parents

As with all chronic illnesses that affect school performance, you and the school nurse will want to meet with the parents early in the year. The parents can help you understand the particular aspects of the child's illness and the implications for school. Since the parents are the real experts on their child, ask them about helpful ways of responding in class. If necessary, set up a regular system of communication with the parents. You will want to contact them if you see that the child is starting to slip in his work, is coughing more than is normal for him, or is extremely tired. Ask the parents if there are other times when they will want to be contacted by the school.

2. Talk Briefly with the Class about Cystic Fibrosis

The other children may become aware of the child's illness because of his coughing episodes and his frequent absences from class. Ask the parents and student for permission to talk with the class about cystic fibrosis, and invite them to participate in the discussion. Let the students know that he may cough frequently and need to leave the class often to go to the bathroom or get a drink of water, but don't dwell on his physical problems; keep the discussion brief. If you observe any teasing of the child with CF, intervene quickly by talking with the student doing the teasing to help him become more understanding.

3. Talk with the Student in Private

Let him know that you are aware of his illness and that you understand that he will have to cough frequently. Emphasize that the coughing will not be a problem and that he is free to leave the room at any time until the coughing fit is over, or if he needs to get a drink of water. Allow him to keep some water at his desk (perhaps in a squeeze bottle) to relieve a persistent cough. You might also keep a box of tissues on your desk in case he runs out. Reassure him that you understand that he may be especially tired some days from coughing fits during the night and that you will work with him and his parents to help him make up work missed because of school absence.

4. Treat Him Like a Normal Student Who Happens to Have Cystic Fibrosis

Your expectations for a student with CF should be the same as for his classmates. If you treat him as sickly, he will come to view himself as different. If you treat him as normal, he will come to see himself as normal. Expect him to complete the same homework assignments, conform to the same standards of behavior, and perform the same classroom responsibilities that you have established for all your students (with some exceptions where there is a specific reason for making an adjustment). And do not let him use his illness to get out of tasks that he dislikes.

5. Allow the Child to Leave the Classroom at Any Time

The student with CF may need to leave the class frequently, either because of persistent coughing or because he needs a drink of water to loosen respiratory secretions. He may also need to use the bathroom more often than his classmates. Allow him to have a permanent pass or arrange for him to give you a subtle signal to let you know he is leaving the room.

6. Make It Comfortable for the Child to Cough

It is important that the child with CF cough as much as possible because the coughing helps to dislodge the mucus from the lungs. He needs to expel the mucus rather than swallow it. As a result, you want to encourage his coughing rather than stifle it. The child should not use cough suppressants. If his coughing is disruptive to the class, allow him to leave the room until the episode is over. Some teachers of CF children have even designed behavior modification programs in which they have prompted them to cough and then rewarded them for the behavior.

7. Adapt Physical Education Activities When Necessary

Keep in mind that physical exercise usually helps the child with CF by stimulating coughing and promoting overall fitness. There may be days, however, when he will be unable to engage in vigorous physical exercise because of fatigue or weakness from failure to absorb essential nutrients. Try to involve him in the physical education class by having him participate in a way that is not physically taxing (for example, keeping score, serving as referee, or being responsible for the equipment).

8. Be Flexible in Allowing Him to Make up Missed Work Due to Absences

The child with CF is likely to be absent more than average due to his disorder. Allow him adequate time to make up the work when he is feeling better. You might send the work home with a friend or sibling or arrange for the parents to pick it up. Make sure the student is clear about what he needs to do and when the work is to be returned. You may want to give him a second set of books to keep at home if he is absent frequently. (Make a note in your calendar to get them back at the end of the school year.) If he is out for long periods, the school should arrange for him to receive instruction at home or in the hospital so that he does not fall behind. Encourage the students to send cards to him if he is out for an extended period. If your schedule allows, you might even pay him a visit. These gestures will help to boost the child's spirits and give him a feeling of acceptance by his classmates, which is often lacking with children with CF.

9. Consider Eligibility for Special Services under Section 504

A student with cystic fibrosis is likely to qualify for eligibility under Section 504, a federal law that mandates that public schools provide accommodations for students with disabilities. See the chapter on asthma for a fuller discussion of this law.

FOR FURTHER INFORMATION

Harris, A., and Super, M. (1995). *Cystic Fibrosis: The Facts.* New York: Oxford University Press.

Orenstein, D. M. (1997). *Cystic Fibrosis: A Guide for Patient and Family* (2d ed.). Philadelphia: Lippincott-Raven.

Shapiro, B. L., and Heussner, R. C., Jr. (1991). *A Parent's Guide to Cystic Fibrosis.* Minneapolis: University of Minnesota Press.

ORGANIZATIONS

Cystic Fibrosis Foundation
6931 Arlington Road, Suite 200
Bethesda, MD 20814
1-800-344-4823
1-301-951-4422

See also:
   Asthma

DIABETES

Diabetes is a chronic disease that impairs the body's ability to use food properly. It is caused by the inability of the pancreas to produce sufficient insulin, a hormone needed to convert sugar into energy for use by the body. When a person lacks insulin, sugar builds up in the bloodstream, but is unavailable for use by the body as fuel. To avoid physical problems from the accumulation of sugar, the child with diabetes must take daily injections of insulin. Diabetes is not contagious, and therefore cannot be passed from student to student.

There are two major types of diabetes. The type that most often develops in children is called insulin-dependent diabetes, formerly called juvenile diabetes. It is one of the most common chronic childhood disorders in this country, affecting an estimated 800,000 Americans. This chapter will focus on insulin-dependent diabetes only (which will be referred to simply as diabetes).

The onset of diabetes may be sudden or gradual. It may cause a child to display the following behaviors:

- frequent urination

- extreme thirst

- weakness and fatigue

- increased appetite accompanied by unexplained weight loss

- impaired vision

- nausea

If you notice that one of your students is displaying some or all of these behaviors, talk with the school nurse and inform the parents.

Diabetes can have extreme consequences if not managed properly. A high level of sugar in the bloodstream can cause problems during adulthood with a person's eyes, kidneys, nerves, and heart. If the sugar level drops too low (for example, because the person has taken too much insulin), hypoglycemia can result, with symptoms of fatigue, hunger, shakiness, and nervousness. In extreme cases, diabetes can even be life threatening.

TREATING DIABETES

Blood sugar levels that are either too high or too low can cause the child to become sick. The overriding goal in treating a child with diabetes is to keep her blood sugar level as normal as possible. This requires constant care and attention. While there is no cure for diabetes, it can be controlled. This is done in three ways: insulin injections, dietary restrictions, and regular exercise. Controlling diabetes is a matter of constantly balancing these three factors. As a general rule, insulin and exercise make the blood sugar level go down, and food makes the blood sugar level go up.

Insulin is typically administered by injection and is usually given two or three times a day. It can also be administered by pump, a relatively new, computerized device about the size of a beeper that delivers a steady dose of insulin through a plastic tube inserted through the skin. The insulin helps to maintain a normal level of blood sugar by allowing the cells to absorb and use the sugar in the bloodstream. The age of children who can give themselves injections varies; some can do this as early as age 7, while others may not be ready until the age of 12. Even the most responsible student will need reminders on occasion, however, so you or the school nurse must keep track of her injections. In terms of diet, a child with diabetes can usually eat the same nutritious foods as other children, although concentrated sweet foods are generally prohibited. She will be provided with a specific food plan and will have to learn to monitor what she eats. She also must be consistent in when and how much she eats. Regular exercise is an important part of the child's treatment program as well, because it helps to lower sugar levels in the blood by burning sugar without insulin.

People with diabetes may need to test the level of sugar in their blood several times a day to determine if it is too high or too low, and to see if any modifications in insulin, diet, or exercise are needed. Many children are able to conduct this test on their own. It involves taking a drop of blood from the finger, placing it on a coated strip, and measuring the amount of sugar with a small device called a glucose meter, or with the use of a color-coded chart. The child's treatment program will specify when she is to test her blood sugar. Most likely, she will do this before lunch and before any strenuous physical activity. The child's doctor may request that she record the results of the tests in a "diabetes diary" to assist in making adjustments in the treatment regimen. Be aware that your school district may have a policy about where children can conduct blood tests.

MANAGING AN INSULIN REACTION

A child may have what is called an insulin reaction when her blood sugar level falls too low. Very low blood sugar is called hypoglycemia, and it is the most common problem associated with diabetes. This may result from too much insulin, too much exercise (without a snack ahead of time), or too little or delayed food. Many children can sense that they are having a reaction and will eat something on their own to raise their blood sugar level, or they will alert you. With younger children, you are likely to be the first to notice an insulin reaction. You should be especially vigilant about watching the student before a meal or after a strenuous physical activity. The signs of an insulin reaction, which may appear rapidly, vary with each child and may include the following:

- sudden and extreme hunger

- perspiration

- pale complexion

- poor coordination

- sleepiness

- dizziness and confusion

- headache and nausea

- irritability

- trembling hands and feet

- rapid pulse

Take the signs of an insulin reaction seriously, as a child experiencing very low blood sugar can lose consciousness or go into convulsions if not treated. Once you conclude that the child is having an insulin reaction, act quickly.

Developing a Plan

The parents and school personnel should work out a plan (see How Teachers Can Help) at the beginning of the school year to describe what should be done if the child has an insulin reaction in school. A child may sense that her blood sugar is low and terminate an insulin reaction by taking some fast-acting sugar that she carries with her or gets from the teacher's snack supply. Usually, the insulin reaction is mild and the child improves quickly with a sweet snack. The list of acceptable snacks should be approved by the child's doctor and may include sugar cubes, fruit juice, non-diet soda, or hard candy. The child may also take glucose tablets when blood sugar is low.

If the child does not improve within 10 or 15 minutes, she may need to be given additional sugar or administered glucagon, a hormone that raises blood sugar. A school nurse should not administer glucagon without consulting with and getting approval from a physician. If the symptoms still remain, this may be the time to contact the parents or obtain medical help. You will also want to get emergency help if the child loses consciousness or cannot swallow. (In either case, do not force the child to eat or drink.) Make sure not to leave the child alone while she is experiencing an insulin reaction. If the child needs to go to the nurse's office, have another student accompany her.

After the child starts to feel better, she should be given unsweetened foods (for example, milk, bread, cereal, or crackers) to avoid a recurrence. Once she feels better, she may be able to return to normal school activities, although she may not perform optimally for a couple of hours, and you should not give her a test after the episode. You or the school nurse should inform the parents of the incident.

When blood sugar is very high, the child is said to have hyperglycemia. A child with hyperglycemia will display some of the following symptoms: excessive thirst, frequent urination, sleepiness, weakness, lack of appetite, and impaired vision. In severe cases of hyperglycemia, the child can develop a serious complication called diabetic coma, but this occurs over a period of several hours or days and is unlikely to be a problem that teachers will confront. If you are confused about whether the child is manifesting signs of high or low blood sugar, a test of her blood sugar can provide the answer. If the problem is high blood sugar, you may want to give the child a sugar-free beverage, although you should first check the school plan about what to give the child.

HOW TEACHERS CAN HELP

Diabetes is a serious disease with potentially significant physical complications. It can, however, be managed with close attention and monitoring, so teachers should not press the panic button if one of their students has diabetes. By following some basic guidelines, described below, school personnel should be able to handle almost any situation that arises in the classroom, and children who conscientiously follow their treatment program should be able to participate in virtually all school activities.

1. Find out the Relevant School Policies

Your school district may have policies for dealing with children with diabetes. For example, some schools require blood sugar testing to be done in the nurse's office, while others allow it to be done in the classroom. The school nurse should be familiar with these policies.

2. Develop a Written Plan with the Parents and School Nurse

Meet with the parents before or soon after school begins to spell out in writing how the school will manage the child with diabetes. The school nurse, and possibly the principal, should be in attendance. In addition, the child should be encouraged to attend and participate. Other school staff involved with the child should also attend or at least be informed of the plan. You and the school nurse will want to ask many questions of the parents about the specific nature of the child's disorder and helpful ways of responding. Figure 3-1 (next page) provides a list of questions to guide you in gathering information and developing a school plan. You, the nurse, and the parents should keep copies of the plan.

If the child qualifies for special services in school under Section 504 (see chapter on asthma for discussion of Section 504), this plan may meet the criteria for a 504 plan. A 504 plan must include a list of accommodations the school will make to deal with a child's disabilty. In the case of a child with diabetes, this may include the following provisions:

- Child will be allowed to eat snacks and lunch at specific times and given sufficient time to finish food.

- Child will be allowed to test blood sugar level and administer insulin at a specific time and place, and will be given assistance, if necessary.

Figure 3–1

INFORMATION TO OBTAIN WHEN A CHILD HAS DIABETES

➡ **Personal Information**

Home phone number?

Mother's work number? Work schedule?

Father's work number? Work schedule?

Name of doctor? Phone number?

Emergency contact? Relation to child? Phone number?

➡ **Food**

Will the child need to eat snacks during the day?

What types of snacks are permitted?

At what time daily will the child need to eat snacks?

Are there other occasions when snacking may be necessary?

Will the child carry snacks with her at school?

Will the parents be sending in snacks for the teacher to store for the child?

What time does the child need lunch?

➡ **Physical Activity**

Are there any physical restrictions?

Will the child need a snack before gym class?

Does the child plan to play on any school athletic teams? Which sport?

Has the coach been notified of the child's diabetes and guidelines for care? If not, who will notify him?

Will the child have snacks available during practices or games?

FIGURE 3–1 *(cont'd)*

⇒ **Insulin**

Will the child take insulin during the day?

When is insulin to be given? In what amount?

Can the child give self injections?

If not, who is to administer?

Where is the child to receive the insulin injection?

Where will supplies for the insulin injections be kept?

⇒ **Testing Blood Sugar Level**

Will the child need to test blood sugar during the school day?

What time?

Are there other occasions when testing is necessary?

Where is the child to conduct the test?

Can the child test self?

If not, who will do the testing? How will the person be trained?

What device is used to do the test?

Where will it be kept?

⇒ **Insulin Reaction (Low Blood Sugar)**

What specific behaviors will signal that the child is having an insulin reaction?

What steps should the staff member take in response to an insulin reaction?

What foods (and how much) should be given to the child during an insulin reaction?

Is it permissible to give a second snack? When?

What foods are off-limits during an insulin reaction?

Is glucagon to be given to the child during an insulin reaction?

Figure 3–1 *(cont'd)*

Under what circumstances?

Who is to administer the glucagon?

What should be done if the child is still having a reaction after 10 or 15 minutes?

Should the child be given anything to eat or drink after the reaction is over? If so, what?

How should the child signal you that he or she is having an insulin reaction?

What are the signs for this child of high blood sugar?

What steps should be taken if the child has high blood sugar?

➡ **Miscellaneous**

Who is to receive copies of this plan?

Who is to be informed of the elements of this plan?

Under what circumstances should the parents be notified?

Under what circumstances should medical attention be obtained?

■ Child will be allowed to go to the bathroom or water fountain whenever she requests it.

■ Child will be allowed to participate in all school and after-school activities, and arrangements will be made to have snacks and lunch at designated times.

■ Child will not be penalized for absences due to diabetes, and the school will provide opportunities for the child to make up the work.

Keep in mind that this meeting is also an opportunity to reassure the parents, who are probably anxious, of your concern for their child and your willingness to ease her adjustment to your class. The child may also need to be reassured by you and the school nurse that the school will be able to help her deal with any diabetes-related problems.

3. Make Sure That All School Personnel Working with the Child Are Informed

Because the child can exhibit diabetes-related problems in various school settings, from the classroom to the ballfield to the cafeteria, school staff who are in a supervisiory capacity with this child must be apprised of her medical condition and steps to take if she has an insulin reaction. The staff members to be informed may include not only her various teachers but also the bus driver, librarian, lunchroom and playground aides, and staff in the after-school program. Some or all of these staff members may need to attend the planning meeting with the child's parents.

4. Help Your Other Students Understand Diabetes

Obtain the parent's permission before you do this. You or the school nurse may lead the discussion, or you may ask the parents or even the student with diabetes to talk to the class. This presentation, which should be brief and matter-of-fact, and allow for questions, will demystify diabetes and help classmates understand when the child with diabetes conducts a blood test, eats a snack, or refuses cake during a class party. This discussion may even be a relief to the child in that she no longer feels she must keep a secret of her diabetes. If the child and her parents feel comfortable, you may even suggest that the child demonstrate how she measures her blood sugar level and how she takes insulin. A younger child might want to show her classmates the equipment she uses during Show and Tell. You might even suggest that an older child do a science project on diabetes as a way of educating her classmates (for example, comparing blood sugar levels after eating different foods or engaging in different activities).

5. Adapt to the Child's Dietary Needs

A child with diabetes will probably need to eat snacks in the morning and afternoon. It is important that the child snack at the prescribed time to maintain the proper blood sugar balance. While she is likely to carry some form of sugar with her (for example, hard candy), you may want to keep a supply of snacks that the parent has sent in. The child may also need to eat lunch at a specific time (most likely the early lunch). The child may bring her own lunch, or she may select foods that are acceptable from the school lunch menu. While many children are good at monitoring their food intake, a cafeteria aide should be informed of the child's dietary restrictions and be asked to keep an eye on the student and ensure that she has enough time to finish her meal. The aide should alert the teacher or nurse if the child does not eat lunch, since this can throw off her blood sugar level.

6. Make Special Provisions for Holidays and Parties

Holiday celebrations and parties in school may be difficult for the child with diabetes, since the food may be off-limits to her. Let the parents know about the party ahead of time so that they can send in some special food for their child, and perhaps the entire class (for example, popcorn or pretzels). The child with diabetes may sometimes be able to have a sweet food at a school party, although you should obtain the parents' permission before allowing this. An occasional cupcake is unlikely to be harmful and will help the child feel more a part of the celebration. Similarly, you must make arrangements during assemblies and field trips to ensure that the child gets her snack and has lunch at the proper time.

7. Monitor the Impact of Physical Activity on the Child

In general, children with diabetes can participate in all school activities as long as they adhere to their treatment program. This includes physical education class and sports. Because physical exercise can lower blood sugar, avoid scheduling physical education class right before lunch, when the blood sugar level may already be somewhat low. The child may need to have a snack just before strenuous exercise to compensate for the sugar that will be burned up during the activity. If the child with diabetes plays on a school team—and many do—the coach and trainer should be aware of her condition and be informed of how to handle an insulin reaction. Fast-acting sugar should be available to the student during practices and games. The parents will want to check with the doctor whether the child with diabetes will need to check her blood sugar before, during, or after the physical activity; under what conditions she cannot participate; and whether the insulin needs to be adjusted because the sport is particularly strenuous (for example, soccer). The child will also have to be accommodated if the sports event changes her snack or lunch schedule.

8. Treat the Child as Normally as Possible

While the child with diabetes has a medical condition that warrants close monitoring, in most respects she has the same concerns and needs as other children. Children with physical problems are often defined by their disease. Remind yourself that she is not a "diabetic" but rather a child with diabetes. You should have the same academic and behavioral expectations for her as for other students, and you should avoid singling her out for special treatment or drawing attention to her condition. (For example, if your class has a snack time, you might schedule it at the same time the child with diabetes eats her snack.) While this may seem obvious to the experienced teacher, parents have reported teachers telling their other students: "Cynthia is eating the snack because she is sick."

At the same time, you don't want to hide her diabetes. Rather, you want to deal with it in a matter-of-fact way. In this way, you will be a role model for your other students about how to relate to the child.

9. Be Sympathetic without Being Overprotective

The child with diabetes faces struggles beyond the normal challenges of growing up. She must be vigilant about her physical condition and her diet, and she may be aware of the physical problems she is likely to face later in life. Self-esteem may suffer as a result of feelings of being different from other children. Teenagers may have a particularly hard time as they try to balance the physical and nutritional demands of their disease with the social and emotional demands of adolescence, and you may find that they are not adhering to their treatment program. The child with diabetes may need more than the usual amount of support, understanding, and sympathy. At the same time, you don't want to shower her with excessive concern or attention, excuse her from the normal classroom responsibilities, or keep her from attending school functions. The risk is that by shielding her from the normal challenges of childhood, or by doing for her what she can do on her own, you will encourage her to become excessively dependent and develop feelings of inadequacy. Children with diabetes, perhaps more than other children, must learn to become resourceful and independent.

FOR FURTHER INFORMATION

Edelwich, J., and Brodsky, A. (1986). *Diabetes: Caring for Your Emotions As Well As Your Health.* Reading, MA: Addison-Wesley.

Johnson, R. W., et al. (1994). *Managing Your Child's Diabetes.* New York: MasterMedia Ltd.

Loring, G. (1991). *Parenting a Diabetic Child.* Los Angeles: Lowell House.

ORGANIZATIONS

American Diabetes Association
1660 Duke Street
Alexandria, VA 22314
1-800-232-3472
1-703-549-1500

Juvenile Diabetes Foundation International
120 Wall Street
New York, NY 10005-4001
1-800-223-1138
1-212-785-9500

National Diabetes Information Clearinghouse
1 Information Way
Bethesda, MD 20892-3560
1-301-654-3327

EPILEPSY

Epilepsy, also called a seizure disorder, is a common neurological condition characterized by brief disturbances in the electrical activity of the brain. When the brain is working normally, millions of electrical impulses pass between nerve cells in the brain and to all parts of the body. When a person has epilepsy, the brain cells malfunction, releasing bursts of unusually intense electrical energy. This "overload" may give rise to temporary changes in a person's consciousness, movements, or sensations. This is called an epileptic seizure. When the electrical bursts subside, the brain returns to normal functioning.

Epilepsy affects about one percent of the population—approximately two million people nationwide. While it can develop at any age, epilepsy primarily affects children and young adults. It is important that teachers be knowledgeable about epilepsy, because they are likely to have students with this disorder and they are often the first to recognize its symptoms. In addition, a student with epilepsy can present significant problems of classroom management. Seizures can be a scary experience for teachers, especially if they have not been prepared for what they may see and what they should do.

The cause of epilepsy cannot be found about half the time. In some cases, epilepsy results from a problem that impairs the electrical system of the brain, including a head injury, lack of oxygen during birth, a brain tumor, a stroke, lead poisoning, or an infection of the brain. Epilepsy may exist as a separate disorder, or it may accompany other disorders that affect the brain, such as cerebral palsy, autism, or mental retardation. Epilepsy is not contagious; it cannot be passed on to other students.

Epilepsy is diagnosed by reviewing the child's medical history, gathering information about her specific behaviors before and during the apparent seizure, and doing some medical tests. If the child is suspected of having had a seizure, she will probably be given an electroencephalogram (EEG). This painless test records the child's brain waves through small wires pasted to her head. A neurologist examines the brain waves to look for patterns characteristic of epilepsy. CT and MRI scans may also be used to look for underlying physical conditions of the brain that can cause a seizure.

TYPES OF SEIZURES

Epilepsy is a general term for over twenty different types of seizure disorders. The seizures can take very different forms, depending on how much of the brain is involved and the location of the problem. There are two primary kinds of seizures: partial seizures, involving only a portion of the brain, and generalized seizures, involving the whole brain.

Partial seizures may result in sudden jerking movements of the limbs or distortions of the way things look, sound, taste, smell, or feel. With some partial seizures, the child does not lose consciousness but is unable to control the jerking motions. This may cause the student considerable fear and distress, so you must be very reassuring and supportive. With other partial seizures, the child may lack awareness of her surroundings during the minute or two that the seizure lasts. Seemingly in a daze, she may be unresponsive and move about aimlessly and clumsily. She may smack her lips, speak in a garbled manner, begin to play with her clothes, and in some cases even start to remove them. After the seizure ends, the child is likely to be confused and not remember the episode. If this happens to one of your students, make sure to explain what happened and help reorient her. These kinds of seizures can be mistaken for a substance abuse problem or acting-out behavior.

Generalized seizures include absence seizures (also called petit mal seizures) in which the child stares blankly into space for a few seconds, after which she regains full awareness. She may blink rapidly, her mouth and limbs may twitch, and she may drop whatever she is holding. She may stop in the middle of a sentence, seem to "space out" for a few seconds, and then resume speaking without an awareness of what has happened. These seizures can occur frequently during the course of a day (sometimes as often as 100 times a day) and may cause students to miss portions of the classroom lesson. Children who have these kinds of seizures are often thought to be daydreaming. If you observe one of your students frequently displaying blank stares, try talking with her during these moments. If she seems unaware of your voice, doesn't respond to a hand on her shoulder, and shows other signs of an absence seizure, inform the nurse and also contact the student's parents with your concerns. You might suggest that the parents talk with the child's physician, but *do not offer a diagnosis.*

Another type of generalized seizure, the grand mal seizure, is the one most people identify with epilepsy. This seizure takes the form of a convulsion in which the child typically loses consciousness for one to three minutes and falls to the ground or slumps over. She may experience a stiffening of the body, jerking motions, and occasional loss of bladder or bowel control. She may also stop breathing for a few seconds, causing the skin to become bluish or pale. If this happens, there is no need for alarm; normal breathing almost always starts again on its own quickly. (If it does not, CPR is called for.) After regaining consciousness, the child is likely to feel sleepy and confused, and will not recall the seizure.

TREATMENT FOR EPILEPSY

When treating a child with epilepsy, the goal is to prevent seizures with as few side effects as possible. Epilepsy may be treated through medication, surgery, or a special high-fat diet, with medication the most common treatment and typically the first to be tried. The medication will vary with the kind of seizure, and must be tailored to the individual. Approximately twenty medications have been approved for the treatment of epilepsy. It may take weeks, and sometimes months, to identify the best medication or combination of medications to achieve the right balance of seizure control and minimal side effects. The most common side effect of the various medications is drowsiness; the student may have difficulty focusing in class and may even nod off on occasion.

Epilepsy can usually be controlled effectively with antiseizure medication, although it does not work with all children with epilepsy, and it certainly is not a cure. The key to the medication's effectiveness is that it must be taken exactly as prescribed. Many children will need medication for a long period. If they remain free of seizures for two or more years, their doctors may gradually withdraw them from medication. Most then remain free of seizures.

Because the medication can have unpleasant side effects, some children will skip doses or take less than is prescribed. Some may even stop taking the medication altogether. Doing this can lead, on rare occasions, to a condition called *status epilepticus,* in which the child experiences continuous seizures and which requires emergency treatment. If the student is taking medication in school, the school nurse is usually responsible for ensuring that she takes the medicine properly. As the student gets older, she should be expected to become more responsible for knowing when to go to the nurse's office to take the medication.

Because of the advances made in the treatment of epilepsy, children with this disorder can live relatively normal lives and in many cases be seizure free. They can be successful students and participate in physical activities, and it need not deter them from success later on. Indeed, many people with epilepsy, from Socrates to Thomas Edison, accomplished great things despite having epilepsy.

WHAT TO DO IF A STUDENT HAS A SEIZURE

If one of your students begins to have a seizure, use the following guidelines in dealing with the problem. First, take note of what you should not do:

- DON'T panic. The seizure is likely to last only a couple of minutes and the child will feel no pain during the seizure.

- DON'T try to restrict or restrain her movements or try to bring her out of the seizure by throwing cold water on her or shaking her. The seizure must run its course and cannot be stopped. There is no need for concern that the child will harm anyone, although she may lash out instinctively if held down.

- DON'T force her mouth open or try to hold onto her tongue. It is a myth that a person having a seizure can swallow her tongue. In fact, it is physically impossible.

- DON'T put anything in the child's mouth, including fluids or medicine.

  The following are things that you should do:

- Calmly reassure the other students that she will be fine in a few minutes.

- Ease the child gently into a lying position, removing any nearby hard or sharp objects that could hurt her. Cushion her head with a flat, soft object (for example, a folded jacket) or your hands, so it will not hit the floor if her body jerks. If she is wearing glasses, remove them.

- Roll her gently on her side so that her airway is clear and any fluid or saliva in her mouth can drain easily.

- Remain nearby until the child awakens and becomes oriented. As she regains consciousness, be supportive, since the child may be confused and embarassed, but avoid conveying worry and anxiety.

- Allow the child to rest or go to sleep. Children will vary in how much time they need to recover from the seizure. She should be encouraged to stay in class if she feels up to it. If she goes to the nurse's office, suggest that she return as soon as she feels ready. If she continues to feel groggy and confused after resting, the nurse may decide to call the parents to arrange for her to go home.

- Whether the child goes home or not, inform her parents that she had a seizure.

On rare occasions, immediate medical attention, including perhaps calling an ambulance, may be warranted. These include the following:

- A child without a history of epilepsy has a seizure.

- A grand mal seizure lasts more than five minutes.

- A seizure continues nonstop (*status epilepticus*).

- A child has two consecutive seizures without regaining consciousness.

- A child fails to regain consciousness after she stops shaking.

The child may also need medical attention if she has hit her head and experienced some of the following signs: unconsciousness, vomiting, persistent headache, impaired vision, and dilation of the pupils. Some children who have frequent seizures and are prone to falling may wear a helmet in school for protection.

While you may feel overwhelmed by the prospect of having to deal with a student's seizure and a potential medical emergency, remember that your job is to get help for the student, not to treat her. Begin with the school nurse, who should inform the principal and contact the parents and doctor when necessary. The decision to seek medical help should rest with the principal or nurse rather than the teacher.

SCHOOL IMPACT

Children with epilepsy can experience a variety of school-related problems as a result of their disorder. While they show the same range of cognitive ability as other children, they are prone to problems in processing and retaining information, memory, fine-motor skills, and attention. These difficulties may be due to the same abnormal brain activity or injury that caused the seizures. The way in which learning is disrupted depends on the location in the brain of the abnormal activity. For example, if the seizure originates from the right side of the brain, the child may have problems recognizing shapes and patterns, or may confuse math symbols. Verbal skills are more likely to be affected if the seizure occurs on the left side of the brain.

The antiseizure medication can also impede a student's school performance. It may make her drowsy and lethargic so that she has difficulty staying on task and can't work as quickly as other students, even though she may understand the work. She may perform poorly on timed tests. The medication may have a particularly dramatic effect on the student during the initial medication period, when the doctor is trying out different medications or dosages to arrive at the best treatment. If you notice that the student is often sleepy or inattentive, alert the parents.

A child may also miss more classroom instruction than average because of the epilepsy. This may result from frequent visits to the doctor or from episodes of petit mal seizures in class that keep her from portions of the classroom lessons. Her attention to task may also suffer in class from anxiety about having a seizure in school. As a result of these school absences or attentional lapses, the student with epilepsy may experience gaps in basic information or skills. If this is a problem, you may have to provide extra assistance to the student to fill in the gaps or get her back on track.

The social and emotional problems some children with epilepsy experience in school may be more disturbing than the academic problems. A child who has seizures may be perceived as odd by her classmates, who may respond by keeping their distance from her or subjecting her to ridicule. The child with epilepsy may contribute to her own social isolation by withdrawing from classmates because of embarrassment about her seizures or fears of peer rejection. The medication may reinforce the child's feelings of being different from her peers by causing slurred speech and facial blemishes. The child's self-esteem and social confidence may plummet and she may be unable to concentrate on schoolwork. Epilepsy may be particularly hard on teens, for whom peer acceptance is so important, and you may see signs of anger and hostility in reaction to the disorder.

Occasionally, students with epilepsy will exhibit behavior problems in school. These problems may be related to the seizures or to the medication they are taking (for example, hyperactivity, irritability, and temper outbursts).

They may also be due to emotional problems associated with epilepsy (for example, anger or low self-esteem). Or they may be unrelated to the epilepsy. Try to identify the basis of the problem and respond accordingly. If you conclude that the problems are a result of the epilepsy, do not discipline or punish the student. Rather, try to make classroom adjustments to lessen the problem or adjust your expectations of the student. If you conclude, however, that the behavior problems are unrelated to the epilepsy, use the same disciplinary measures you would apply to other students. There is no reason for concern about the impact on the child; teacher discipline will not trigger a seizure.

PARTICIPATING IN SCHOOL ACTIVITIES

Many children with epilepsy are able to participate in the full range of school activities, including physical activities. In fact, children are less likely to have seizures when involved in physical activity. At the same time, you need guidance from the child's doctor about any restrictions in physical activities. Gymnastics and swimming require particular caution. Generally, a child with epilepsy will be allowed to swim, but she should always be in the company of adults who know of her condition and can rescue her if she has a problem in the water. Some children with epilepsy even play football, although doctors have expressed concern that head injuries from contact sports could cause seizures.

Students with epilepsy should take the academic portion of driver's education class even if their seizures are poorly controlled. If they are able to gain control of their seizures later on, they may be allowed to drive. States typically allow licensed drivers with a history of epilepsy to drive if they can demonstrate that the epilepsy has been under control for a specific period (although insurance premiums are likely to be much higher than average).

HOW TEACHERS CAN HELP

While you cannot prevent the occurrence of a seizure, you can help to lessen its impact on the student's social and emotional well-being. Some strategies are listed below.

1. Gather Information from the Parents

As with other physical problems, school staff must meet with the child's parents at the beginning of the school year to learn key information about her disorder. The child should be encouraged to attend this meeting. You may want to ask the parents the following questions:

- What kind of seizures does your child have?

- How often does she have the seizures? Under what circumstances? How long do they last?

- Does she take antiseizure medication? What are the potential side effects? Does she need to take the medication in school? What time?

- Does she ever lose control of her bladder or bowel functions? (If so, suggest that the parents send in a change of clothing.)

- Does she have any physical restrictions?

- Does she have any learning problems due to the epilepsy?

- Under what circumstances should medical help be obtained?

- Under what circumstances do you want to be called by the school?

While open and ongoing communication between the parents and teacher is essential for the child's school adjustment, some parents are reluctant to discuss their child's disorder with the teacher for fear that the child will be stigmatized and ostracized. This reluctance may reflect negative experiences parents have had previously with teachers. If you sense that the parents are cautious in talking with you, try to gain their trust by letting them know through both your words and your actions that you are understanding of their child's special needs and sensitive to her feelings.

2. Talk with the Child

If the student did not attend the meeting with the parents, let her know that you are aware of her disorder and know what to do in case she has a seizure. Feel free to ask questions and encourage her to ask questions of you. You want to convey confidence to the child that you and other school staff can handle any situation that arises. You also want to convey a message of acceptance, which is an important issue for many children with epilepsy. Talk about specific situations that may arise, discussing how you might handle them and asking for suggestions from the student. Ask her if she can anticipate a seizure and, if so, to alert you so that you can take steps to protect her.

3. Talk with the Class

If the child is likely to have a seizure in class, it is important that you and the school nurse talk with your students. Make sure you obtain the parents' permission to discuss her condition with her classmates and invite them to participate. You can have this discussion with the child present or absent, depending on her preferences. In either case, let her know what you plan to tell the class. As you talk to the class, keep in mind that the experience of seeing a classmate have a seizure can be frightening and make them feel vulnerable. They may wonder, Could this happen to me? The fear they experience from seeing a seizure may develop into a fear of the child. Your comments can help relieve their concerns and dispel their fears.

Here are some key points to discuss during the presentation:

- Describe what epilepsy is in terms your students will understand, noting that it is a physical problem that can be helped by medication.

- State that epilepsy is not a contagious disease, and that they are in no danger of catching it.

- Describe what the child's seizure will look like.

- Tell them that a child having a seizure experiences no pain, that the seizure will pass after a few minutes, and that they are in no danger of being hurt by the child.

- Inform them what they should do if the child does have a seizure, emphasizing that their responsibility is to inform you immediately and to stay calm.

- Let them know that the child will return to her normal state after the seizure ends.

- Ask if the students have any questions or comments.

4. Help the Child Become Accepted by Her Peers

Because children with epilepsy are often perceived as strange, and shunned by their peers, you may want to help foster her acceptance by other students. First and foremost, model for your class your acceptance of the student. Treat her as you treat other students but create opportunities to showcase her strengths and talents. The child may need some help with basic social skills, so keep an eye out for how she handles peer situations and give her some pointers on how she might deal with various situations. She may need some prodding to interact with peers, especially if she has had hurtful experiences with other children. Try to arrange interactions with children who will be accepting and in which she is likely to have some success or enjoyment. Similarly, avoid situations in which the student may be rejected. (For example, don't have children select classmates for games if you expect she will always be chosen last.)

5. Avoid Overprotecting the Student

In an effort to shield children with epilepsy from physical risk and embarrassment, parents and teachers may discourage or even prevent them from participating in a range of school activities. When parents and teachers are overprotective, children with epilepsy learn to rely on others to solve problems and never learn to trust their own instincts. They learn to view themselves as different, and come to expect preferential treatment. While you certainly want to offer emotional support for the student and minimize the risk of physical problems, you also want to give her opportunities to deal with situations on her own, so that she learns to become resourceful and independent. This means encouraging her to participate in as many school activities as her doctor allows. When she does not participate in an activity, she loses out on the opportunity to benefit from that experience, learn from her mistakes, and develop social skills. Similarly, the student with epilepsy should have the same classroom responsibilities as other students.

6. Don't Let the Student Use the Seizures as an Excuse

Children with physical problems may use their condition as an excuse to avoid school responsibilities they dislike. If you conclude that a student with epilepsy is able to do the activity, let her know that you expect her to complete it in the same manner as her classmates. This means, for example, that she should be expected to turn in work on time and according to your instructions, unless there are specific reasons for making an adjustment. Similarly, you should have the same standards for classroom behavior for her as for other students, unless her behavior is a direct result of the epilepsy.

7. Monitor the Child's Understanding

Children with epilepsy may have problems with concentration in class, especially if they are prone to absence seizures in which they "blank out" for a few seconds at a time. If so, you must monitor their understanding to make sure that they understand your directions and have not missed out on crucial information.

8. Watch for Side Effects from the Medication

If the student is on medication, the school nurse or parents should inform you about the possible side effects. The most common side effects with antiseizure medication are drowsiness and lethargy, although you may also observe slurred speech, slowed performance, hyperactivity, irritability, nausea, and clumsiness. Let the parents know if you observe any of these behaviors on a consistent basis. Also, inform them if you notice a decline in the child's academic performance, attention span, or classroom behavior. Your observations may suggest to the doctor a need to change the type or amount of medication. You may have to provide the student with additional time to complete classwork or tests due to the medication's side effects.

9. Make Notes of What Happened during the Seizure

Observe the child carefully during the seizure. Jot down the date and time of the seizure, the length of time she is unconscious, and her specific behaviors before, during, and after the seizure. This information may be helpful to the parents and doctor in tracking the disorder as well as in monitoring the effects of the medication.

10. Consider Referring the Child for Special Education

Most children with epilepsy are able to learn effectively in regular classes, and thus should not be referred for special education or lower-level classes simply because of their disorder. If, however, you see signs of learning or attentional problems that are interfering with a child's academic performance, consider suggesting to the principal that the student be referred for evaluation by the school's evaluation team to determine eligibility for special education. If the student is not a candidate for special education but needs school accommodations because of her disability, she may be eligible for these special services under Section 504. (See the chapter on asthma for a fuller discussion of Section 504.)

FOR FURTHER INFORMATION

Devinsky, O. (1994). *A Guide to Understanding and Living With Epilepsy.* Philadelphia: F.A. Davis Company.

Freeman, J. M.; Vining, E.; and Pillas, D. J. (1997). *Seizures and Epilepsy in Childhood* (2d ed.). Baltimore: Johns Hopkins University Press.

Michael, R. J. (1995). *The Educator's Guide to Students With Epilepsy.* Springfield, IL: Charles C. Thomas.

Reisner, H. (1990). *Children With Epilepsy.* Rockville, MD: Woodbine House.

ORGANIZATIONS

Epilepsy Foundation of America
4351 Garden City Drive
Landover, MD 20785
1-800-EFA-1000
1-301-459-3700

The Epilepsy Foundation of America offers videos on epilepsy for elementary and secondary teachers as well as a variety of helpful publications. A publication entitled *School Alert Teacher Information Packet* is especially helpful.

See also:
   Asthma
   Autism
   Cerebral Palsy
   Low Self-Esteem

HEARING IMPAIRMENT

Hearing impairment is a general term that describes all types of hearing losses. A child who is hearing impaired is either hard of hearing—meaning she can hear some sounds, or deaf—meaning she can hear virtually no sounds, even with the use of a hearing aid. It has been estimated that 2 to 3 percent of school-aged children have some kind of hearing impairment. The majority of these students will have mild-to-moderate hearing losses, and will attend regular classes.

A hearing problem may be present at birth, or it may develop at any point during the life span. It can be caused by heredity, illness, trauma, birth complications, or medication taken by the mother during pregnancy or the child during infancy. In addition, children can develop a hearing loss as a result of exposure to extremely loud noises. In many cases, physicians are not able to pinpoint the precise cause of the hearing impairment. While a hearing loss can be inherited, most deaf parents have children with intact hearing and most deaf children have parents with intact hearing.

KINDS AND DEGREES OF HEARING IMPAIRMENT

There are three major kinds of hearing impairment. A *conductive* hearing loss results from a problem with the outer or middle ear, and usually does not involve a serious loss. It is most commonly caused by a middle ear infection, referred to as *otitis media*. A conductive hearing loss can often be corrected through medication (antibiotics) or surgery (inserting a tube in the ear to drain fluid). If it cannot be corrected, a hearing aid can usually improve the child's hearing. A *sensorineural* hearing loss is caused by a malfunction in the inner ear or in the nerve that supplies it. The loss may range from mild to profound and can rarely be corrected through surgery. A child with this kind of loss will often use a hearing aid. The third kind of hearing impairment is a *mixed* hearing loss, in which the child has characteristics of both conductive and sensorineural hearing loss. The hearing loss can be in one ear (a unilateral hearing loss) or both ears (a bilateral loss).

If you have a student with a hearing impairment, she may be described as having a specific degree of hearing loss. The degree of loss is determined

317

by how loud a sound must be for the child to hear it. Loudness is measured in decibels, abbreviated dB. A normal-hearing person can detect sounds as low as 0 dB, and normal speech ranges from 40 to 60 dB. Sounds above 90 dB can be uncomfortably loud and in some cases painful. The categories of hearing loss are listed below:

- *Slight Loss:* May have problems with faint or distant speech. May miss teacher instructions if given too quickly or if classroom is noisy. Lowest sounds child can hear are 15 to 25 dB.

- *Mild Loss:* May have difficulty understanding normal speech. Speech may be delayed, but should develop normally with proper treatment. May miss much of class discussion in noisy setting. Hearing aid or FM trainer is likely to be helpful. Lowest sounds heard are 25 to 40 dB.

- *Moderate Loss:* May have difficulty understanding even loud normal speech. Will often have speech delay and articulation problems. Will probably benefit from hearing aid and FM trainer, as well as speech and language therapy. May need extra help in reading and language arts. Lowest sounds heard are 40 to 60 dB.

- *Severe Loss:* Can hear only very loud speech. Child's speech will be immature and vocabulary will be limited. Voice may sound abnormal. Will have speech delay and articulation difficulties. Will require hearing aid as well as speech and language therapy. May require special class or school. If in regular class, will probably need individualized instruction in academic subjects. Lowest sounds heard are 60 to 90 dB.

- *Profound Loss or Deafness:* Will not be able to understand speech, even with the use of a hearing aid. Will obtain most information through visual means. Will have severe speech and language deficit and will probably need to learn sign language. Will typically attend special school. Child cannot hear sounds below 90 dB.

DETECTING A HEARING PROBLEM

Because a hearing problem is an invisible disorder that rarely causes pain or discomfort, it may go undetected for a long period. It may also be mistaken for other problems. A child with a mild hearing loss may be perceived as inattentive, uncooperative, or stubborn. In extreme cases, the child with a hearing loss may be misdiagnosed as having problems ranging from emotional disturbance to autism to mental retardation.

Early detection is essential. If a hearing loss goes undetected, the child will not receive potentially significant help in the form of medication, surgery, or a hearing aid. As a result, she may be denied exposure to speech during the critical language-learning years (birth through age 6) and suffer a delay in speaking. While a child with a severe or profound hearing loss will be identified well before she begins public school, a mild hearing loss may not be recognized until she begins school. Mild hearing problems may become apparent only amid the tumult of a classroom setting. Teachers can thus play an important role in identifying mild hearing problems.

You may see in some of your students the following signs of a possible hearing problem that suggest the need for further evaluation:

- is delayed in acquiring speech

- has a history of ear infections

- displays speech articulation problems

- watches the teacher intently when he is talking

- often asks teacher to repeat what she has said

- consistently turns one side of head toward source of sound

- speaks very loudly or softly

- gives irrelevant or unusual responses to questions

- holds hand behind ear when listening

- does not seem to hear person talking from behind her

- does not turn in reaction to loud noise

If one of your students shows a pattern of these difficulties, talk to the school nurse about screening her hearing. Most states require that schools screen students' hearing at least one or two times during elementary school, but the nurse will also screen the hearing of children at risk for hearing problems. The most common type of testing used by school nurses is pure-tone audiometry. Typically, if a child is not able to hear 30 dB at any frequency on this screening, she will be referred for further evaluation by a certified audiologist or a physician.

HEARING AIDS AND FM TRAINERS

Most children with a hearing loss can benefit from a hearing aid. Children of any age can use them successfully, so it is essential that they begin to use them as soon as the loss is detected to minimize impact on language development. A hearing aid is basically a miniature amplification system containing a microphone, a loudspeaker, and a power source. Typically, a child will wear an aid in each ear. The two most common types of hearing aids used by children are body-level aids and ear-level aids. The body-level aid consists of a small box clipped to the clothing that attaches by a cord to a receiver placed in the ear. The ear-level aid is a one-piece unit that fits in or behind the ear and generally is more effective than a body-level aid.

While a hearing aid is an essential tool for most children with hearing impairments, it does not restore normal hearing in the same way that glasses restore normal vision. A hearing aid will increase the intensity but not the clarity of the sound. In addition, it will amplify all sounds—even those that are undesirable such as shuffling of feet, moving of furniture, and wadding of paper. As a result, a child using a hearing aid may still have difficulty hearing teacher or student comments because of the background noise. Children with hearing aids may also have difficulty hearing sounds from a distance.

Another device that can improve a child's hearing in the classroom is the FM trainer. This is a wireless amplification device that transmits speech directly from the teacher's microphone to the child's hearing aid without interference from classroom noise. Students, as well as speakers at assemblies, may also use the FM trainer. In addition, the teacher can use the FM trainer to enhance the child's understanding of sound from tape recorders, projectors, and televisions by placing the device next to the speakers. The trainer must be charged every evening.

SCHOOL IMPACT

While a hearing impairment does not affect a child's reasoning capacity, it can impede her speech and language development by limiting her auditory experience. As a result, the child with a hearing impairment is more prone than average to problems with language-related skills such as reading and writing. As a general rule, the more severe the hearing impairment, the greater the learning problem.

Reading, a skill involving auditory discrimination, is particularly affected by hearing problems. The child with a hearing problem is likely to learn best using approaches that emphasize the visual approach to word recognition, rather than phonics. Stress the visual characteristics of words, as well as the use of context clues for identifying words. The "language experience" and "whole word" approaches are examples of methods of reading instruction that de-emphasize the use of phonics. While phonics should be downplayed, it should not be ignored. Hearing-impaired students need exposure to letter sounds, but they will probably have more difficulty using phonics to decode words than students with intact hearing because they may not consistently hear the differences in letter sounds.

Children with severe or profound hearing losses are likely to receive educational services during their preschool years. When a child with a hearing impairment, whether mild or severe, reaches kindergarten age, the school and the parents must arrange a suitable educational program. This decision should be based on the degree of the child's hearing impairment, her language development, and her method of communication. Many children with mild or moderate hearing losses will be able to attend regular classes, although they will surely need some individualized instruction from a special education teacher—either in the classroom or in a separate setting. They may also require speech and language therapy to improve their articulation and extend their vocabulary. For students who are deaf or have severe hearing losses, an interpreter may be required to enable them to participate in regular classes.

The method of communication generally varies with the degree of hearing loss. Students with mild or moderate hearing impairments will probably communicate orally—through speaking, lipreading, and using their residual hearing. Students with more severe hearing impairments may communicate manually—through sign language and fingerspelling. Many will use a combination of oral and manual means of communication, referred to as Total Communication. Sign language is a visual means of communication using manual symbols to convey words and concepts. American Sign Language, the language used by many deaf Americans, is a complete language with its own vocabulary, grammar, and syntax. Facial expressons also help convey meaning. Fingerspelling is a manual representation of the alphabet in which each letter is conveyed by a specific shape of the hand. This process of "air writing" is used in conjunction with sign language when a sign either does not exist or is not known.

Children with hearing impairments may present behavior problems in school. Their difficulty in understanding and communicating can generate intense stress and frustration, which may surface in school in the form of acting-out behavior, temper outbursts, and low motivation. Some react in the opposite direction by withdrawing and isolating themselves from their peers. While you can use the same disciplinary practices with hearing-impaired students that you use with your other students, bear in mind that such problems as speaking out of turn or talking to classmates when you are talking may be a direct result of the student's hearing problem. The child may simply not know that another person is speaking.

You may also notice that the child with hearing problems fatigues easily and has difficulty concentrating. This is to be expected. The act of trying to decipher what the teacher is saying while filtering out background noise and attending to visual cues can sap the child's energy and cause her to be inattentive on occasion. Try to give her some listening breaks.

HOW TEACHERS CAN HELP

The more severe the hearing impairment, the more accommodations you will have to make in the classroom. Try to implement the following strategies in a way that calls minimal attention to the hearing-impaired child.

1. Seat the Child near You

Place her at the front of the class so that she can easily see you but also see her classmates by turning around. Avoid placing her near noise sources in the classroom (for example, near the doorway or next to the heater), which will compete with your voice. Seat her so that her better ear is closer to you. Do not move around the room excessively while instructing the class, even if the child has a hearing aid. Children with a hearing aid hear best when the speaker is within 10 feet. If the class is small and there are frequent class discussions, you may want to arrange the class in a semicircle so that the hearing-impaired child can see all of her classmates. Or you might allow her to move around the classroom so that she can hear the questions and comments of other students.

2. Communicate in a Way That Maximizes the Child's Hearing

The following teacher strategies will enhance the child's hearing within the classroom:

- Check that the student is paying attention before you start speaking. If necessary, get her attention with a touch on the shoulder or a gesture.

- Make sure you are facing the class and your mouth is not obstructed when speaking.

- Speak clearly but naturally, reinforcing your comments by repeating or rephrasing. Speaking unnaturally may suggest to other students that the hearing-impaired child is slow.

- Do not overenunciate or exaggerate your mouth movements.

- Do not shout, especially if the student has a hearing aid or FM trainer, because it can hurt her ears. Rather than raising your voice, move closer to the student.

- Try to keep the classroom noise to a minimum, because a hearing aid will amplify all noise.

- Let the student know when another student is talking by pointing to the speaker or saying her name.

- Make sure that only one person speaks at a time.

- Repeat questions asked by other students, especially if they are sitting behind the hearing-impaired student.

- If the student does not understand you, repeat or rephrase what you have said, using simpler sentences and different vocabulary. You might also slow down your pace but without exaggeration. If this does not work, write it down.

- If you have difficulty understanding the student, ask her to repeat herself or write it down rather than making her think you understood.

- Periodically summarize the main points of your lesson.

3. Reinforce Your Oral Communication with Visual Aids

At the beginning of the school year, you might give the student a schedule of her day, with room numbers and teachers' names. Write on the board key information, including a brief outline of the lesson, new vocabulary, classwork and homework assignments, test and project dates, and important school announcements. Alternatively, you might give your students a handout with an outline of the class lesson and new vocabulary, or use an overhead projector to emphasize key points. Hands-on activities and visual demonstrations are also useful with hearing-impaired students, as they are with all students.

4. Enhance the Student's Ability to Lipread

While lipreading is usually associated with children with severe hearing impairments, children with mild hearing losses may also lipread because they miss specific sounds, even with a hearing aid. It is important that you avoid standing in front of the window because the resulting shadow on your face will make it harder for the student to read your lips. Try to position yourself so that your face is well lit and visible almost all the time. Remember that if you switch off the lights (for example, to show a filmstrip), the child will not be able to read your lips. Even under the best of conditions, lipreading does not ensure complete understanding. Only about one third of English sounds are visible on the lips, so many words look exactly the same to the lipreader.

5. Try to Reduce Background Noise

Encourage your students to be quiet without insisting upon silence. Ideally, a classroom with a hearing-impaired student should be located away from such noisy areas of the school as the cafeteria, the playground, the gymnasium, and shop classes. Classroom noise can also be reduced by installing wall-to-wall carpeting, sound-absorbing ceiling tile, and draperies. Special classroom lighting is also available to enhance the child's vision, which is so important to the hearing-impaired child.

6. Monitor the Student's Understanding

A child with a hearing loss may hear some sounds clearly but miss other sounds. As a result, she may misunderstand certain words in addition to not hearing others. Encourage her to tell you when she does not understand what someone has said. In addition, you will want to check periodically to make sure she understands what you have said. Do this in a way that does not single her out or embarrass her. If you are not sure whether she understood the directions, you might ask her to repeat them to you. (Occasionally ask other students to repeat directions as well.) The child's responses during class may give you some clues about her understanding. If she often asks you for information you have already given, if her questions or comments are unrelated to what is being discussed, or if she sits passively in class with a blank stare and rarely participates, this may signal that she is lost or confused. Similarly, it may reveal an unsuspected problem.

7. Encourage the Student to Participate in Class

Provide a climate in which a hearing-impaired student feels comfortable talking in class. If she is reluctant to participate, you might let her know before class that you would like to call on her for a specific question, so that she has a chance to rehearse her answer. When she does speak up, reinforce her comments with positive statements and an encouraging smile. Also, encourage her to participate in school activities and after-school activities. This may require that you assume the role of a social director. The student may need some help with social skills, so you may want to give her some tips on what to say and do with her peers.

8. Have the Student Teach the Class Some Sign Language

If you have a hearing-impaired child in your class who uses sign language, have her teach you and her classmates how to sign some basic words. You may be surprised by how fast your students learn the signs. This will help promote the child's self-esteem by presenting her as competent in a skill not possessed by her classmates. In addition, other children may be more understanding of the difficulty of having to communicate nonverbally.

9. Assign the Child a Classroom "Buddy" with Intact Hearing

Find a responsible student who will not feel burdened by the task of helping out a classmate. She may even feel a sense of importance from this responsibility. Let her know that her job is to alert the hearing-impaired student of instructions, page numbers, and classroom or schedule changes, and to inform her when other students are reading aloud. If the hearing-impaired student is looking down when the teacher is talking, the buddy should tap her on the shoulder to get her to look up.

10. Arrange for the Child to Obtain Class Notes from Others

The child with a hearing impairment will have a difficult time taking notes at the same time that she is trying to lipread. Enable the student to give her full attention to the teacher by giving her a copy of your notes or arranging to photocopy another student's notes that you have checked for accuracy.

11. Make Sure the Child's Hearing Aid Works Properly

The hearing aid should be checked every morning to make sure it is turned on and has sufficient power and clarity. The parents can show you how to do this simple task. Suggest to the parents that they send in extra batteries to be kept at school. (Keep them out of reach of young children, since they can be toxic if swallowed.) The older child should assume responsibility for checking the hearing aid, but you may need to do this for the younger child. Encourage the student to let you know if her aid is not working.

12. Make Use of the Computer

Computer-assisted instruction is well suited for use with the hearing impaired because of the visual approach to instruction and its ability to move at the pace of the student.

13. Make Adjustments When Showing Films or Videos

Try to obtain videos and filmstrips that are captioned. If this is not possible, check that the sound quality is optimal and have the student sit near the speakers. If she relies on lipreading, provide assistance in situations where lipreading is difficult or impossible (for example, movies or audiotapes). This may mean giving her a script or summary, or even using an interpreter. If the child is using an FM trainer, you should be able to connect the projector (audio output) to the trainer.

14. Make Sure That the Child's Vision Has Been Checked

The child with hearing problems will rely on her vision to pick up cues from the environment. This is particularly true of the child with a severe hearing loss who lipreads. A visual problem may limit the information she gains from use of her eyes and place her at an even greater disadvantage.

15. Make Optimal Use of an Interpreter

The role of the interpreter is to convey in sign language everything you say in class, not to provide her own explanations. Meet with her ahead of class to review the lesson and key vocabulary. When using an interpreter, speak in a clear voice at a normal rate, directing your comments to the students rather than the interpreter. Bear in mind that the interpreter will need occasional breaks. To obtain the name of an interpreter in your area, contact the Registry of Interpreters for the Deaf (1-301-608-0050) or consult the Yellow Pages.

16. Obtain Help from Others

Keep in mind that you are a part of a team that is available to help the child. This may include a teacher of the hearing impaired or deaf, a resource room teacher, a speech-language pathologist, an educational audiologist, and an interpreter. Do not hesitate to call upon them for assistance. Consulting with teachers is part of their job. Your best resource, of course, may be the student's parents. Communicate regularly with them and consider sending them advance notice of materials to be covered during the coming week.

FOR FURTHER INFORMATION

Maxon, A. (1992). *The Hearing-Impaired Child: Infancy Through High School Years.* Boston: Andover Medical Publishers.

Medwid, D. J. (1995). *Kid-Friendly Parenting With Deaf and Hard-of-Hearing Children.* Washington, DC: Clerc Books.

Moores, D. F. (1995). *Educating the Deaf: Psychology, Principles, and Practices.* Boston: Houghton Mifflin.

Ross, M. (ed.) (1990). *Hearing-Impaired Children in the Mainstream.* Parkton, MD: York Press.

Wilson, J. J. (1996). *The Classroom Notetaker: How to Organize a Program Serving Students With Hearing Impairments.* Washington, DC: Alexander Graham Bell Association for the Deaf.

ORGANIZATIONS

Alexander Graham Bell Association for the Deaf
3417 Volta Place, NW
Washington, DC 20007-2778
1-202-337-5220

National Association of the Deaf
814 Thayer Avenue
Silver Spring, MD 20910-4500
1-301-587-1788

National Information Center on Deafness
Gallaudet University
800 Florida Avenue, NE
Washington, DC 20002-3695
1-202-651-5051

See also:
    Auditory Processing Problem
    Reading Disability
    Speech and Language Problems
    Spelling Problem

Spina Bifida

Spina bifida is a birth condition characterized by the incomplete development of the spine. Literally meaning "open spine," spina bifida results from the failure of the spine to close properly during the early stages of pregnancy. It occurs in one of every 1,000 newborns, making it the most common permanently disabling birth defect.

While there is no cure for spina bifida, medical advances enable persons with this condition to live long and productive lives. Many children with spina bifida are able to be educated in regular classes. At the same time, children with spina bifida can have significant physical complications as well as learning problems, so it is important that teachers with a student with this condition learn about its classroom implications.

PHYSICAL COMPLICATIONS

There are three types of spina bifida, and children with this problem can present very diverse medical and academic profiles. Some children with spina bifida may be indistinguishable physically and academically from their classmates; others may have significant medical and learning problems. Those who do have physical complications may experience some of the following problems: complete or partial paralysis of the lower extremities, loss of bladder and bowel control, and loss of skin sensation. In addition, most children born with spina bifida also develop hydrocephalus, the accumulation of fluid in the brain, which may give rise to learning problems and even mental retardation if untreated.

Various medical procedures may be necessary to correct these problems, including surgery on the spine, leg, or foot; insertion of a shunt (tube) to drain fluid from the brain to the abdomen or chest; and management of bladder and bowel functioning. Because of these surgical procedures, the student with spina bifida may be absent from school for long periods.

A child with spina bifida will often need crutches, braces, or a wheelchair to get around due to the paralysis of the lower extremities. If so, his school must be adapted to allow him access to different parts of the school. (Section 504 of the Rehabilitation Act of 1973 requires that public schools be accessible to the disabled.) This may mean adding a ramp, moving a course to ground level, or installing an elevator. Students with spina bifida who have motor problems may also receive physical therapy, occupational therapy, and adaptive physical education, which may be provided in the school.

Many children with spina bifida lack bladder and bowel control as a result of nerve damage, and may require the use of diapers. Bladder management procedures may have to be developed for use at school. Some require the insertion of a tube to allow the child to empty his bladder, a process called catheterization. For students with spina bifida who require catheterization at school, and who are eligible for special education, it must be provided at public expense. This is a result of a 1984 United States Supreme Court ruling that "clean intermittent catheterization" is necessary to help the child benefit from and have access to special education, and thus must be provided by school districts in the same way they provide transportation to special education students.

Catheterization is a painless procedure that provides comfort to children with bladder difficulties, lessens the chance of an accident, and helps prevent infection. It is usually done once a day in school at about noon and takes just one or two minutes to perform. The ideal is for the child to catheterize himself. Children as young as 6 or 7 can learn to perform this procedure, while others may not be comfortable with self-catheterization until the age of 10. If the child is unable to catheterize himself, the school nurse is the most appropriate school staff member to perform this procedure. It is an easy procedure to perform and can be learned in about 20 minutes. Some teachers have learned the procedure. Even under the best of circumstances, however, accidents will happen, since the child with nerve damage lacks control. You might suggest that the child wear a watch with an alarm that goes off when catheterization is needed.

SCHOOL IMPACT

Most students with spina bifida have average intelligence, although their ability levels can range from intellectually gifted to mentally retarded. Their verbal skills are usually better than their nonverbal skills. They may be articulate and use sophisticated vocabulary, but their verbal facility may camouflage some non-verbal deficiencies.

Many children with spina bifida display poor visual-perceptual and perceptual-motor skills, so tasks requiring eye-hand coordination can be more difficult for them than for their peers. They may be slow to perform tasks involving their arms or hands. This may manifest itself in the form of problems with handwriting as well as self-care tasks. For example, students with spina bifida may have difficulty finishing written assignments on time and completing tests within the allotted time. They may also struggle in learning to catheterize themselves because of their fine-motor difficulties. In addition, some may have problems learning to manipulate a wheelchair or a walker.

In terms of academic skills, children with spina bifida tend to be more proficient in reading and spelling than in other academic areas. Math is often their most difficult subject. Research suggests that as many as 75 percent of children with spina bifida have difficulties with math. They may experience a range of other school-related problems, although the profile of problems will differ for each child. Difficulties may surface in the following areas: retention of information, expressive and receptive language, memory, attention, impulsivity, sequencing, organization, and reasoning. These difficulties may be apparent even when the child is of average or above-average intelligence. In terms of motivation and behavior, students with spina bifida do not appear to be different from other students. Studies indicate that children with spina bifida generally work as hard as other students and do not present behavior problems beyond the norm.

HOW TEACHERS CAN HELP

If you are feeling apprehensive at the prospect of coping with the problems of a child with spina bifida, bear in mind that he is unlikely to have all of the physical and academic problems described above. If he does present a wide array of problems that seem daunting, remember that you are not alone in handling his problems. The nurse, parents, and child's physician are key members of the team working with the student, and you can call upon them for assistance. In addition, if a student with spina bifida has many physical complications, the school may provide a full- or part-time teacher aide to assist him.

You can take the following steps in the classroom to ease the child's adjustment:

1. Maintain Ongoing Communication with the Student's Parents

When you and the school nurse meet with the parents, preferably before school begins, you may want to ask the following questions:

- Does your child use crutches, braces, or a wheelchair?

- Does he lack sensation in any areas of his body?

- Does he have control of his bladder? His bowels?

- Will he alert his teacher when he has lost control of his bladder or his bowels?

- Should he be encouraged to have a bowel movement at a particular time during the day?

- Does he wear diapers? Will you be sending in a change of clothing or extra diapers?

- Does he need to be catheterized during the school day? At what time? Can he do this himself?

- Will he be taking medication in school? What kind, and what is the dosage? What are the potential side effects?

- Does he have a shunt? What signs will I see that suggest that the shunt is not functioning properly?

- Does he have any restrictions in his diet?

- Does he have any physical restrictions?

- What particular school-related problems is he likely to have? What have you found to be helpful ways of dealing with these problems?

- Under what circumstances do you want to be contacted?

2. Anticipate Potential Obstacles if the Student Uses a Wheelchair

Make sure that field-trip destinations can accommodate individuals in wheelchairs.

3. Be Alert for Signs of a Problem with the Shunt

If the student does have a shunt, you must ensure that he avoids rough physical activity that could knock the shunt out of place. Also, be aware of the possibility of shunt failure. The following symptoms could suggest a malfunctioning shunt and should be referred to the school nurse: headache, nausea, vomiting, neck pain, drowsiness, loss of appetite, irritability, and visual disturbances. A blocked shunt may also cause a seizure. In addition, consider contacting the parents if you notice some regression in the child's academic or social functioning (for example, deterioration in handwriting or social withdrawal). That, too, could signal a problem with the shunt or another physical concern. The child with spina bifida may also take medication. If so, find out from the nurse the potential side effects of these medications and alert parents if you observe them.

4. Monitor the Child for Injuries in Areas of the Body Where He Lacks Sensation

If he lacks sensation in parts of his body, he could injure himself without being aware of it. For example, a child lacking sensation below the waist might sit on a pencil and poke himself, yet not be aware of it. Similarly, he might develop sores from the braces but not know it. If he is wheelchair-bound, he may be prone to develop pressure sores. To avoid this, remind the student to shift positions often while sitting in the wheelchair.

5. Show Sensitivity to the Child's Physical Problems

Having bowel and bladder problems can be emotionally difficult for a child, especially when classmates become aware of these problems. Be understanding of the child's feelings and concerns and try to minimize peer problems. Encourage the child to develop an awareness of odor if he is incontinent and to alert the teacher that he needs to leave the room. Suggest a quick and easy signal that he can use to inform you that he will be out of the class.

6. Promote Self-Care Skills

As with many children with orthopedic handicaps, children with spina bifida may become excessively dependent on others to do things they are capable of doing themselves. It is important to their self-esteem, as well as their general functioning, to become as independent as possible in caring for themselves. Encourage the child to handle as much of his bladder and bowel management as he can and praise him for his efforts. If the student needs help changing clothes in school, give some assistance, but avoid doing it for him. In addition, try to involve him in the activities of the classroom as much as possible, so that he feels a sense of belonging and classmates perceive him as a regular participant. This is crucial to his personal and social growth.

7. Consider Modifying the Student's Handwriting Requirements

See the discussion of handwriting in the chapter on Tourette syndrome, in the How Teachers Can Help section.

8. Consider Eligibility for Special Services

The student with spina bifida may have academic problems that warrant special education. If you believe that these problems warrant individualized instruction, talk with your principal about referring him for evaluation by the school district's evaluation team. If found eligible for special education, he may be recommended for a regular class (with or without resource room help), or he may be found to need a more restrictive setting such as a full-time special education class. As an alternative to the special education route, you may want to refer him for a Section 504 evaluation, so that he is eligible for special services and school accommodations to compensate for his disability. (See the chapter on asthma for a discussion of Section 504.)

FOR FURTHER INFORMATION

Bloom, B. A., and Seljeskog, E. S. (1988). *A Parent's Guide to Spina Bifida.* Minneapolis: University of Minnesota Press.

Rowley-Kelly, F. L., and Reigel, D. H. (eds.) (1993). *Teaching the Student With Spina Bifida.* Baltimore: Paul H. Brookes.

ORGANIZATIONS

Spina Bifida Association of America
4590 MacArthur Boulevard, NW, Suite 250
Washington, DC 20007-4226
1-800-621-3141
1-202-944-3285

The Spina Bifida Association of America has booklets available for parents and teachers, including *Learning Disabilities and the Person With Spina Bifida* and *Parent/Teacher Packet.*

See also:
    Asthma
    Cerebral Palsy
    Handwriting Problem
    Tourette Syndrome

TOURETTE SYNDROME

Tourette syndrome (TS), also called Tourette's syndrome, is a neurological disorder that can baffle and frustrate the most experienced teachers. It is characterized by tics, which can take the form of repeated and involuntary rapid body movements (motor tics) or uncontrollable verbalizations (vocal tics). While it is not uncommon for children to have a single tic for a short period (called transient tic disorder), the child with TS typically exhibits multiple tics involving parts of the face or body as well as vocal sounds. This disorder can present significant issues of classroom management for the teacher and important issues of self-esteem and peer acceptance for the student.

Tourette syndrome was first described in 1825 by Georges Gilles de la Tourette, a French neurologist for whom the disorder was named. A hereditary disorder, TS is transmitted by a single abnormal gene that causes changes in one or more neurotransmitters in the brain. A person who inherits this gene has a 50 percent chance of passing it on to his or her child. About a third of those who inherit the gene do not exhibit symptoms of the disorder. Boys are three times more likely than girls to have TS.

BEHAVIORAL AND ACADEMIC PROFILE

While the symptoms of TS vary from person to person, most people with this disorder have mild cases. The majority of students with TS will be able to learn effectively in regular classes, and most will lead productive and independent lives as adults. The symptoms generally lessen with age. Research indicates that 20 to 30 percent of children with TS outgrow this problem in their teens or early twenties.

The behaviors you see with TS will differ with each child, and in most cases will be relatively mild. Typically, a child with TS will exhibit such behaviors as rapid blinking of the eyes, twitching of the mouth, or jerking of the head. Sometimes, the behaviors are more complex and disruptive, such as kicking, touching other people, or jumping. Involuntary vocalizations might include meaningless sounds or such noises as repeated throat clearing, grunting, or yelping—or using words or phrases out of context and in a repeated manner. On rare occasions, the person with TS will use socially inappropriate or offensive language involuntarily (for example, obscenities). Called *coprolalia,* this use of offensive language is actually quite rare, although it has been sensationalized in the media.

These behaviors may wax and wane in intensity and may be replaced by other behaviors. They may even disappear for weeks or months at a time— and they are not always present. For example, many persons with TS do not exhibit tics during sleep or periods of intense concentration. A surgeon with TS reports that he is able to operate for hours at a time without displaying any tics.

While these behaviors are involuntary and unintentional, it is not true that people with TS lack complete control of these behaviors. It is more like an irresistible urge, similar to the urge to scratch a mosquito bite. Many can suppress the tics for a short period of time, but eventually they must be released. When they are finally expressed, there may be an even stronger outburst than if expressed immediately. In school, a child may be able to hold off on releasing the tics until he can get to the privacy of a bathroom or the nurse's office.

Tourette syndrome may affect a child's school performance. While children with TS typically fall within the same IQ range as other children, many have learning and attentional problems. They may find it hard to persist with tasks for concentrated periods, stay in their seats, and organize their work. By some estimates, about half of children with TS meet the criteria for attention deficit disorder (ADD) and, in fact, many TS children are misdiagnosed as having ADD. This can cause a problem because stimulant medication often prescribed for ADD can increase tics.

Students with TS may also have problems controlling their impulses; they may be easily frustrated and quick to lose their temper. Some may exhibit aggressive or socially inappropriate acts and thus have difficulties gaining acceptance from peers. They may also be prone to obsessive thoughts or compulsive behaviors. For example, a student learning to write letters may go over a letter so many times that his pencil tears a hole in the paper.

The social and emotional problems that often accompany TS can be more distressing for the student than the physical symptoms or the academic difficulties. Many children with TS often go undiagnosed for years. During that time, they may be seen as having psychological or emotional problems. Some teachers may perceive the child as simply nervous. Others may view him as seeking attention. Still others may view him as an obnoxious child who is determined to make life miserable for teachers. The child's parents may even see the child as strange or oppositional and treat him punitively in a misguided and futile effort to get him to stop. The ridicule and rejection a child is likely to receive from peers may be the most hurtful of all—especially during adolescence when peer acceptance is so important.

Some persons with Tourette syndrome find out only as adults what was plaguing them as children. Jim Eisenreich, a professional baseball player, began showing signs of the disorder at the age of 6 in the form of twitches and snorting noises. He was 23 years old when he learned that what he had was TS. Even then, the team he was playing for believed that he was only suffering from "stage fright" and kept him from taking medication to alleviate the symptoms.

DIAGNOSING AND TREATING TOURETTE SYNDROME

TS is diagnosed by observing the child's behaviors and reviewing the history of their onset. There are no medical tests to detect TS, although the child may undergo tests to rule out other problems. It is not surprising, then, that most cases of TS are not initially discovered by a physician. The diagnosis often comes as a relief for many persons with TS, because they finally have an explanation for their unusual behavior, as well as a medical opinion that their behaviors are unintentional and uncontrollable. Prior to receiving the diagnosis, many with TS come to accept the perceptions of others that they are different or even disturbed.

Because the diagnosis of TS relies largely on behavioral observations, teachers can play a key role in detecting this disorder. In fact, teachers are often the first to spot the problem. If you observe a student in your class displaying behaviors suggestive of Tourette syndrome, begin to observe him systematically, jotting down the form and frequency of the tics, and the situations and times they occur. You may also consider asking the school nurse or school psychologist to observe the child. If you continue to have concerns after seeking an additional opinion, contact the parents to inform them of your observations.

While there is at present no cure for TS, medication can be helpful in lessening its more extreme symptoms. Halperidol is often the medication of choice because of its effectiveness in reducing tics. But the medications typically prescribed can have significant side effects and thus are reserved for the more severe cases. The medication may cause the child to exhibit drowsiness or sluggish thinking, have memory problems, or withdraw socially. Some children even become school phobic during the initial stage of the medication.

It is important that you be informed when a child is beginning to take medication and that you report any side effects you observe to the parents. The physician may want to alter the medication to lessen the side effects, and will rely partially on reports of the child's classroom behaviors to make this decision. You may be asked by the child's parent or physician to complete a checklist to help monitor his behavior while he is on the medication. In addition to medication, some children with TS have benefited from the use of behavior therapy, relaxation techniques, and biofeedback. Family therapy may also be helpful where the disorder places a strain on family members.

HOW TEACHERS CAN HELP

Teaching a child with TS can be a challenge. While many of his behaviors are not under his control and thus not open to change, there are steps you can take to make the child feel more comfortable in the classroom and accepted by his classmates.

1. Support the Parents

Parents of children with TS may have almost as difficult a time with the child's disorder as does the child. In addition to possibly feeling guilty because of the genetic component to TS, they may be distressed and perplexed by their child's unusual behaviors. Your support and understanding will help ease their discomfort and give them confidence that the child will be treated with care and concern. You will surely want to meet with them early in the year to gain information on the particular problems their child may present, effective and ineffective ways of responding, and potential side effects to any medication he may be taking.

2. Talk with the Student in Private

Let him know that you are aware of his medical problem—that you understand that he lacks control over his tics and that he is not misbehaving. This will be important to the student with TS, since he is probably sensitive to others' perceiving him as strange or uncooperative. Ask him if he has any suggestions about what you can do to make him feel comfortable in class.

3. Talk with Your Class about Tourette Syndrome

Be sure to get permission from the student and his parents before talking with the class, and ask the student whether he would like to be there for the discussion. You may want to invite the student and his parents to join in the discussion, although the presentation should be relatively brief. Classmates are likely to be sympathetic if they come to understand that the child's behaviors have a medical basis and are not under his control. The Tourette Syndrome Association (see address at end of this chapter) offers a brochure called "Matthew and the Tics" for teachers to read to their students, or for students to read on their own. If you observe classmates who are teasing or posing problems for the student with TS, take them aside and try to elicit their understanding and cooperation. If another student is making noises in class, try to get him to stop, because the child with TS may think the student is making fun of him. The students are likely to look to you for guidance about how to respond to the child with TS, so try to model an understanding, accepting approach.

4. Avoid Drawing Attention to the Tics

In most cases, the tics will not be disruptive to your teaching or to the other students. The best response to these tics is no response at all. Drawing attention to the tics will only make the child more self-conscious about his disorder and create a social barrier between him and other students. Where tics are disruptive and hard to ignore, try to find ways to lessen their disruptiveness. (For example, place a piece of foam rubber on the desk of a child who compulsively taps his pencil.)

5. Give the Student Permission to Leave the Classroom at Any Time

The student with TS may be able to hold off on expressing his tics for a short time, but he may need a place he can go to when he feels himself losing control to release his symptoms and avoid the embarrassment of doing so in public. This might be the bathroom, the nurse's office, or a corner of the library. A study carrel in your classroom might provide a modicum of privacy for the student. Arrange a special signal the student can use to alert you that he needs to leave the room.

6. Provide Opportunities for the Child to Release Excess Energy

Like the student with ADD, the student with TS may have difficulty sitting still for a long period. In addition, the tension resulting from having to sit quietly may worsen the TS symptoms. Allow the child to move around at several points during the day by, for example, letting him go to the water fountain or bathroom or serve as classroom messenger.

7. Don't Hesitate to Set Limits

Teachers must walk a fine line with a student with TS, trying to be understanding without being overprotective. In some cases, this may mean disciplining him in the same way you would other students. If you sense that the child is acting inappropriately in a way that is under his control, don't hesitate to set firm limits or use disciplinary measures while suggesting alternative ways of behaving. In addition, allow him to participate in the normal activities of your classroom, including field trips, class plays, and assemblies, and encourage independence and responsibility.

8. Look for Opportunities for the Child to Succeed in the Classroom

The child with TS is often lacking in confidence, and may not feel accepted by his classmates. Take advantage of his strengths and interests to find areas where he can shine in the classroom. For example, if he is a good reader, he may be able to help others in the class who are not. Or if he has a special skill, encourage him to give a demonstration to the class.

9. Make Accommodations if the Student Has Handwriting Difficulties

Many students with TS have poor or illegible handwriting because of problems in controlling the movements of their hands. If so, find ways to limit the amount of material the student must write by hand, or give him extra time. Consider using worksheets that require limited writing, and avoid making him recopy assignments that are done sloppily. Allow him to decide whether he wants to write in manuscript or cursive. You may find that he can use a computer more effectively than he can write by hand. If a secondary school student with TS is not able to take notes in class with sufficient speed, allow him to photocopy another student's notes or provide him with copies of your own notes. If your class includes lectures, offer him the chance to tape your lessons.

10. Provide Test-Taking Alternatives

The student's tics and handwriting difficulties may place him at a significant disadvantage when taking timed tests, so that the test results fail to reflect what the student knows. In addition, the student's vocal tics may be disruptive to other students taking a test. Consider the following options: extra time to complete the test, an alternate test setting such as the resource room or the library, or taking an oral exam rather than a written one.

11. Consider Recommending the Student for a School Evaluation

While most TS students can learn effectively in regular classes, some may warrant special education. The student with TS should be considered for evaluation if the disorder is presenting significant obstacles to learning. If determined eligible for special education, he may receive individualized instruction either in the regular classroom or in a special education class. As an alternative, the student may qualify to receive special accommodations in school through Section 504 (see discussion of Section 504 in the chapter on asthma).

FOR FURTHER INFORMATION

Haerle, T. (1992). *Children With Tourette Syndrome*. Rockville, MD: Woodbine House.

Shimberg, E. F. (1995). *Living With Tourette's Syndrome*. New York: Fireside Books.

ORGANIZATIONS

Tourette Syndrome Association
42-40 Bell Boulevard
Bayside, NY 11361-2820
1-718-224-2999

The Tourette Syndrome Association offers many useful publications for teachers and parents.

See also:
    Asthma
    Attention Deficit Disorder
    Handwriting Problem
    Low Self-Esteem
    The School-Phobic Student

Visual Impairment

Children who are visually impaired have less than normal vision after correction. Their impairment can take a variety of forms. Some have difficulty seeing close up, while others have difficulty seeing far away. Some can see well straight ahead, but have a narrow field of vision. Some can make out the form of a person or object, but cannot identify who or what they are seeing. Some can distinguish light and dark, but see little else. Some—the totally blind—see nothing at all. These students—even those who are blind—often attend regular classes, and may require you to make significant accommodations.

WHAT IS ABNORMAL VISION?

To understand abnormal vision, we must understand normal vision. Vision is typically measured in terms of visual acuity, or how clearly you see. A child with normal eyesight is said to have 20/20 vision. This means that he can see as well from 20 feet away as a person with normal vision can see at 20 feet. The larger the second number, the poorer the child's vision. For example, a child with 20/50 vision can see at a distance of 20 feet only what a normally sighted person can see at a distance of 50 feet. Vision is better than normal if the second number is less than 20. A child's vision is impaired if his acuity is significantly worse than 20/20 or if he has a loss of visual field—the area seen by a person without moving his eyes or head. Typically, most people have a field of vision of almost 180 degrees when looking straight ahead.

The degree of a child's visual impairment depends on the type of problem, the age when the loss occurs, and his environmental experiences. A child who is visually impaired but is able to read either regular or large print is said to be *partially sighted* or to have *low vision*. He may require special education, as well as specialized aids, to use his vision effectively. A child whose vision is 20/200 or less in the better eye with correction is said to be *legally blind*. He should be able to count fingers placed one foot in front of his face but will probably not be able to read regular print. A child is also said to be legally blind if his vision is better than 20/200 but he has a field of vision of 20 degrees or less. A child who is *totally blind* has no vision at all, and will

341

not even perceive light and dark. He will learn through the use of braille or other nonvisual media.

A child can develop a visual impairment for a variety of reasons. Vision may be affected by damage to any of the following components of the visual system: the eye itself; the optic nerve, which carries visual information from the eye to the brain; or the visual cortex of the brain. The eye is a highly complicated organ, and damage to any of its parts—including the cornea, pupil, lens, iris, and retina—may impede vision. A visual impairment may be present at birth or develop later, and may result from disease, heredity, accident, injury, or a congenital defect. Children with multiple disabilities are often visually impaired. Figure 3–2 lists some common myths about vision.

DETECTING A VISUAL IMPAIRMENT

About one in every five children needs glasses, so it is essential that children be screened early for eye problems. In addition, amblyopia can be prevented if treatment is begun by age 3, which reinforces the importance of early identification and preschool screening. The vast majority of vision problems can be detected through the routine screening procedures conducted by pediatricians and schools. Vision screening by the school nurse may also be warranted if a student begins to have unexplained problems with schoolwork.

You may see the following signs of a possible vision problem in the classroom; these signs may suggest the need for a screening or in-depth examination:

- has jerky eye movements
- tilts head consistently to one side
- favors one eye over another
- has difficulty coordinating eye movements (for example, one eye tends to wander)
- holds reading material close to or far from face
- hesitates to participate in visually demanding tasks
- has difficulty reading or copying from chalkboard
- confuses letters while reading (for example, *c* and *e*, or *g* and *q*)

FIGURE 3–2

COMMON MYTHS ABOUT VISION

1. Contrary to common belief, you do not conserve your vision by limiting use of your eyes. You should not discourage your students from using their eyes, although there may be exceptions for particular children.

2. Contrary to common belief, visual problems do not simply get better with time. It is important that children have routine eye exams, especially during the first ten years of life, and receive treatment if necessary as soon as possible.

3. Contrary to common belief, "legally blind" does not mean the absence of vision. In fact, the vast majority of children who are legally blind have some usable vision.

4. Contrary to common belief, a student will not damage his eyes by holding a book close to his face. Indeed, a visually impaired child may need to do this in order to read the print. Similarly, there is little chance of harm to one's eyes from sitting as close as one foot from the TV.

5. Contrary to common belief, children can read in dim light without hurting their eyes. Children's eyes naturally adapt to different light and distance conditons when reading. Some children with such eye conditions as albinism and cataracts may even read more comfortably with dim lights.

6. Contrary to common belief, all visual impairments cannot be corrected by glasses. Some children continue to have limited vision, even with glasses.

7. Contrary to common belief, glasses or contact lenses do not weaken the eyes, nor do they heal eye problems, although they may improve amblyopia. This is a condition in which vision is reduced in one eye because the brain suppresses images from that eye to avoid double vision.

■ rubs eyes often

■ squints or blinks eyes frequently

■ complains often of dizziness or headaches

■ has difficulty aligning written work

Some visual problems can be corrected easily with glasses or contact lenses. If amblyopia has been diagnosed, one eye is frequently patched to strengthen the "lazy eye." At times, eye surgery is required to correct a muscle imbalance or to remove a cataract. If a student in your class has amblyopia and wears glasses, it is important that you encourage him to wear his glasses consistently, because they can improve his vision.

Poor eyesight has been claimed by some to be one of the causes of reading disabilities. Research does not support this. The American Academy of Ophthalmology has issued a statement asserting that learning-disabled children are no more prone to vision problems than normally achieving children. In particular, the tendency to "reverse" letters is not usually caused by a vision problem. Nonetheless, special eye exercises and visual training programs are offered by some optometrists for children with learning disabilities. These programs are of questionable value inasmuch as there is little evidence showing long-term gains in reading skills from these programs.

SCHOOL IMPACT

The educational needs of a visually impaired student will depend on the nature and degree of his impairment, his intellectual ability, and his motivation. Many students with visual problems can perform successfully in regular classes, although you may need to modify the curriculum and adapt your teaching approach. Some students may be able to attend regular classes but need the services of a resource teacher or vision specialist to provide either academic assistance or help in using special aids and materials. Others may require a full-time special education class. Some school districts require that a student's visual acuity be below a specified level to qualify for special education, while others require only that the child have a visual impairment that affects learning and warrants special help or materials.

About half of totally blind children have developmental disabilties, including cerebral palsy, mental retardation, and hearing impairment. The educational programs for many of these students must emphasize daily living skills, communication, mobility, and the use of special aids. These programs will most likely take place in full-time special education classes.

While visually impaired students may be restricted in their ability to obtain information, they may compensate for this limitation by learning to use their other senses efficiently. In particular, they may develop a heightened sense of hearing. They will probably be curious and ask many questions, trying to elicit information that is apparent to their classmates but eludes them. While language development may be delayed with severely visually impaired children, eventually most can be expected to achieve normal language skills by the time they begin kindergarten. You may observe selective weaknesses, however, with visually impaired students. For example, some will have difficulties with abstract reasoning tasks, while others will have problems with such spatial concepts as "above," "below," "behind," and "under."

Visually impaired students often exhibit poor social skills. They may lack understanding of classroom protocol and act in ways that turn off their classmates. Their gestures may be immature and their reactions may be inappropriate. It is not surprising that some children with severe visual impairments have social difficulties, since so much of our social learning derives from visual information. In addition to lacking visual models of social behavior, they may miss critical visual feedback, such as facial expressions and gestures, so that their responses may appear unusual. If a visually impaired student appears unresponsive to another student, it may be because he is unaware of that student's presence. The student may also appear bored or inattentive on occasion; this may signal that he is confused about the lesson or an assignment, or that he simply has difficulty maintaining eye contact.

Students with severe visual problems will need assistance in learning how to get around school. While the goal is to help the child become as independent as possible within the school setting and to allow him to participate in the full range of school activities, this should be balanced with a concern for the student's safety. A vision specialist or an expert in orientation and mobility—typically a professional working for the state, who consults with teachers of students who are visually impaired—may familiarize the student with the layout of the classroom and school, as well as the use of specialized techniques of travel. The student will learn to use all his senses to take in information about the setting so he can negotiate the school environment. He may be provided with a cane as well as an electronic device that allows him to detect nearby obstacles.

Occasions may arise in which you or a classmate must assist the student in getting around. If he is very familiar with the building, you may want to let him walk the halls on his own, and you may be surprised at how well he is able to get around. It is unlikely that a visually impaired student will run into the wall. If he is in an unfamiliar place, offer your arm so that he holds it right above the elbow (a younger child may hold your wrist). Make sure you steer him away from obstacles and tell him whether stairs and curbs are going up or down. When giving directions, use specific and clear language. For example, rather than saying "over there," say "about 6 feet to your left."

The school cafeteria is another potential trouble spot, and thus requires some advance planning. The visually impaired student may need some instruction in lunchroom basics, including the location of the trays and garbage cans, and where to stand on line. He will also need some initial help in finding his seat. The cafeteria workers must be instructed to inform the student of the menu choices, as well as unexpected obstacles in the cafeteria. The student may also need some help figuring out where the food is on his plate. If so, a student or staff member can tell him at what "time" the food is located on his plate (for example, the potatoes are at one o'clock).

AIDS FOR THE VISUALLY IMPAIRED STUDENT

A wide variety of aids, materials, and equipment is available to help visually impaired students compensate for their limitations. Some, like braille, have been around for decades, while others are relatively new—for example, the talking computer. A vision specialist can assist you in obtaining suitable aids for your student or adapting your standard classroom materials. Because of these aids, many visually impaired students can attend regular classes, participate in a range of school activities, and use regular textbooks.

The following is a list of some of the more common aids used by visually impaired students:

■ *Optical aids:* Students can enlarge the print of reading material by using hand-held magnifiers or wearing very thick glasses that magnify what they see. They may also use small telescopes in school to view the chalkboards or class demonstrations. A student using a telescope to see the board should sit in the center row, a few seats back from the front.

- *Large-print books:* While the above optical devices will allow some visually impaired students to use regular-print books, some may still need large-print books. A child with better than 20/200 vision who can read letters a quarter-inch in size should be encouraged to use large-print materials rather than braille. If you have books that must be converted into large type, give copies to the vision specialist, who can determine the required size of print and arrange for the books' conversion.

- *Talking books:* The National Library Service for the Blind and Physically Handicapped lends braille and recorded materials to visually impaired persons at no charge. Recording for the Blind & Dyslexic lends recorded education books, including textbooks, to individuals with "print disabilities." (See addresses of organizations at end of chapter.) These tapes are called "talking books." Give a list of the books you need taped (or enlarged or brailled) to the vision specialist as soon as possible to ensure that the student has the materials in a timely manner.

- *Closed-circuit television (CCTV):* Where large-print books or audiotapes are not available, closed-circuit televisions allow visually impaired students to greatly enlarge printed material and project it onto a television screen. A closed-circuit TV resembles a regular TV with the addition of a camera. It is easy to use: the student places a page of print under the camera and adjusts for focus, brightness, and contrast. An enlarged version will appear on the television screen. The advantage of CCTV is that the student is not restricted to large-print materials.

- *Computer:* Computer technology has opened up a world of information to visually impaired students and greatly expanded the communication options. Computers can modify the size of the print on the screen as well as the contrast and brightness to enhance the student's ability to read the print. They can also be programmed to scan the page at a desired speed and focus on particular parts of the screen. Some computers can even read orally, with speech synthesizers transforming print on the computer screen into speech. In addition, many printers can produce documents in large print. Because of these and other computer innovations, it is important that visually impaired students learn keyboarding, which may be done in a regular or special education class. Third grade is not too early for children to be learning keyboarding skills.

- *Specialized reading aids:* An optacon is a device that converts print into a tactile format, so that it can be read by the visually impaired. Placing acetate over reading material darkens the print and heightens the contrast so the document is easier to read. Bookstands are available to hold a book close to the reader's eyes, thus eliminating the discomfort of having to hold the book.

- *Specialized writing aids:* Various materials can facilitate the writing process for the visually impaired student. Black felt-tip pens produce thick lines that are easy to see. Bold-line paper helps students who have difficulty seeing the lines on regular paper, while raised-line paper makes it easier for students to write on the line or construct a graph.

- *Specialized math aids:* Some teachers may use an abacus to help visually impaired students learn to compute, and concrete objects to help them grasp math concepts. A talking calculator is a regular calculator, except that it communicates through speech your numerical entries and the result.

- *Specialized gym equipment:* The beeper ball is an example of equipment that can be used with students with limited vision. The beeper inside the ball allows a visually impaired child to catch the ball by listening for the sound.

- *Cassette recorders:* Visually impaired students can use cassette recorders to listen to recorded texts, tape and play back lectures, and formulate compositions.

BRAILLE

Many blind people read and write through the use of braille. By moving their fingertips across a series of raised dots that represent letters of the alphabet, blind people can understand printed material. Used throughout the world for over a hundred years, braille is a hard skill to learn. Blind children begin to learn braille when other children are beginning to learn to read. If you have a student who is using braille, it is not necessary for you to know braille, although you may have to arrange for classroom materials and tests to be brailled ahead of time.

Students will require intensive instruction in reading and writing braille, as well as the use of specialized equipment and materials. This instruction should be provided by a vision specialist, who may work at different schools. The student will learn to use aids that enable him to communicate in writing, even with those who do not know braille. He can write in braille using a slate and stylus or a six-key machine called a braillewriter. He can use a computer with a keyboard similar to a braillewriter to take notes or write assignments, and then print them on a regular printer or a brailleprinter. A braille embosser can produce a braille version of print from a regular computer. In addition, a visually impaired student can use a computer for completing tests or writing papers, and then print out and submit the document to the teacher.

HOW TEACHERS CAN HELP

While, as a classroom teacher of a visually impaired student, you do not necessarily require specialized training, you will have to make some accommodations in your teaching approach. You may find it helpful to seek out the services of the vision specialist. Some of the following strategies are intended to be used with students with partial sight, while others are for students who are legally or totally blind.

1. Seat the Child Front Row Center

This is a good rule of thumb with visually impaired students when the board is in the front of the class; however, some visually impaired students do better seated away from the window to reduce glare, while others benefit from being near the window to take advantage of natural light.

2. It Is Okay to Use Vision-Oriented Words Like "See" and "Look"

Children who are visually impaired are just as likely to use these words as children with intact vision. They may use them in casual conversation as in the expression "See you later." It is hard to avoid using them because there are few good substitutes.

3. Let Your Students Know How They Can Help a Visually Impaired Classmate

Talk with the student and his parents and get their permission to have a discussion with the class. Invite them to participate. The student may feel a sense of relief if his classmates are aware of his visual limitations and how they can help him. If he is comfortable, have him demonstrate to his classmates any technology he uses. You might even have your students put on blindfolds for short periods to sense what it is like to have no eyesight. Avoid dwelling on the child's disability, however, because this will accentuate his differences from his peers.

4. Let the Student Know When You Arrive and When You Leave

A visually impaired child may not be aware you are speaking to him unless you let him know. Also let him know when you are about to leave. Otherwise, you may find the child talking when no one is there. Teach your students to follow this rule.

5. Allow the Student to Move around the Class

Once the student learns the layout of the classroom, allow him to move around to get closer to the board, see a demonstration, or obtain materials. Make sure to let him know if any classroom furniture has been moved.

6. Treat a Visually Impaired Child as You Would Other Children

There will no doubt be times when the student will require special assistance, but avoid doing things that make him stand out. Talk directly to a visually impaired student rather than through another person. Speak in a natural manner and a normal volume. Use the same disciplinary measures you use with other students as long as he is not disciplined for behaviors directly related to his visual problems. Do not excuse inappropriate behavior because of his visual impairment.

7. Encourage the Student to Act Independently

Avoid being overly solicitous, and certainly do not show pity. Allow the student to do as much as he can on his own and encourage independence by giving clear and concrete directions. It is hard to watch children with obvious handicaps have difficulty, but they can learn from their struggles. You may be surprised how much a visually impaired student can learn to do on his own, especially with the use of specialized aids. Encourage him to ask for assistance when needed.

8. Find Alternative Ways for the Student to Gain Classroom Information

Taking notes in lecture-type classes may pose a problem for the visually impaired student. Encourage him to use a tape recorder. To help him understand your notes on the board, read them aloud as you write them or ask a classmate to read them to the student. You might give the student a copy of your own notes or have another student's notes photocopied. Make sure that the notes as well as handouts are easy for him to read and in the appropriate print size. If the student needs the notes brailled or enlarged, arrange for this in advance.

9. Describe to the Student Events That He Cannot See

It is hard for people with intact vision to appreciate how much of what goes on in the classroom (and out of the classroom) depends on vision for understanding. You may need to fill in the student's gaps in understanding by letting him know what he is missing. Even ordinary activities may elude the visually impaired student (for example, using a combination lock or seeing the text on a filmstrip). A person's comments may require explanation because the child is unable to see his facial expressions. If the class is watching a movie, help the student understand what he can't see. Read aloud subtitles that accompany filmstrips.

10. Help the Student Blend in with His Classmates

The visually impaired child may need to learn the basics of classroom protocol and social interaction that you take for granted with other students. You may have to encourage him to keep his head up, face the person he is speaking with and use his name, maintain good eye contact, sit and stand straight, not press his eyes, and raise his hand to answer a question. Of course, you will want to make these suggestions discreetly, so the child is not embarrassed. Children with severe visual impairments may display conspicuous classroom mannerisms (sometimes called "blindisms") that alienate their classmates, such as rocking, head weaving, and arm flapping. They may not even realize they are doing this, so you will want to remind them gently.

11. Assign a Buddy to a Student Who Is Visually Impaired

Find a responsible student who is willing to occasionally assist his visually impaired classmate. The buddy's job is to help the student stay on track in class. The buddy might make the visually impaired student aware of information and activities that he has missed and, if necessary, make copies of his class notes for the student, using carbon paper or a copying machine.

12. Help Organize the Student's Desk

Encourage the student to put items in the same place every time, so that he can easily find them. Give him a box or tray to hold small items so they do not fall on the floor. You may find that he needs additional work or storage space, especially if he uses special materials or aids.

13. Give the Child Extra Time When Necessary

Many classroom tasks, from taking of tests to completion of in-class assignments, may take the visually impaired student longer than average to complete. If so, allow him a reasonable amount of extra time (for example, 50 percent more time). As an alternative, you can shorten the assignments (for example, have him do every other math problem or only the more difficult ones). As the student develops adaptive skills for completing academic work, you may want to lessen the extra time or increase the workload so that he gradually approaches the expectations for all students.

14. Use Alternative Methods of Testing the Student

The challenge for teachers is to find ways to assess the student's understanding of the subject matter while working around his visual limitations. If the student has difficulty writing, allow him to type his answers on a computer or take the test orally. If you write test questions on the board, consider reading them to the student or giving him a copy in print or braille. If the student requires large print, you may be able to enlarge the test print using your school's copying machine, or the student may prefer to use optical aids to read the print. Tests and answer sheets will have to be transcribed into braille for some students. As with assignments, the visually impaired student may need extra time to complete the test. Special arrangements will probably have to be made for standardized tests, especially if the tests require that students "bubble" in their responses. If so, you may want to allow the student to mark his answers directly on the test booklet, or give him a different answer sheet where he can circle the correct letter. His responses can later be transferred to the standard answer sheet.

15. Develop a Plan for Fire Drills

You may want to consult the vision specialist and your school administrator in developing this plan. Rather than assigning responsibility to one particular classmate for guiding the student during a drill, suggest that the visually impaired student take hold of the arm of the nearest student and quietly follow him. Inform the class of the procedure ahead of time.

FOR FURTHER INFORMATION

Holbrook, M. C. (ed.) (1995). *Children With Visual Impairments: A Parents' Guide.* Bethesda, MD: Woodbine House.

Mangold, S. S. (1982). *A Teacher's Guide to the Special Educational Needs of Blind and Visually Handicapped Children.* New York: American Foundation for the Blind.

Rogow, S. (1988). *Helping the Visually Impaired Child With Developmental Problems: Effective Practice in Home, School, and Community.* New York: Teachers College Press.

Scott, E.; Jan, J.; and Freeman, R. (1994). *Can't Your Child See? A Guide for Parents and Professionals About Children Who Are Visually Impaired* (3d ed.). Austin, TX: Pro-Ed.

ORGANIZATIONS

American Foundation for the Blind
11 Penn Plaza, Suite 300
New York, NY 10001
1-800-232-5463
1-212-502-7661

National Association for Parents of the Visually Impaired
P.O. Box 317
Watertown, MA 02272-0317
1-800-562-6265

National Association for Visually Handicapped
22 West 21st Street
New York, NY 10010
1-212-889-3141

National Library Service for the Blind and Physically Handicapped
1291 Taylor Street, NW
Washington, DC 20542
1-202-707-5100

Recording for the Blind & Dyslexic
20 Roszel Road
Princeton, NJ 08540
1-800-221-4792
1-609-452-0606

See also:
  Cerebral Palsy
  Handwriting Problem
  Hearing Impairment
  Reading Disability

INDEX

Teacher Notes

Teacher Notes